BUREAU FOR PARANORMAL • RESEARCH AND DEFENSE •

# B.P.R.D. HELL ON EARTH: A COLD DAY IN HELL

created by MIKE MIGNOLA

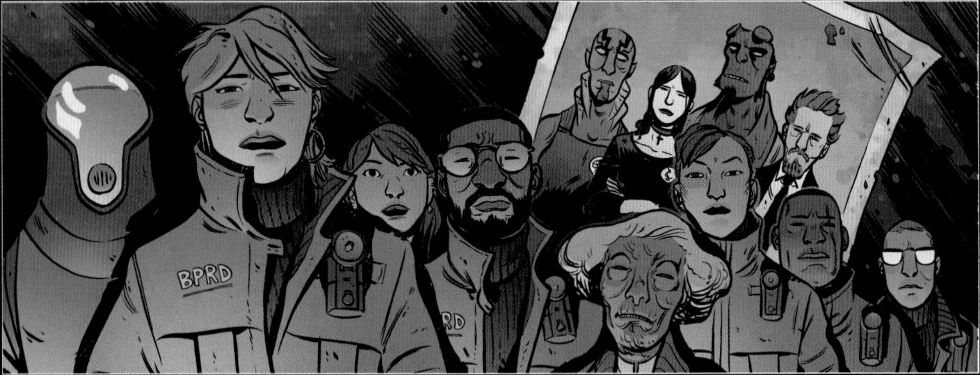
BPRD
RD

Since Liz Sherman destroyed the frog army and the Black Flame in Agartha, the Bureau for Paranormal Research and Defense has seen their charter expanded to oversee international threats, leading to collaborations with Russia's occult bureau. With Liz Sherman and Abe Sapien missing in action, the burden lies upon Kate Corrigan, Johann, and the more conventional agents of the B.P.R.D.

MIKE MIGNOLA'S

# B.P.R.D.™
# HELL ON EARTH
## A COLD DAY IN HELL

story by **MIKE MIGNOLA** and **JOHN ARCUDI**

art for *Wasteland* by **LAURENCE CAMPBELL**

art for *A Cold Day in Hell* by **PETER SNEJBJERG**

colors by **DAVE STEWART**

letters by **CLEM ROBINS**

cover art by **MIKE MIGNOLA** with **DAVE STEWART**

chapter break art by **DAVE JOHNSON**

editor **SCOTT ALLIE**

associate editor **DANIEL CHABON**    collection designer **AMY ARENDTS**

Mike Richardson PRESIDENT AND PUBLISHER · Neil Hankerson EXECUTIVE VICE PRESIDENT
Tom Weddle CHIEF FINANCIAL OFFICER · Randy Stradley VICE PRESIDENT OF PUBLISHING
Michael Martens VICE PRESIDENT OF BOOK TRADE SALES · Anita Nelson VICE PRESIDENT
OF BUSINESS AFFAIRS · Scott Allie EDITOR IN CHIEF · Matt Parkinson VICE PRESIDENT OF
MARKETING · David Scroggy VICE PRESIDENT OF PRODUCT DEVELOPMENT · Dale LaFountain
VICE PRESIDENT OF INFORMATION TECHNOLOGY · Darlene Vogel SENIOR DIRECTOR OF
PRINT, DESIGN, AND PRODUCTION · Ken Lizzi GENERAL COUNSEL · Davey Estrada EDITORIAL
DIRECTOR · Chris Warner SENIOR BOOKS EDITOR · Diana Schutz EXECUTIVE EDITOR · Cary
Grazzini DIRECTOR OF PRINT AND DEVELOPMENT · Lia Ribacchi ART DIRECTOR · Cara Niece
DIRECTOR OF SCHEDULING · Tim Wiesch DIRECTOR OF INTERNATIONAL LICENSING · Mark
Bernardi DIRECTOR OF DIGITAL PUBLISHING

DarkHorse.com    Hellboy.com

This book collects the comic-book series B.P.R.D. Hell on Earth #105–#109, originally published by
Dark Horse Comics.

Published by Dark Horse Books
A division of Dark Horse Comics, Inc.
10956 SE Main Street
Milwaukie, OR 97222

International Licensing: (503) 905-2377

# WASTELAND CHAPTER ONE

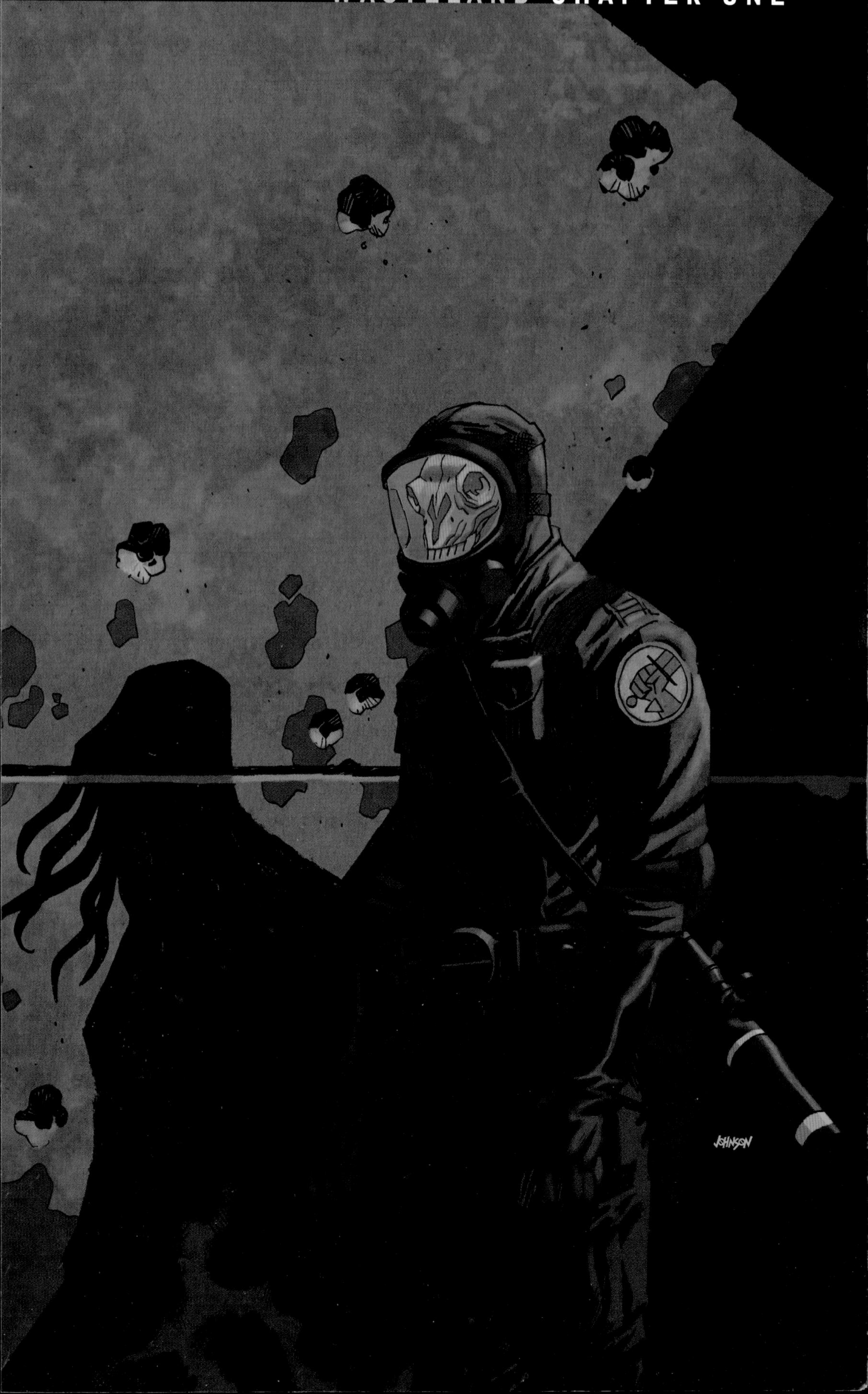
JOHNSON

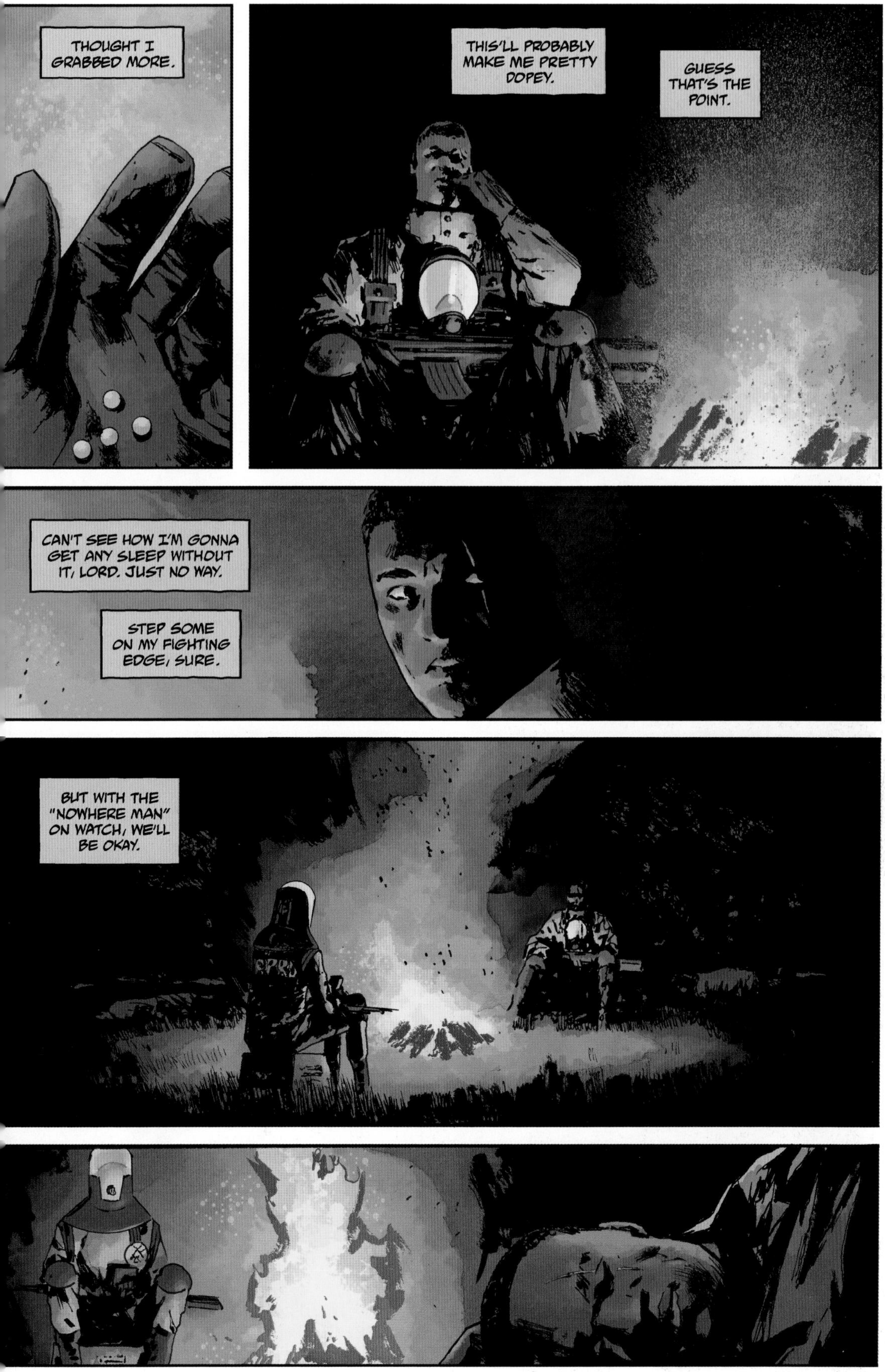
THOUGHT I GRABBED MORE.
THIS'LL PROBABLY MAKE ME PRETTY DOPEY.
GUESS THAT'S THE POINT.
CAN'T SEE HOW I'M GONNA GET ANY SLEEP WITHOUT IT, LORD. JUST NO WAY.
STEP SOME ON MY FIGHTING EDGE, SURE.
BUT WITH THE "NOWHERE MAN" ON WATCH, WE'LL BE OKAY.

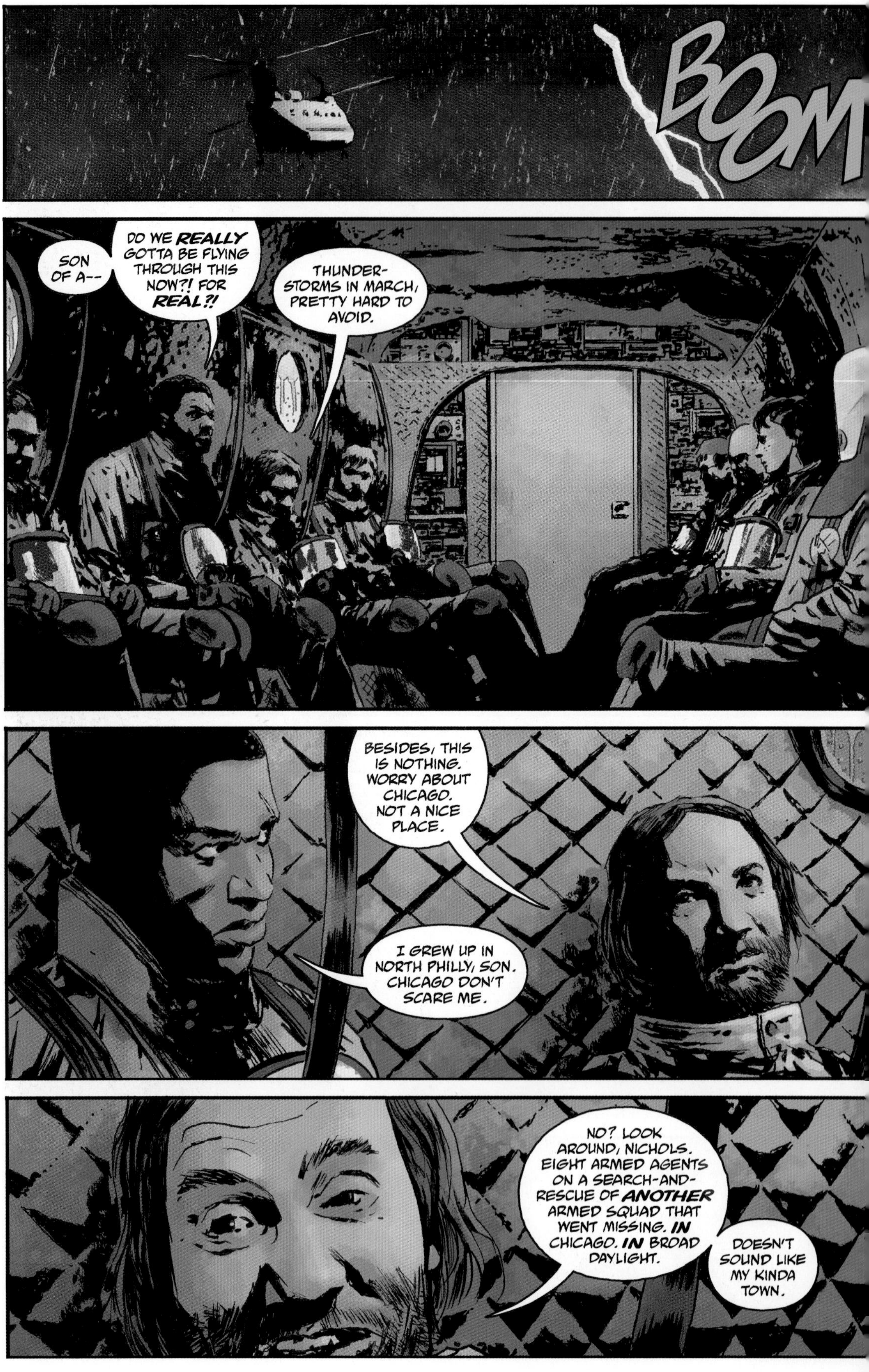
BOOM
SON OF A--
DO WE REALLY GOTTA BE FLYING THROUGH THIS NOW?! FOR REAL?!
THUNDER-STORMS IN MARCH, PRETTY HARD TO AVOID.
BESIDES, THIS IS NOTHING. WORRY ABOUT CHICAGO. NOT A NICE PLACE.
I GREW UP IN NORTH PHILLY, SON. CHICAGO DON'T SCARE ME.
NO? LOOK AROUND, NICHOLS. EIGHT ARMED AGENTS ON A SEARCH-AND-RESCUE OF ANOTHER ARMED SQUAD THAT WENT MISSING. IN CHICAGO. IN BROAD DAYLIGHT.
DOESN'T SOUND LIKE MY KINDA TOWN.

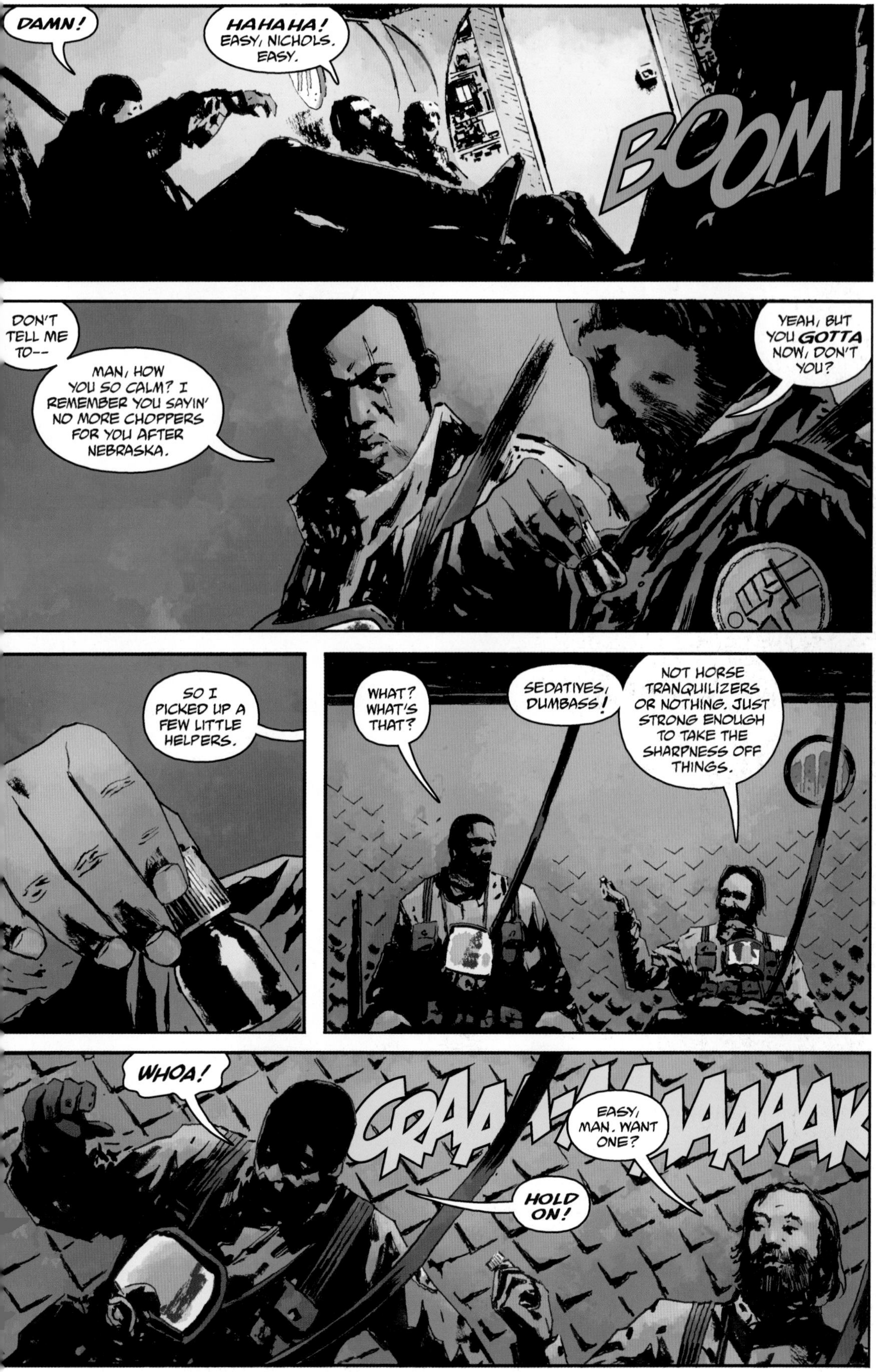
DAMN!
HAHAHA! EASY, NICHOLS. EASY.
BOOM!
DON'T TELL ME TO--
MAN, HOW YOU SO CALM? I REMEMBER YOU SAYIN' NO MORE CHOPPERS FOR YOU AFTER NEBRASKA.
YEAH, BUT YOU GOTTA NOW, DON'T YOU?
SO I PICKED UP A FEW LITTLE HELPERS.
WHAT? WHAT'S THAT?
SEDATIVES, DUMBASS!
NOT HORSE TRANQUILIZERS OR NOTHING. JUST STRONG ENOUGH TO TAKE THE SHARPNESS OFF THINGS.
WHOA!
CRAAA-AAAAAAK
EASY, MAN. WANT ONE?
HOLD ON!

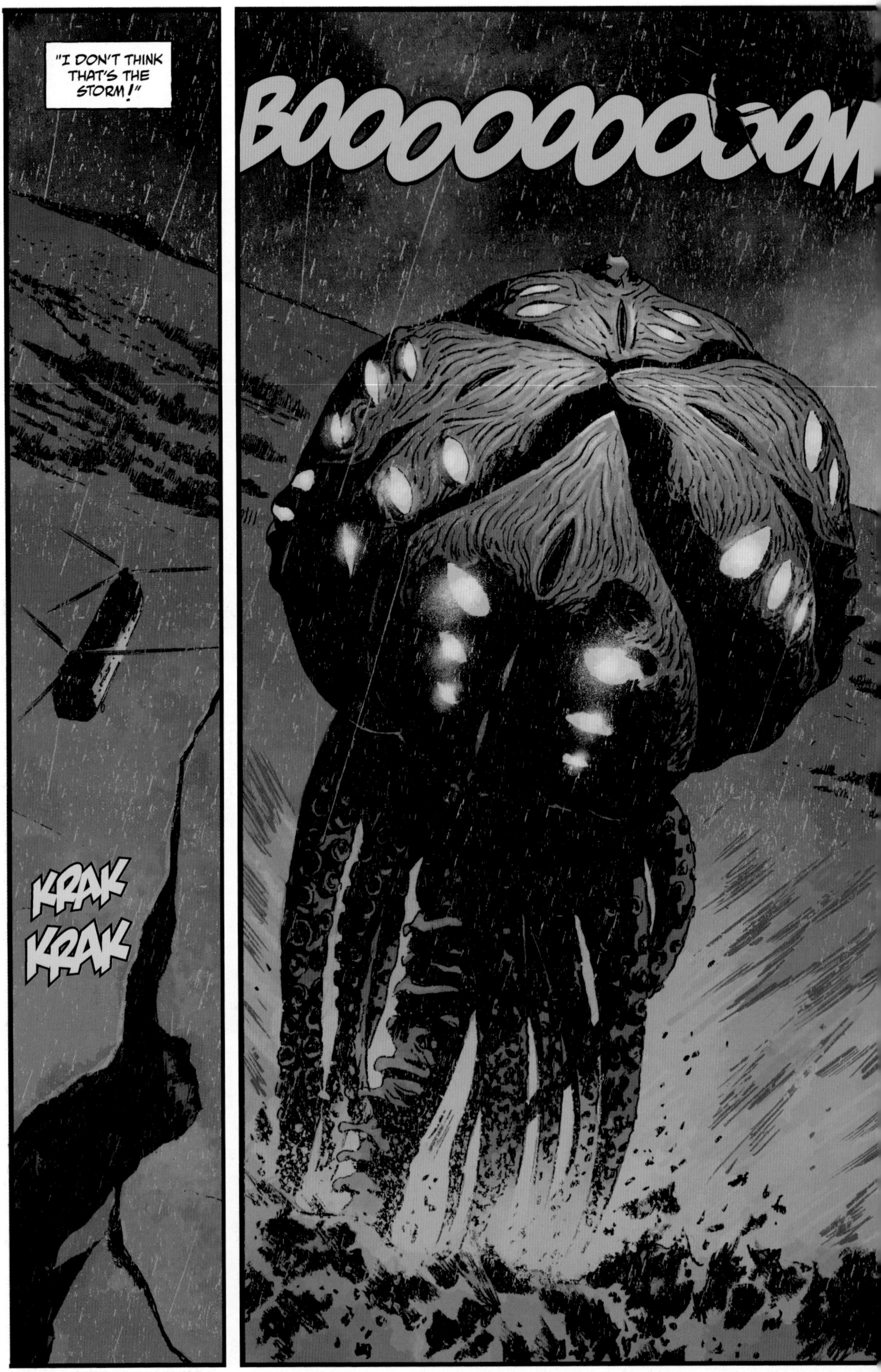
"I DON'T THINK THAT'S THE STORM!"
BOOOOOOOOOM
KRAK
KRAK

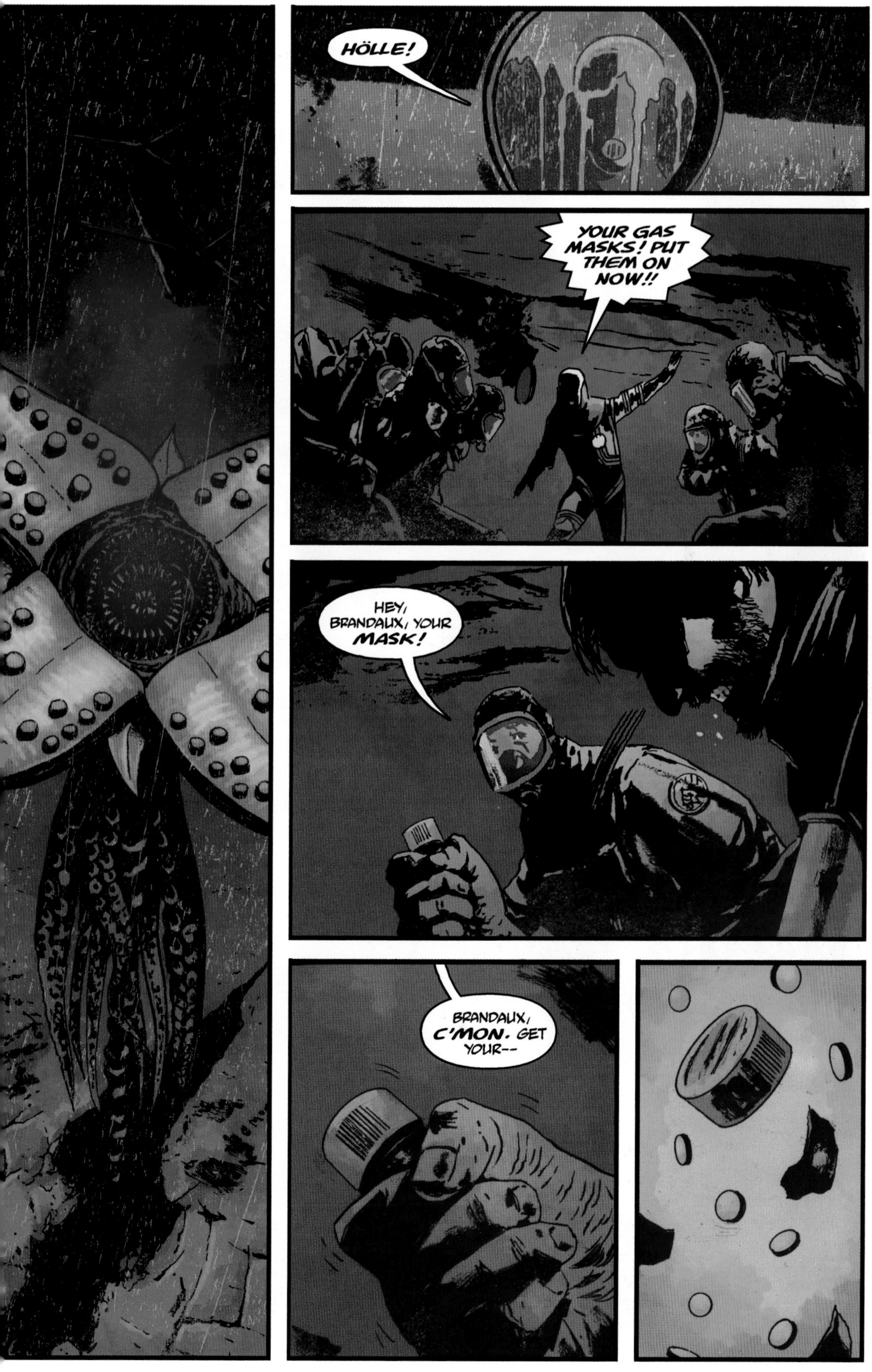
HÖLLE!
YOUR GAS MASKS! PUT THEM ON NOW!!
HEY, BRANDAUX, YOUR MASK!
BRANDAUX, C'MON. GET YOUR--

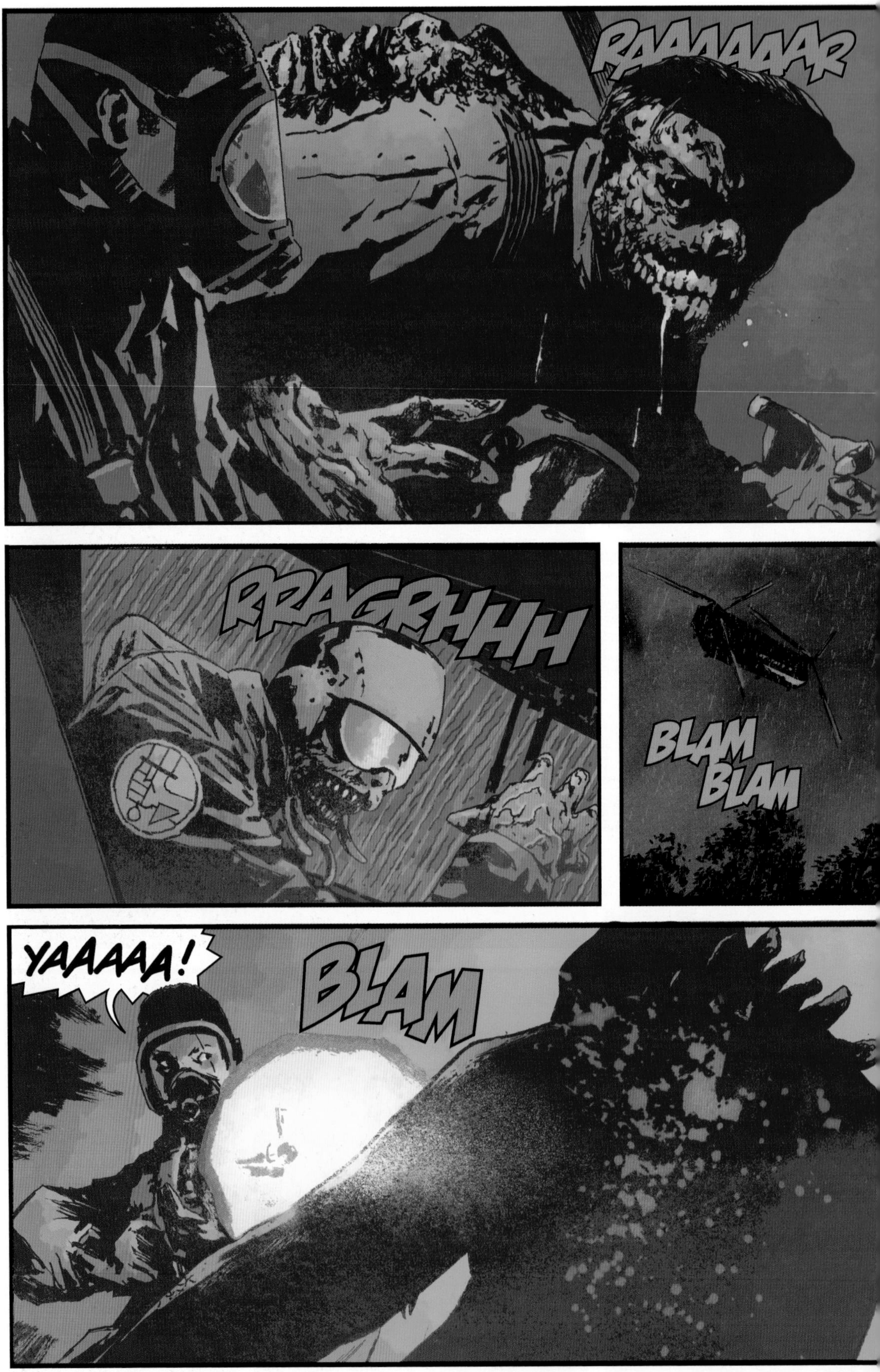

RAAAAAAR
RRAGRHHH
BLAM
BLAM
YAAAAA!
BLAM

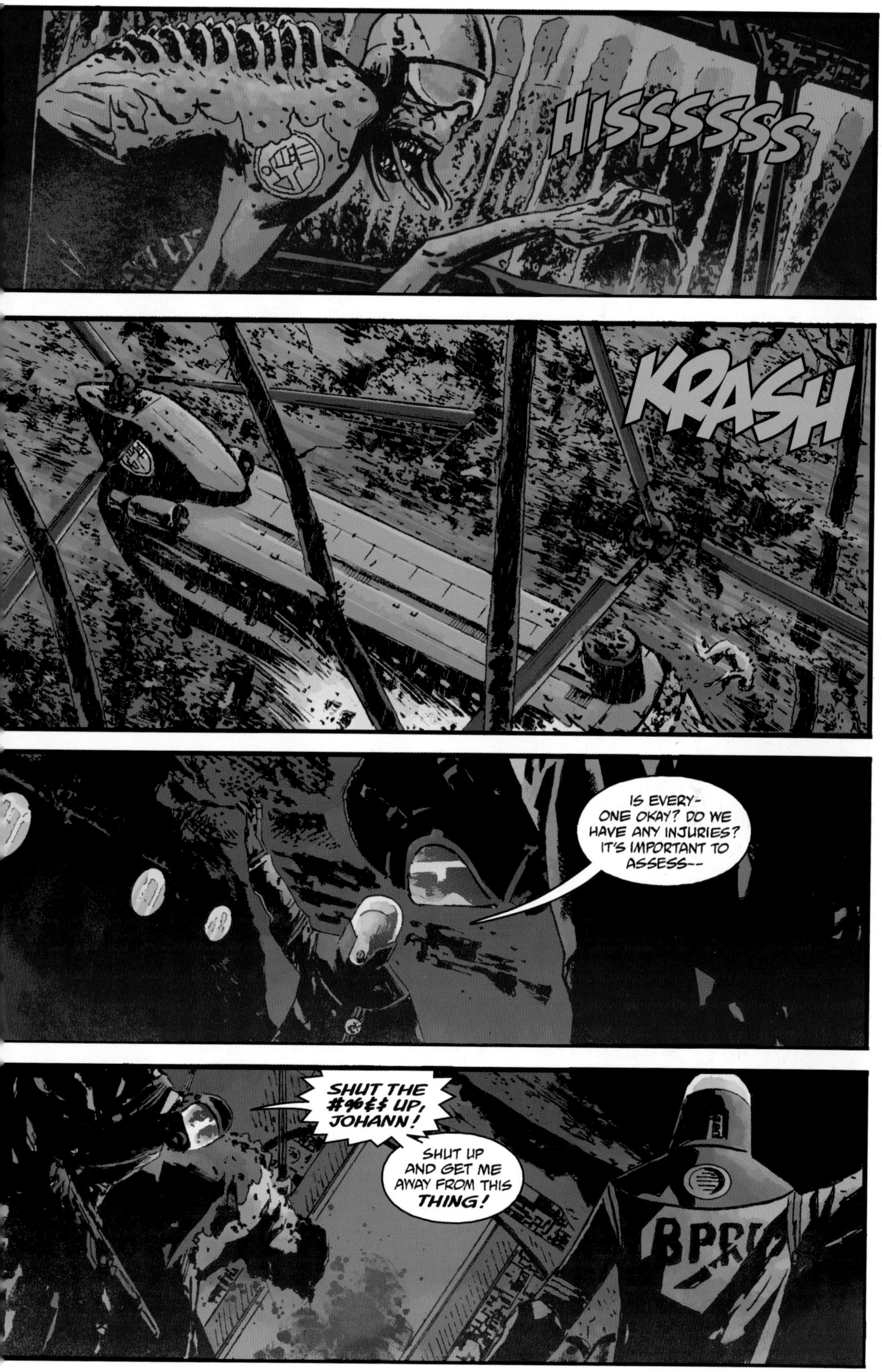

HISSSSSS
KRASH
IS EVERY-ONE OKAY? DO WE HAVE ANY INJURIES? IT'S IMPORTANT TO ASSESS--
SHUT THE #%&$ UP, JOHANN!
SHUT UP AND GET ME AWAY FROM THIS THING!
BPRD

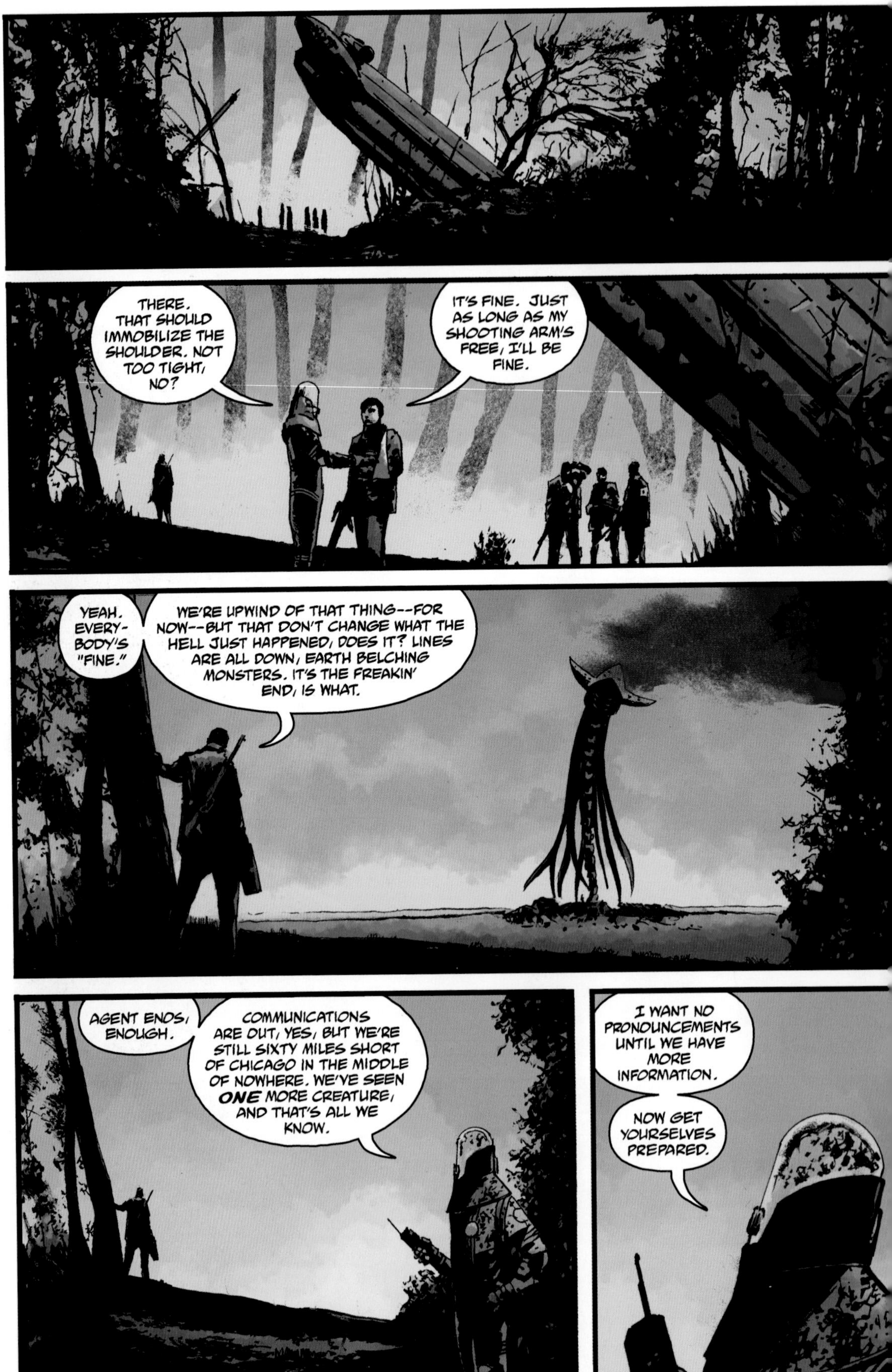
THERE. THAT SHOULD IMMOBILIZE THE SHOULDER. NOT TOO TIGHT, NO?
IT'S FINE. JUST AS LONG AS MY SHOOTING ARM'S FREE, I'LL BE FINE.
YEAH. EVERYBODY'S "FINE."
WE'RE UPWIND OF THAT THING--FOR NOW--BUT THAT DON'T CHANGE WHAT THE HELL JUST HAPPENED, DOES IT? LINES ARE ALL DOWN, EARTH BELCHING MONSTERS. IT'S THE FREAKIN' END, IS WHAT.
AGENT ENOS, ENOUGH.
COMMUNICATIONS ARE OUT, YES, BUT WE'RE STILL SIXTY MILES SHORT OF CHICAGO IN THE MIDDLE OF NOWHERE. WE'VE SEEN ONE MORE CREATURE, AND THAT'S ALL WE KNOW.
I WANT NO PRONOUNCEMENTS UNTIL WE HAVE MORE INFORMATION.
NOW GET YOURSELVES PREPARED.

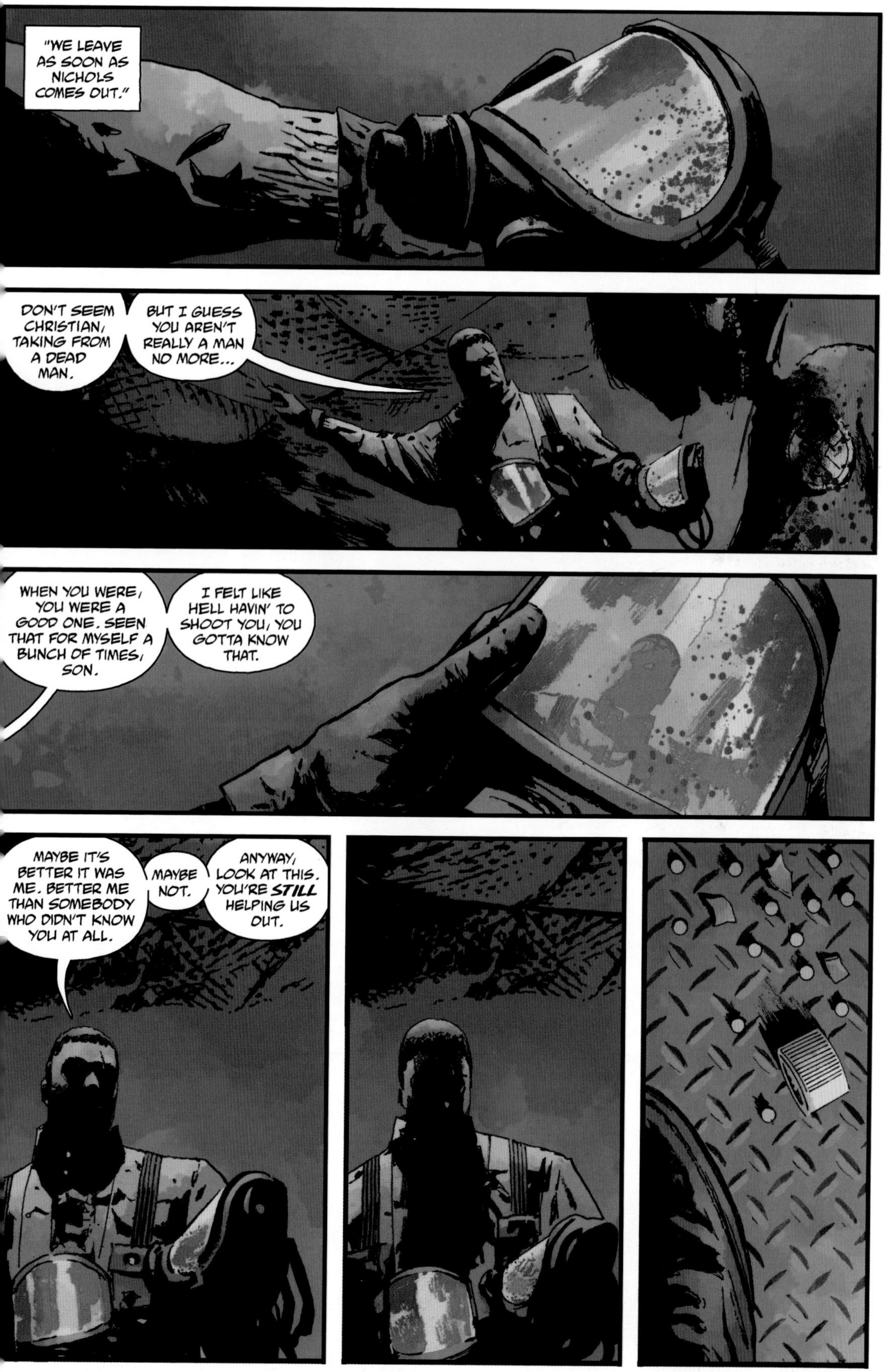
"WE LEAVE AS SOON AS NICHOLS COMES OUT."
DON'T SEEM CHRISTIAN, TAKING FROM A DEAD MAN.
BUT I GUESS YOU AREN'T REALLY A MAN NO MORE...
WHEN YOU WERE, YOU WERE A GOOD ONE. SEEN THAT FOR MYSELF A BUNCH OF TIMES, SON.
I FELT LIKE HELL HAVIN' TO SHOOT YOU, YOU GOTTA KNOW THAT.
MAYBE IT'S BETTER IT WAS ME. BETTER ME THAN SOMEBODY WHO DIDN'T KNOW YOU AT ALL.
MAYBE NOT.
ANYWAY, LOOK AT THIS. YOU'RE STILL HELPING US OUT.

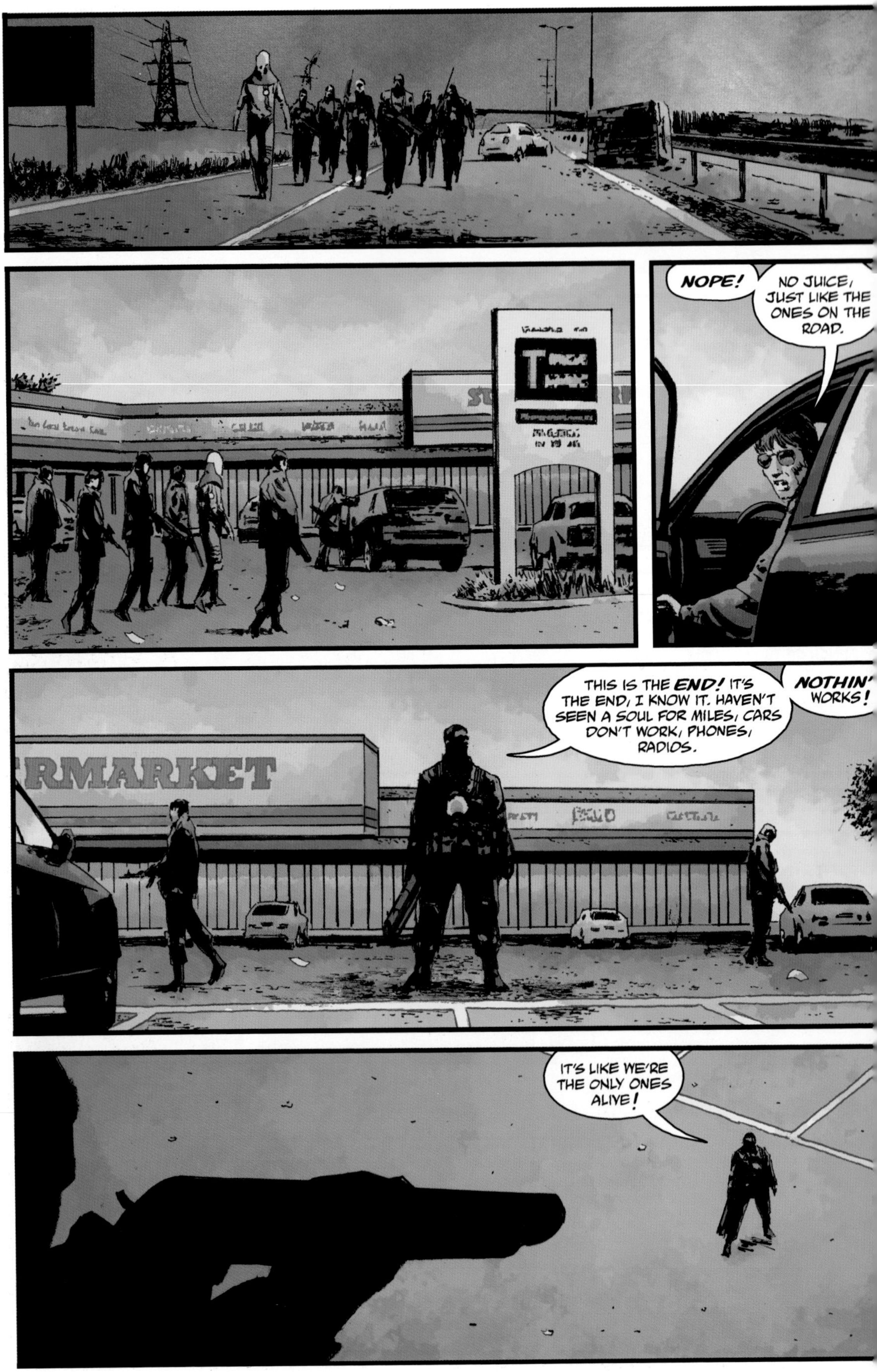
NOPE!
NO JUICE, JUST LIKE THE ONES ON THE ROAD.
THIS IS THE END! IT'S THE END, I KNOW IT. HAVEN'T SEEN A SOUL FOR MILES, CARS DON'T WORK, PHONES, RADIOS.
NOTHIN' WORKS!
RMARKET
IT'S LIKE WE'RE THE ONLY ONES ALIVE!

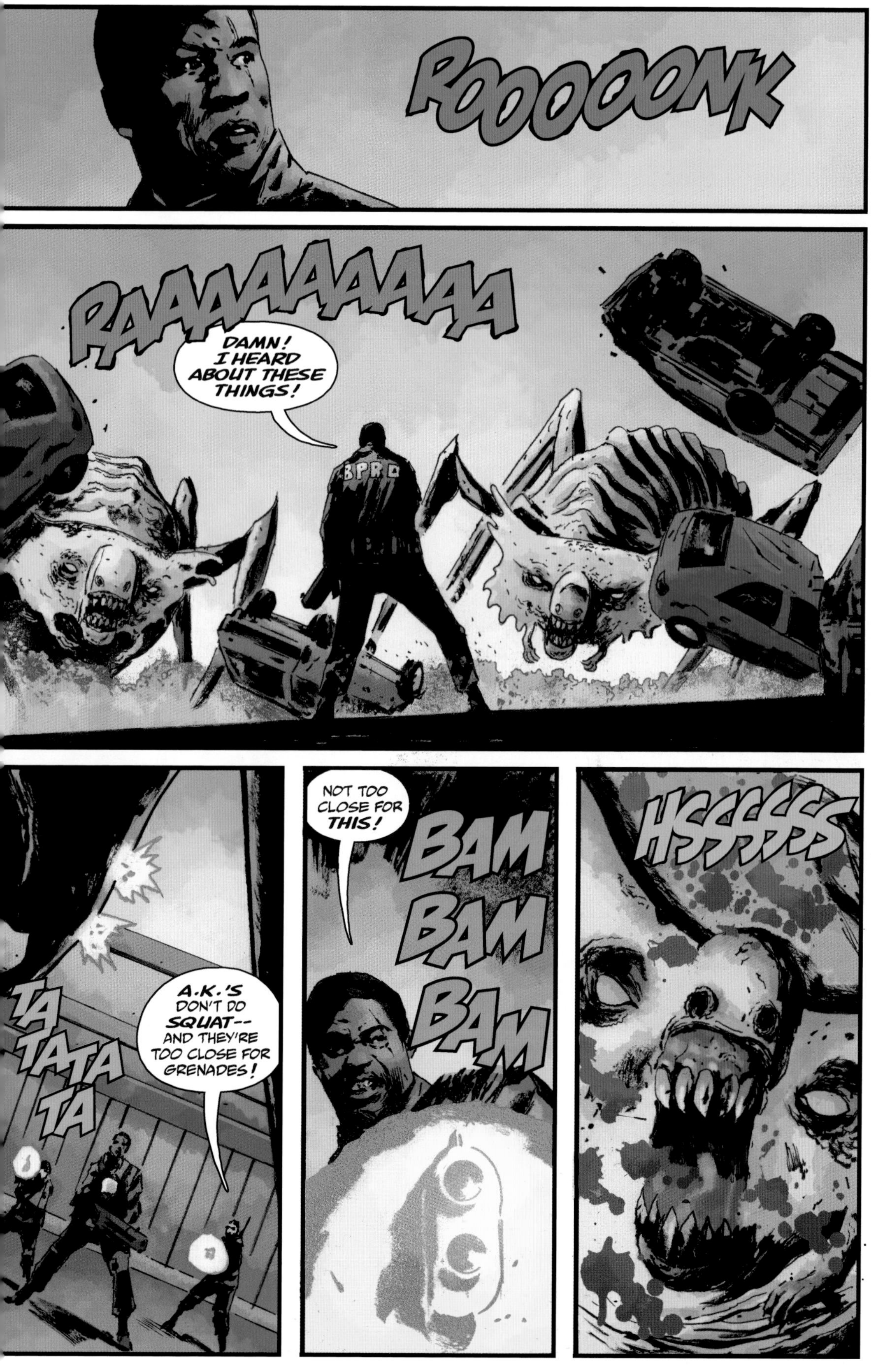
ROOOOONK
RAAAAAAAAA
DAMN! I HEARD ABOUT THESE THINGS!
TA TATA TA TA
A.K.'S DON'T DO SQUAT-- AND THEY'RE TOO CLOSE FOR GRENADES!
NOT TOO CLOSE FOR THIS!
BAM BAM BAM
HSSSSS

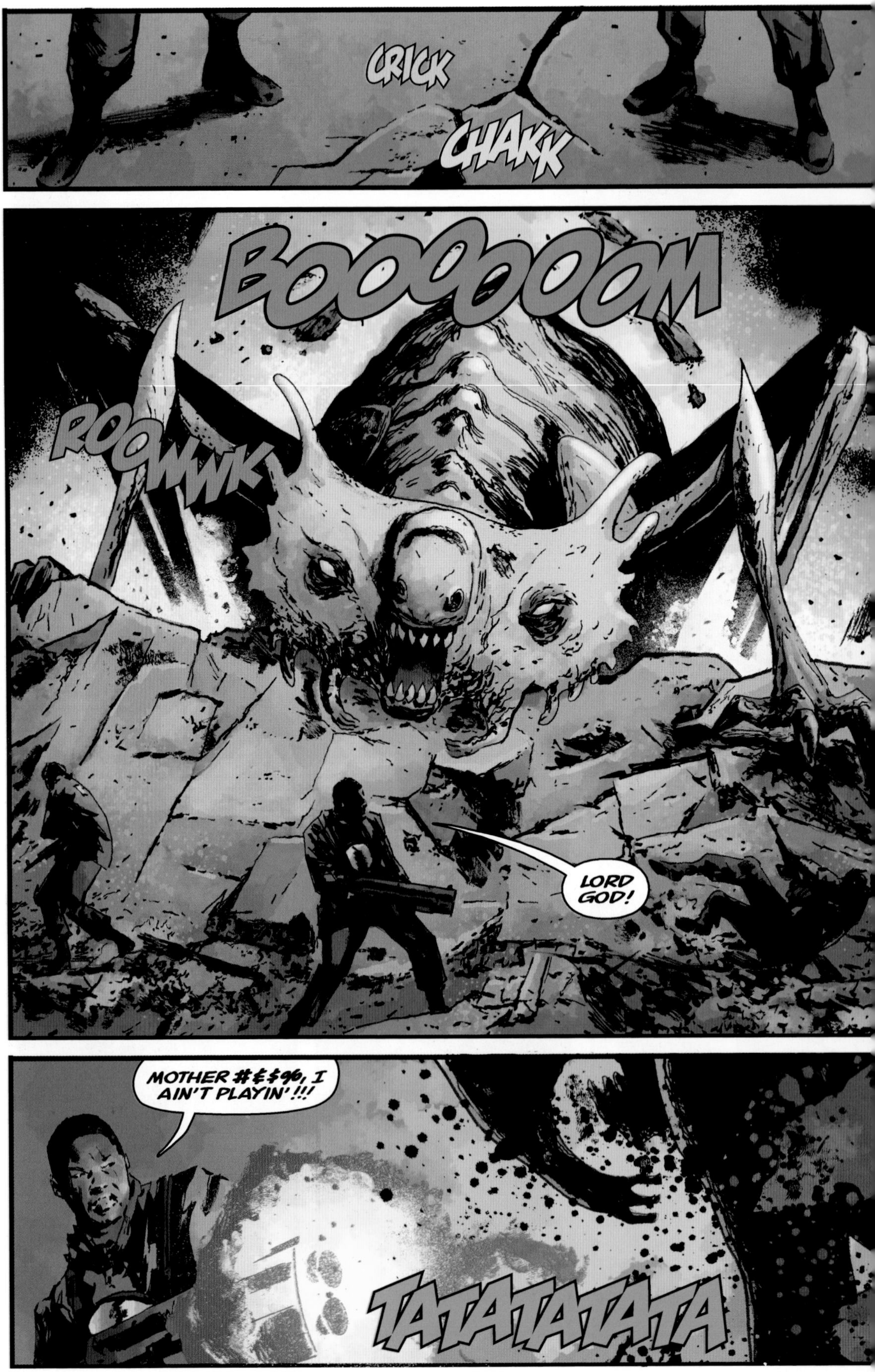
CRICK
CHAKK
BOOOOOOM
ROOWWK
LORD GOD!
MOTHER #&$%, I AIN'T PLAYIN'!!!
TATATATATA

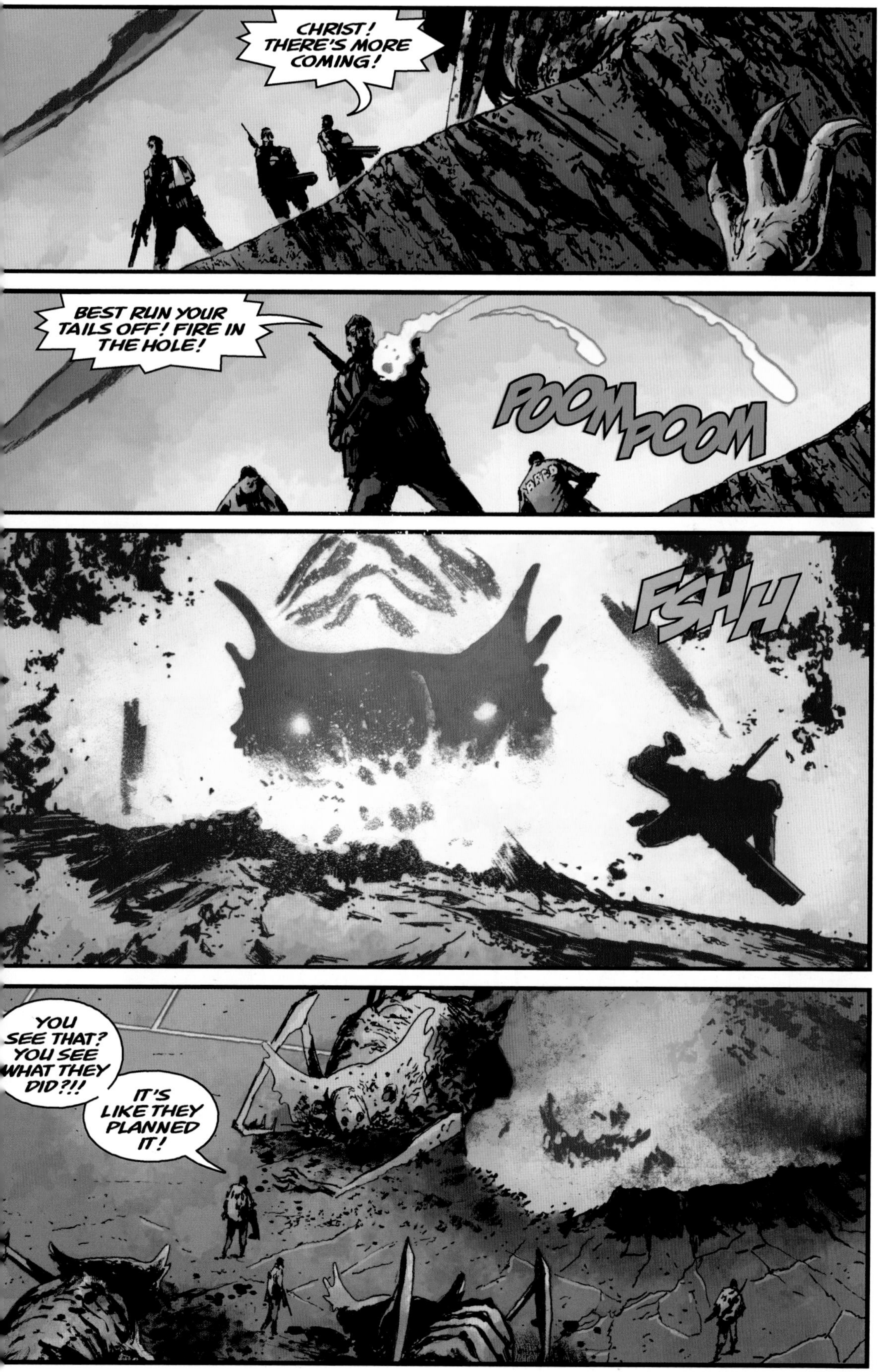
CHRIST! THERE'S MORE COMING!
BEST RUN YOUR TAILS OFF! FIRE IN THE HOLE!
POOM POOM
FSHH
YOU SEE THAT? YOU SEE WHAT THEY DID?!!
IT'S LIKE THEY PLANNED IT!

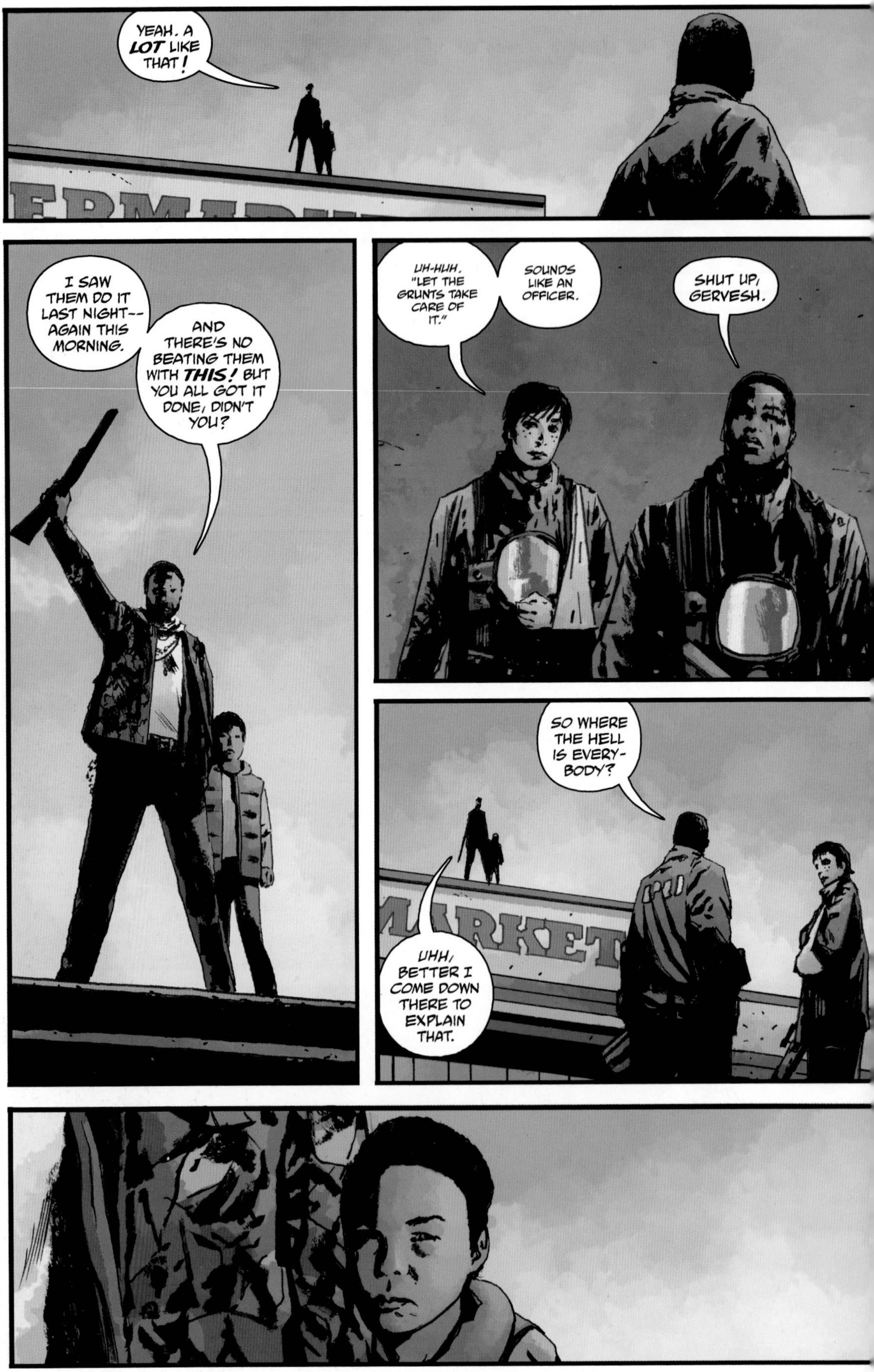

YEAH. A LOT LIKE THAT!
I SAW THEM DO IT LAST NIGHT-- AGAIN THIS MORNING.
AND THERE'S NO BEATING THEM WITH THIS! BUT YOU ALL GOT IT DONE, DIDN'T YOU?
UH-HUH. "LET THE GRUNTS TAKE CARE OF IT."
SOUNDS LIKE AN OFFICER.
SHUT UP, GERVESH.
SO WHERE THE HELL IS EVERY-BODY?
MARKET
UHH, BETTER I COME DOWN THERE TO EXPLAIN THAT.

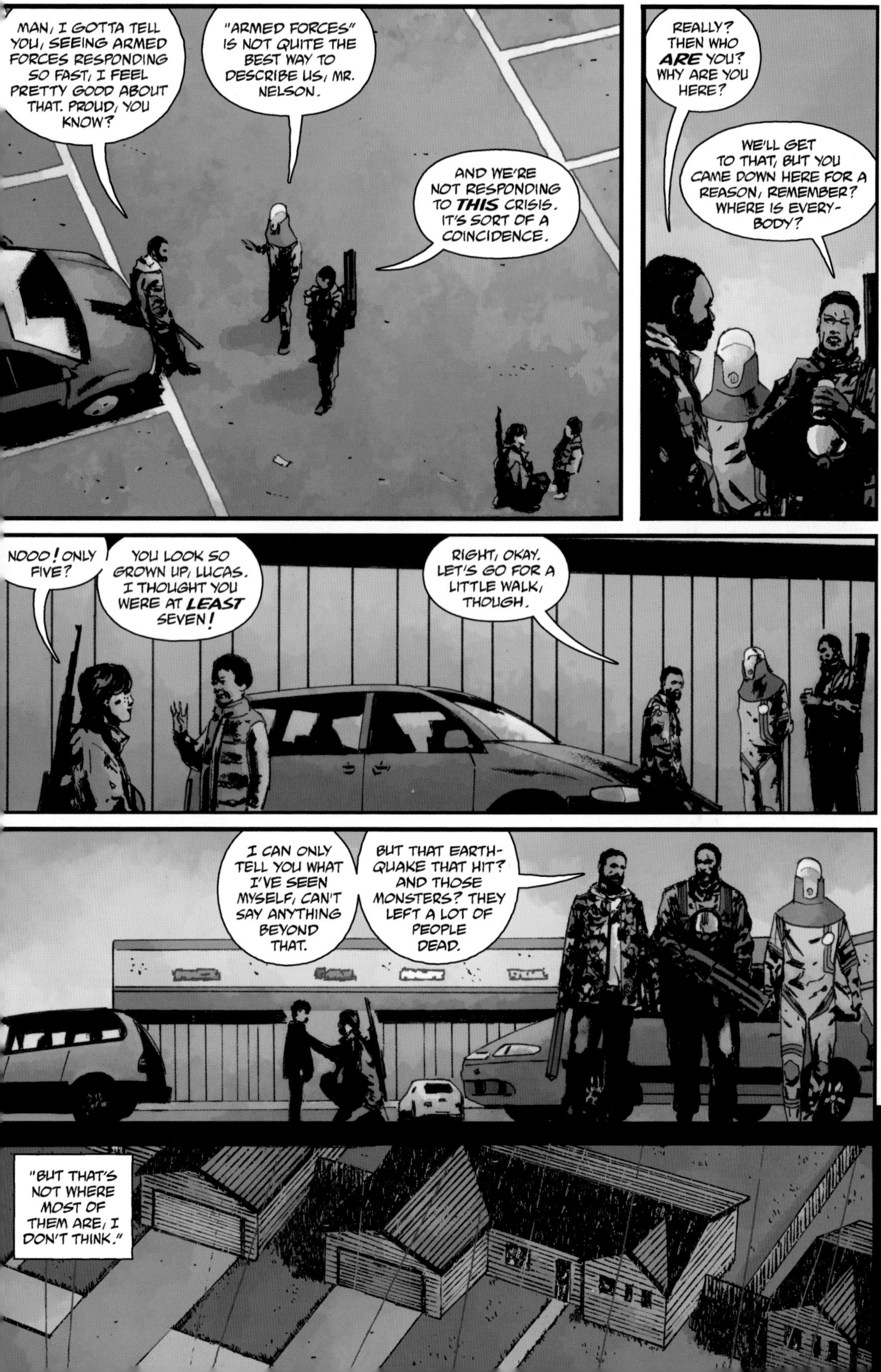
MAN, I GOTTA TELL YOU, SEEING ARMED FORCES RESPONDING SO FAST, I FEEL PRETTY GOOD ABOUT THAT. PROUD, YOU KNOW?
"ARMED FORCES" IS NOT QUITE THE BEST WAY TO DESCRIBE US, MR. NELSON.
AND WE'RE NOT RESPONDING TO THIS CRISIS. IT'S SORT OF A COINCIDENCE.
REALLY? THEN WHO ARE YOU? WHY ARE YOU HERE?
WE'LL GET TO THAT, BUT YOU CAME DOWN HERE FOR A REASON, REMEMBER? WHERE IS EVERY-BODY?
NOOO! ONLY FIVE?
YOU LOOK SO GROWN UP, LUCAS. I THOUGHT YOU WERE AT LEAST SEVEN!
RIGHT, OKAY. LET'S GO FOR A LITTLE WALK, THOUGH.
I CAN ONLY TELL YOU WHAT I'VE SEEN MYSELF, CAN'T SAY ANYTHING BEYOND THAT.
BUT THAT EARTH-QUAKE THAT HIT? AND THOSE MONSTERS? THEY LEFT A LOT OF PEOPLE DEAD.
"BUT THAT'S NOT WHERE MOST OF THEM ARE, I DON'T THINK."

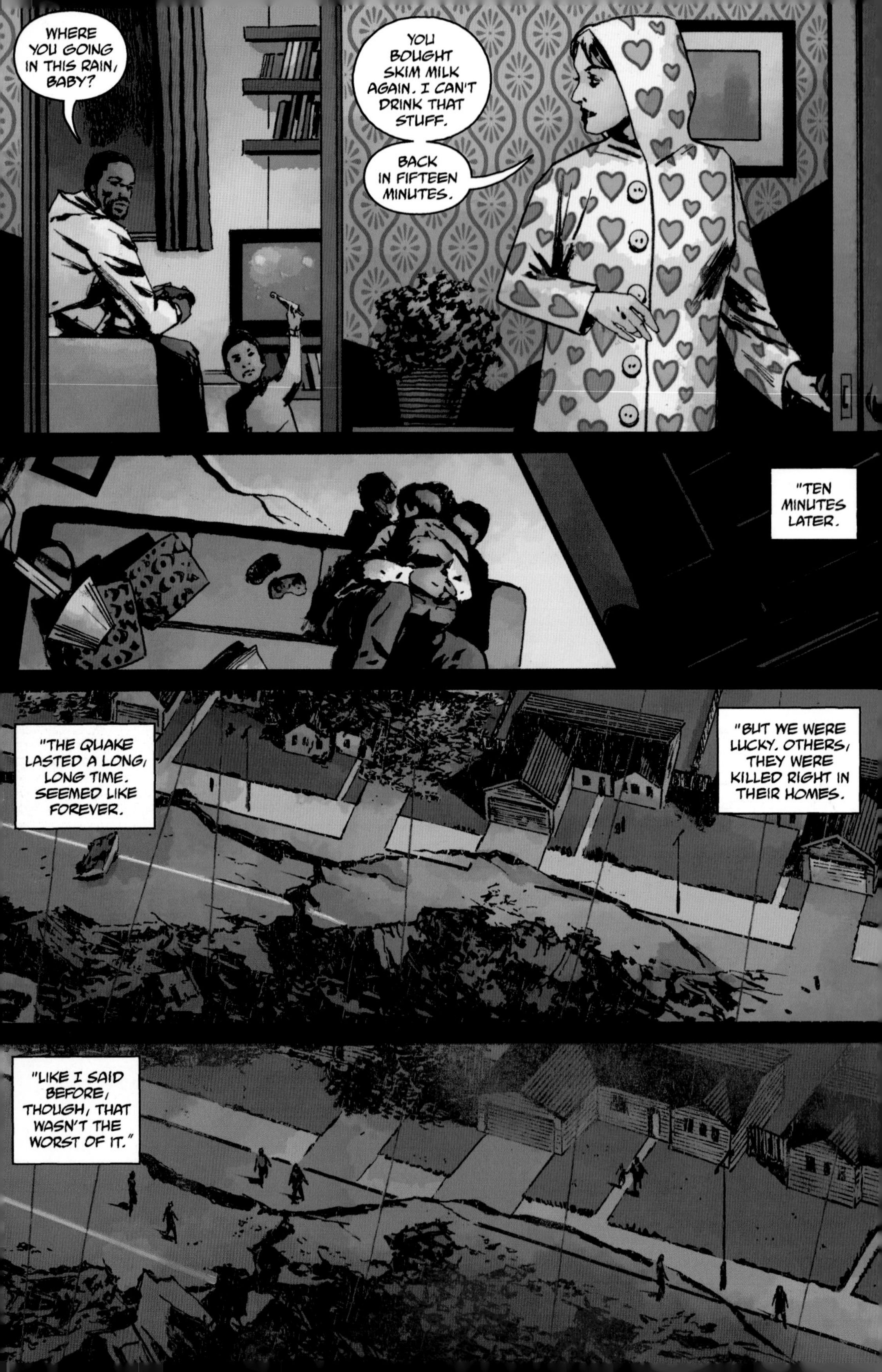
WHERE YOU GOING IN THIS RAIN, BABY?
YOU BOUGHT SKIM MILK AGAIN. I CAN'T DRINK THAT STUFF.
BACK IN FIFTEEN MINUTES.
"TEN MINUTES LATER.
"THE QUAKE LASTED A LONG, LONG TIME. SEEMED LIKE FOREVER.
"BUT WE WERE LUCKY. OTHERS, THEY WERE KILLED RIGHT IN THEIR HOMES.
"LIKE I SAID BEFORE, THOUGH, THAT WASN'T THE WORST OF IT."

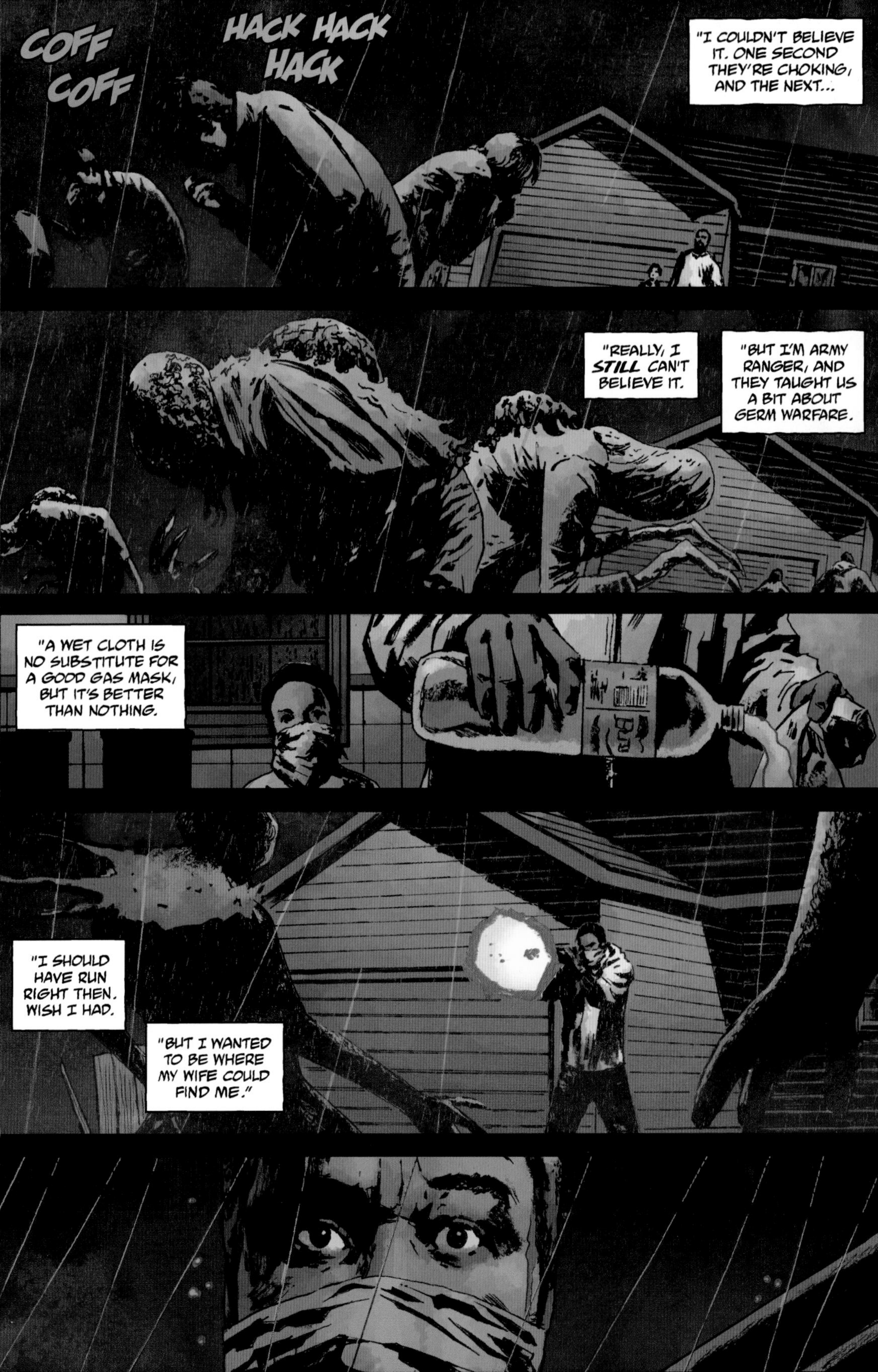
COFF COFF
HACK HACK HACK
"I COULDN'T BELIEVE IT. ONE SECOND THEY'RE CHOKING, AND THE NEXT...
"REALLY, I STILL CAN'T BELIEVE IT.
"BUT I'M ARMY RANGER, AND THEY TAUGHT US A BIT ABOUT GERM WARFARE.
"A WET CLOTH IS NO SUBSTITUTE FOR A GOOD GAS MASK, BUT IT'S BETTER THAN NOTHING.
"I SHOULD HAVE RUN RIGHT THEN. WISH I HAD.
"BUT I WANTED TO BE WHERE MY WIFE COULD FIND ME."

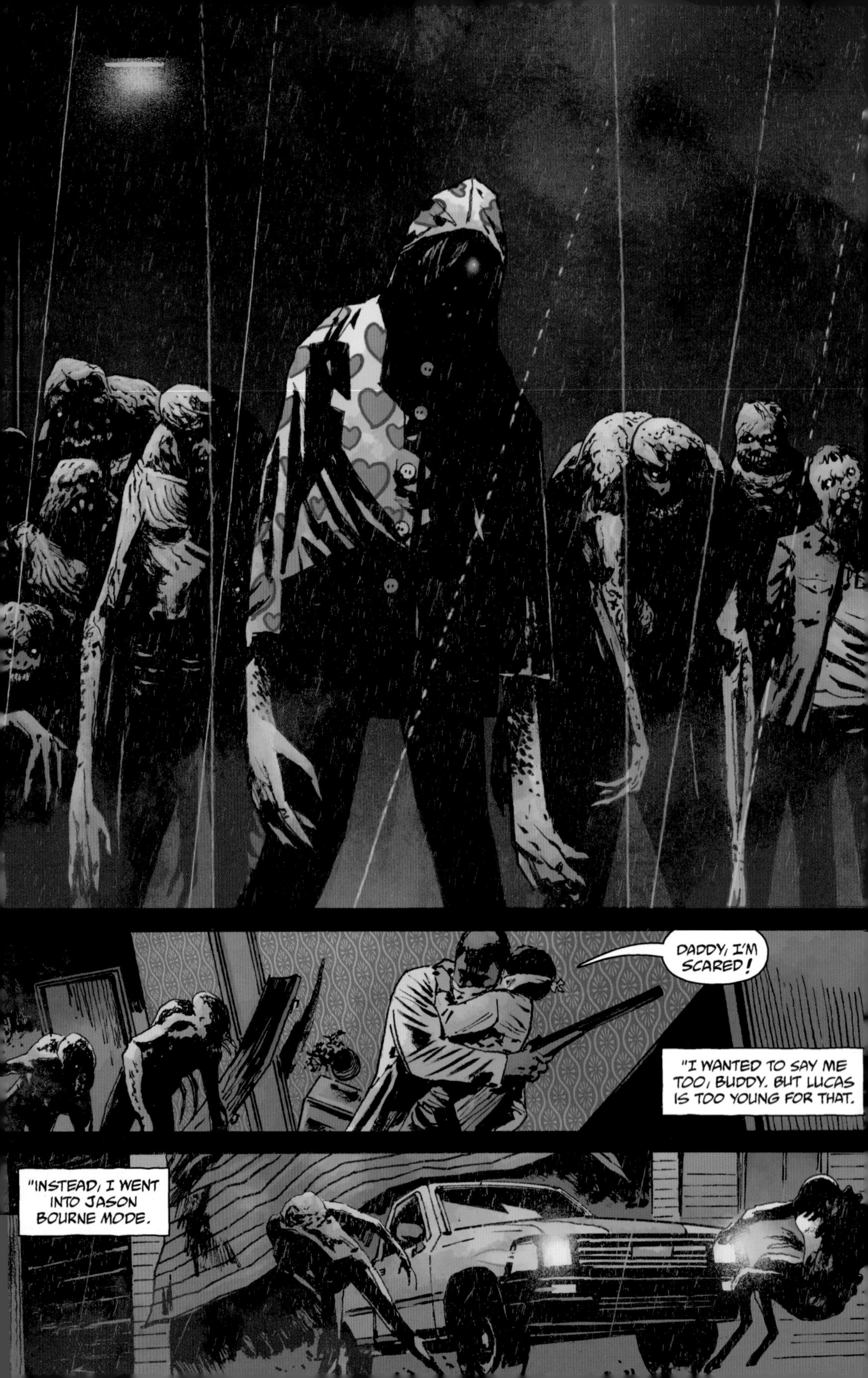
DADDY, I'M SCARED!
"I WANTED TO SAY ME TOO, BUDDY. BUT LUCAS IS TOO YOUNG FOR THAT.
"INSTEAD, I WENT INTO JASON BOURNE MODE.

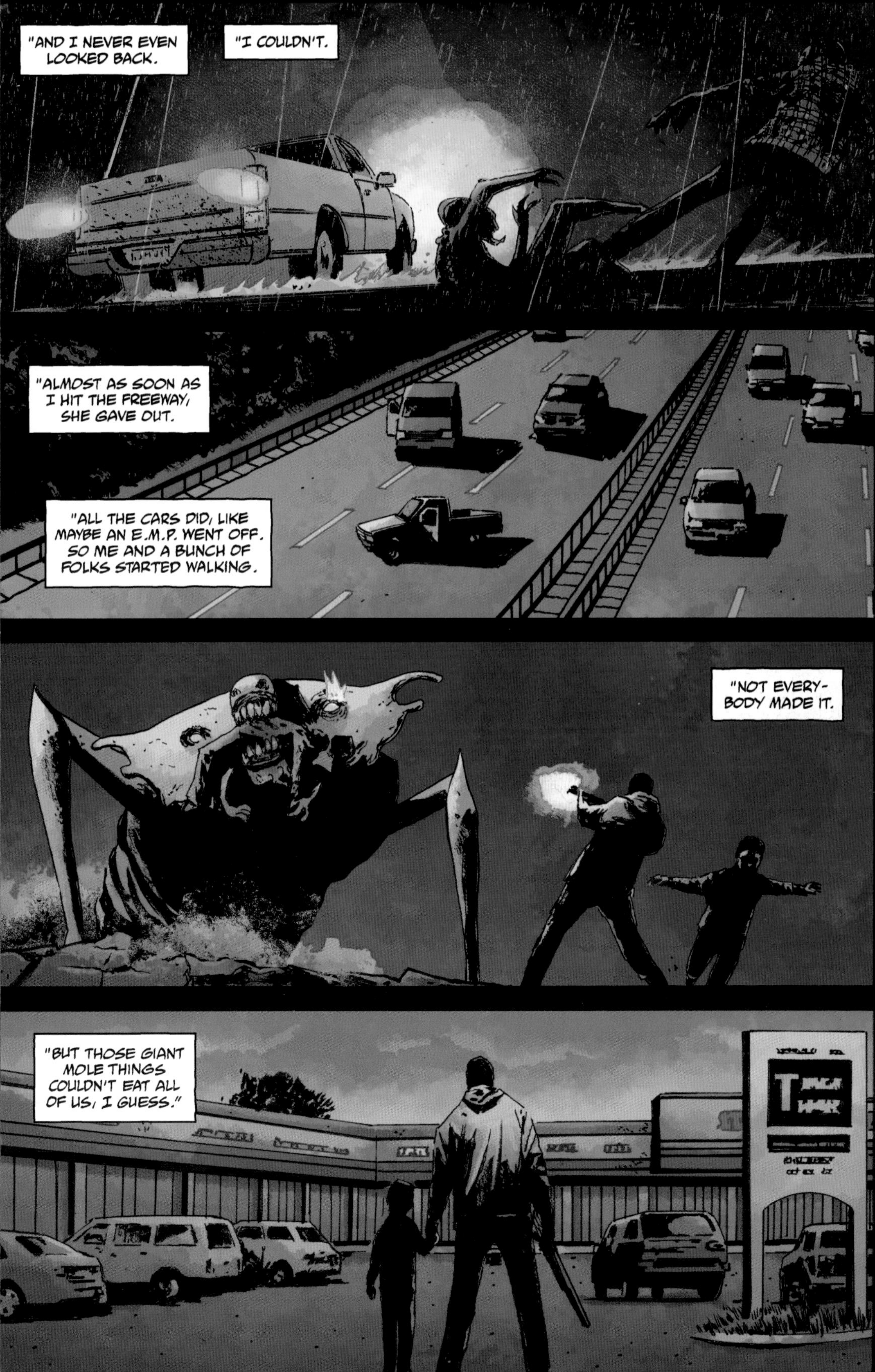
"AND I NEVER EVEN LOOKED BACK.
"I COULDN'T.
"ALMOST AS SOON AS I HIT THE FREEWAY, SHE GAVE OUT.
"ALL THE CARS DID, LIKE MAYBE AN E.M.P. WENT OFF. SO ME AND A BUNCH OF FOLKS STARTED WALKING.
"NOT EVERY-BODY MADE IT.
"BUT THOSE GIANT MOLE THINGS COULDN'T EAT ALL OF US, I GUESS."

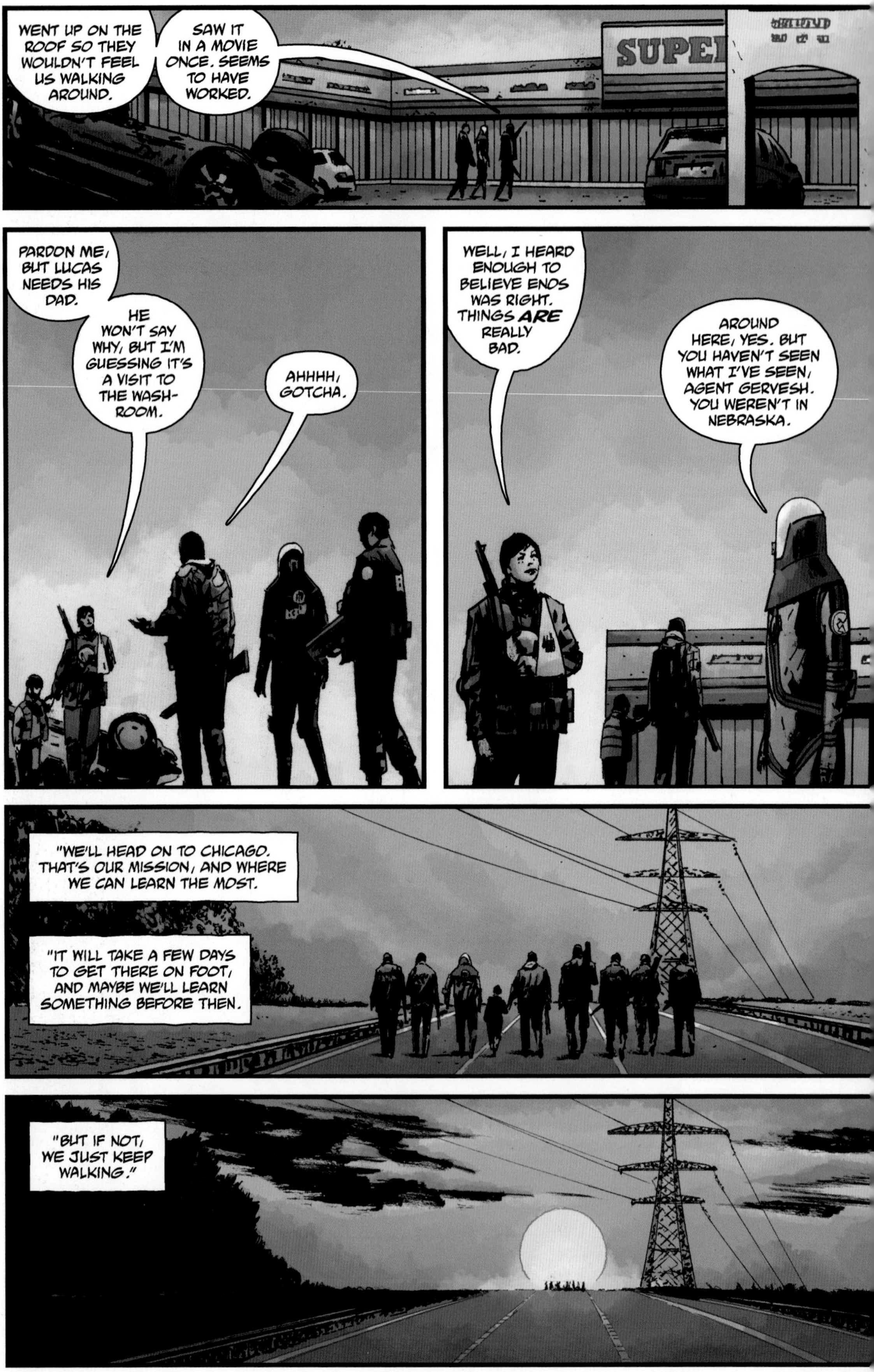

WENT UP ON THE ROOF SO THEY WOULDN'T FEEL US WALKING AROUND.
SAW IT IN A MOVIE ONCE. SEEMS TO HAVE WORKED.
SUPE
PARDON ME, BUT LUCAS NEEDS HIS DAD.
HE WON'T SAY WHY, BUT I'M GUESSING IT'S A VISIT TO THE WASH-ROOM.
AHHHH, GOTCHA.
WELL, I HEARD ENOUGH TO BELIEVE ENDS WAS RIGHT. THINGS ARE REALLY BAD.
AROUND HERE, YES. BUT YOU HAVEN'T SEEN WHAT I'VE SEEN, AGENT GERVESH. YOU WEREN'T IN NEBRASKA.
"WE'LL HEAD ON TO CHICAGO. THAT'S OUR MISSION, AND WHERE WE CAN LEARN THE MOST.
"IT WILL TAKE A FEW DAYS TO GET THERE ON FOOT, AND MAYBE WE'LL LEARN SOMETHING BEFORE THEN.
"BUT IF NOT, WE JUST KEEP WALKING."

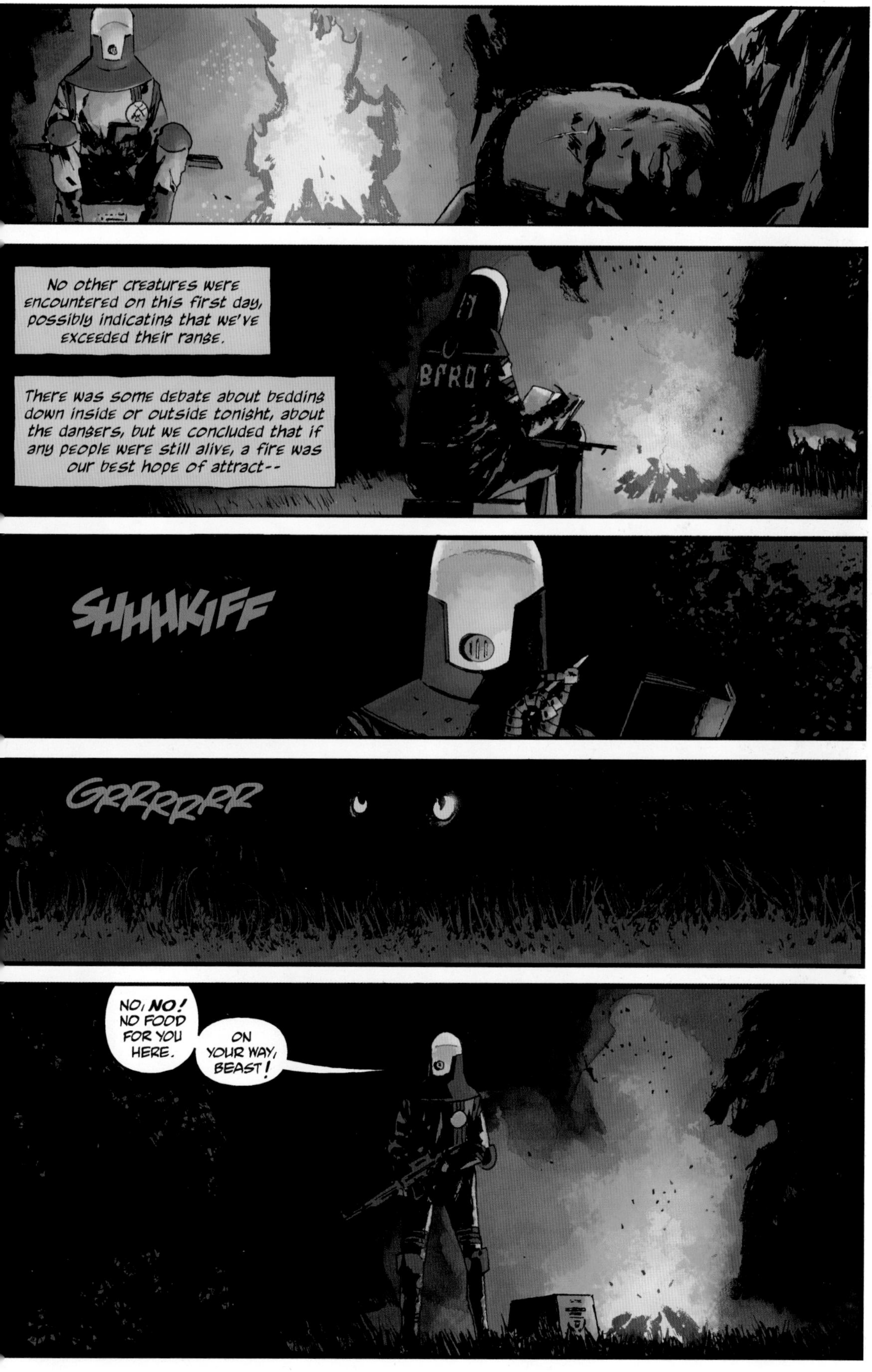
No other creatures were encountered on this first day, possibly indicating that we've exceeded their range.
There was some debate about bedding down inside or outside tonight, about the dangers, but we concluded that if any people were still alive, a fire was our best hope of attract--
SHHHKIFF
GRRRRRR
NO, NO! NO FOOD FOR YOU HERE.
ON YOUR WAY, BEAST!

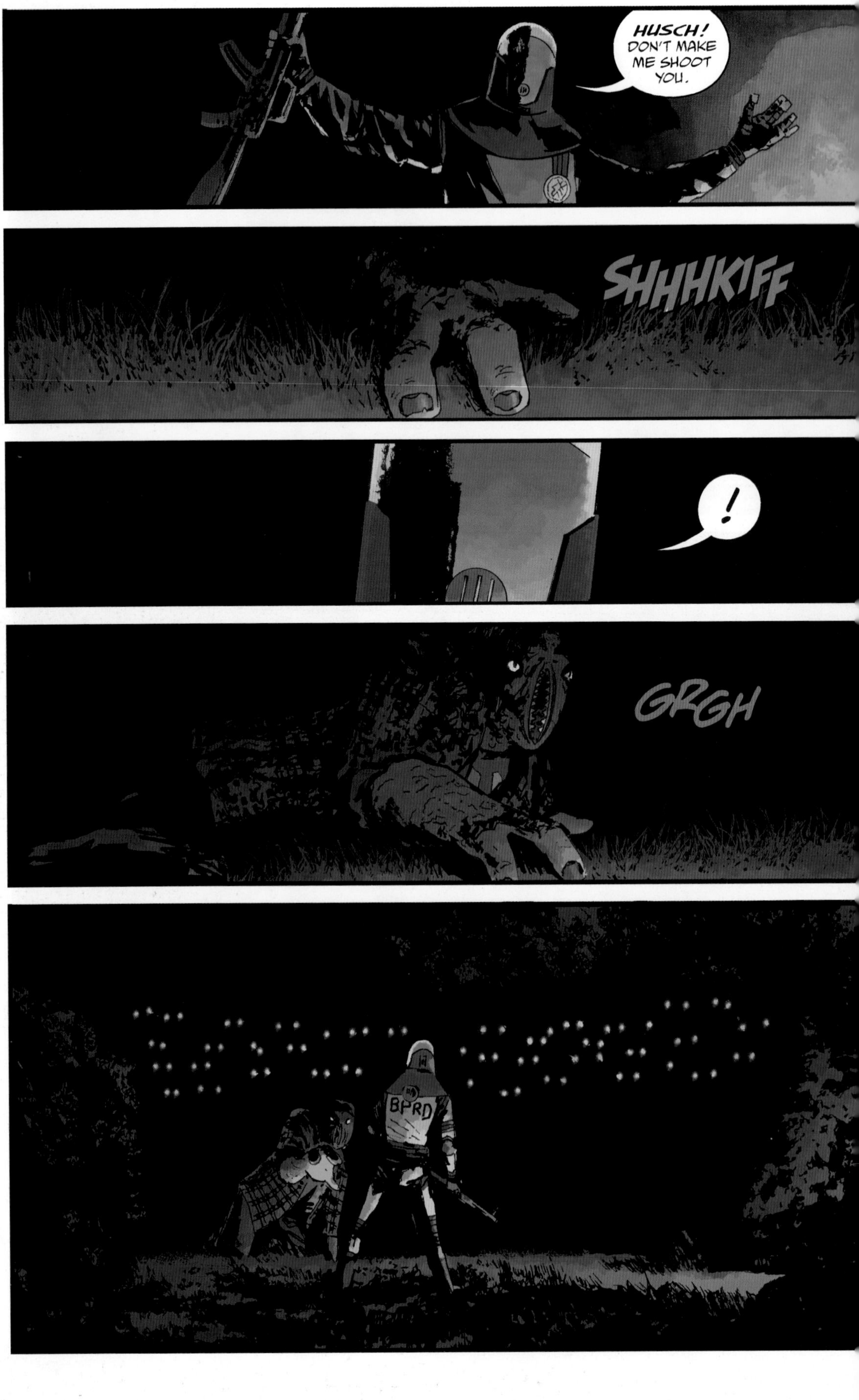
HUSCH! DON'T MAKE ME SHOOT YOU.
SHHHKIFF
!
GRGH
BPRD

# WASTELAND CHAPTER TWO

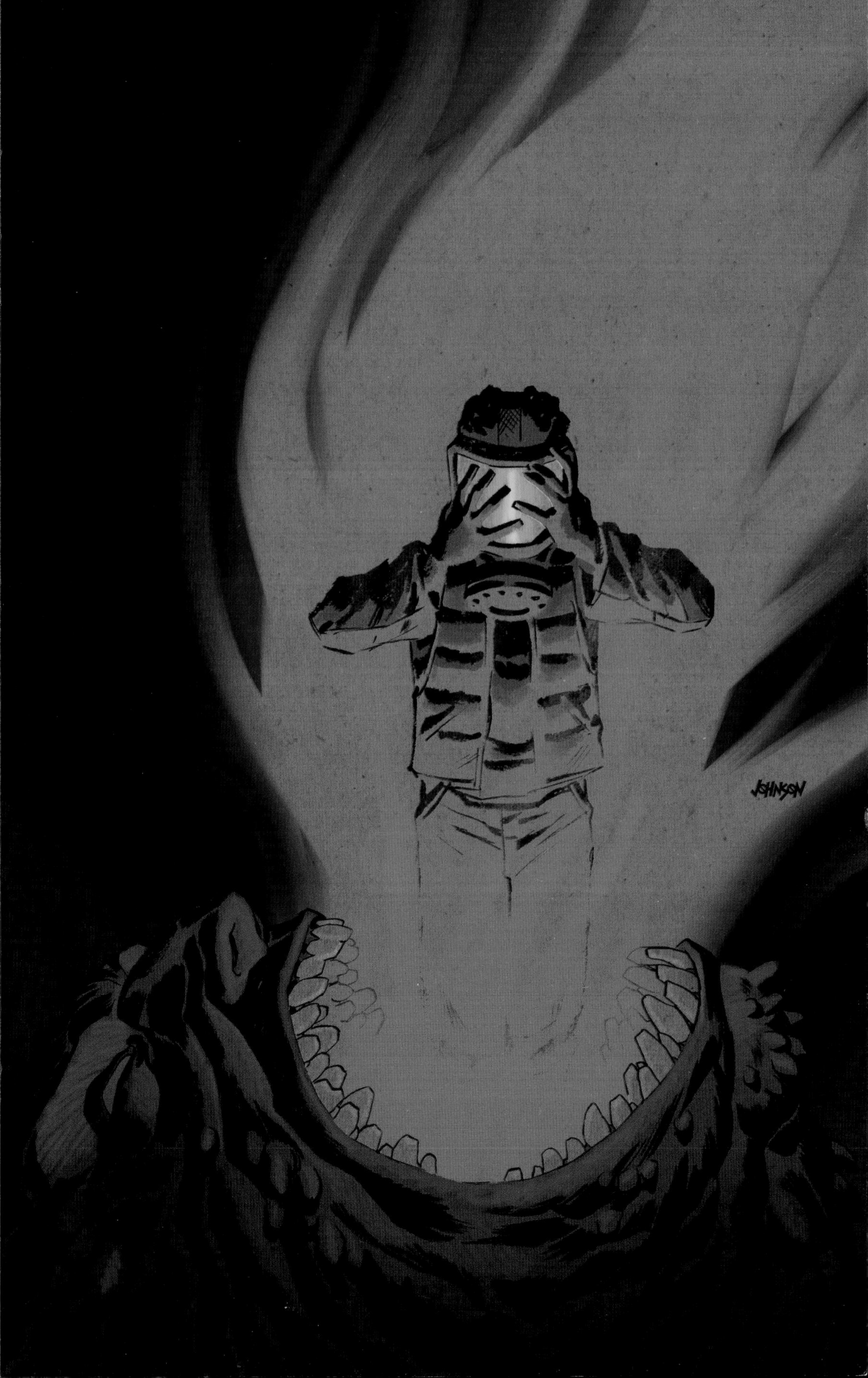
JOHNSON

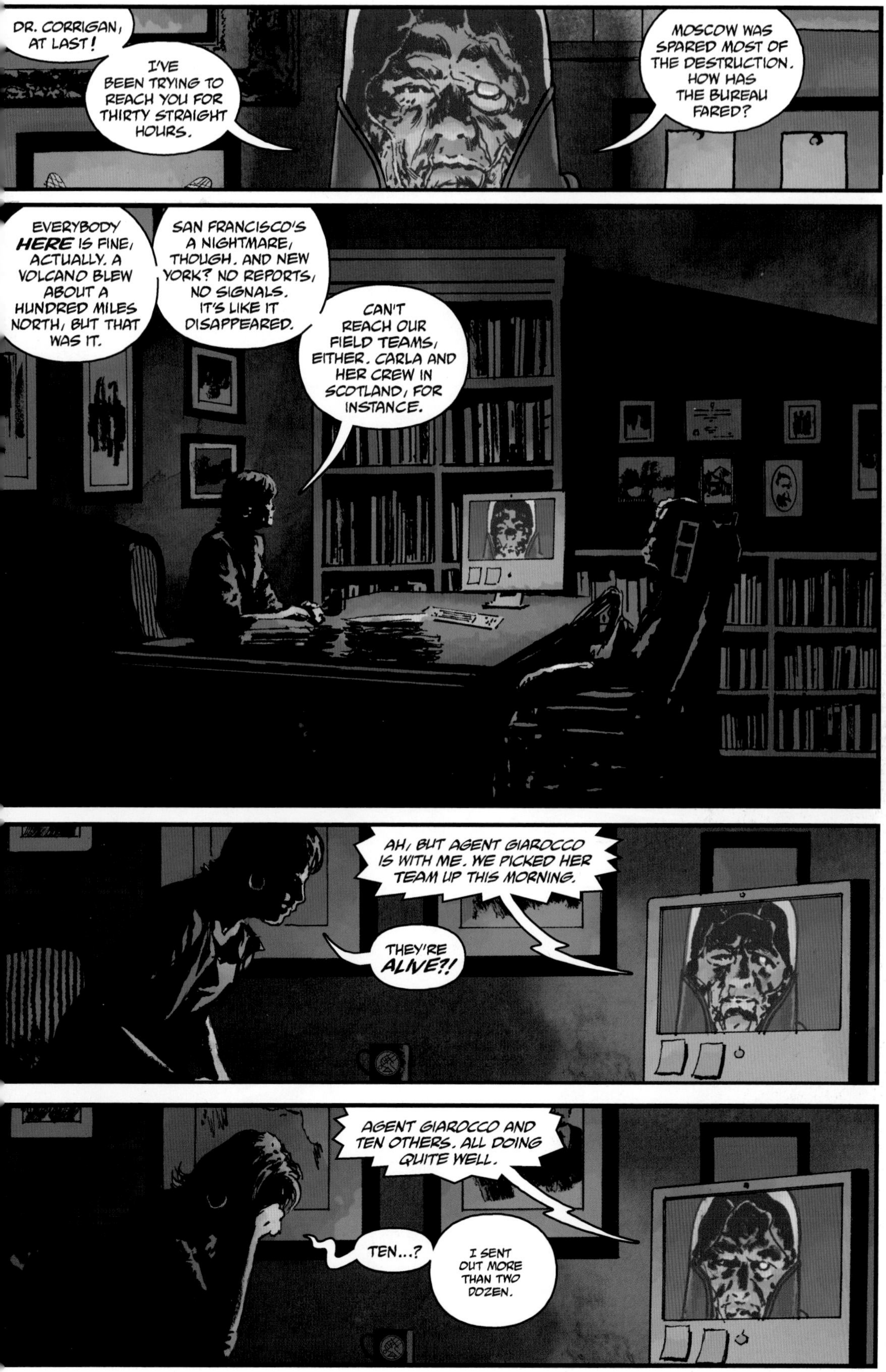

DR. CORRIGAN, AT LAST!
I'VE BEEN TRYING TO REACH YOU FOR THIRTY STRAIGHT HOURS.
MOSCOW WAS SPARED MOST OF THE DESTRUCTION. HOW HAS THE BUREAU FARED?
EVERYBODY **HERE** IS FINE, ACTUALLY. A VOLCANO BLEW ABOUT A HUNDRED MILES NORTH, BUT THAT WAS IT.
SAN FRANCISCO'S A NIGHTMARE, THOUGH. AND NEW YORK? NO REPORTS, NO SIGNALS. IT'S LIKE IT DISAPPEARED.
CAN'T REACH OUR FIELD TEAMS, EITHER. CARLA AND HER CREW IN SCOTLAND, FOR INSTANCE.
*AH, BUT AGENT GIAROCCO IS WITH ME. WE PICKED HER TEAM UP THIS MORNING.*
THEY'RE ***ALIVE?!***
*AGENT GIAROCCO AND TEN OTHERS. ALL DOING QUITE WELL.*
TEN...?
I SENT OUT MORE THAN TWO DOZEN.

TEN IS BETTER THAN NINE. IT'S A PHILOSOPHY THAT WILL SERVE US WELL GOING FORWARD.

YOU'RE RIGHT, YES. AND THANK YOU. THANK YOU FOR PICKING THEM UP.

THAT MAN LAZAR, THE ONE CARLA WAS AFTER, IS THERE ANY EVIDENCE *HE* HAD ANYTHING TO DO WITH THIS CATACLYSM?

NONE. LAZAR IS DEAD. KILLED BY AN ERUPTION RIGHT THERE IN THE HIGHLANDS AS AGENT GIAROCCO WATCHED.

IF ANY ONE THING *DID* CAUSE THIS, WE MAY NEVER KNOW WHAT IT WAS.

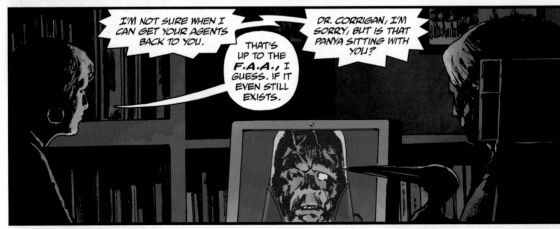

I'M NOT SURE WHEN I CAN GET YOUR AGENTS BACK TO YOU.

THAT'S UP TO THE *F.A.A.*, I GUESS. IF IT EVEN STILL EXISTS.

DR. CORRIGAN, I'M SORRY, BUT IS THAT PANYA SITTING WITH YOU?

YES, DIRECTOR NICHAYKO. AWFUL CIRCUMSTANCES UNDER WHICH TO MEET.

BUT I'M HAPPY WE DO MEET NONETHELESS. JOHANN TOLD ME QUITE A BIT ABOUT YOU WHEN HE WAS HERE.

JOHANN...

I'M SORRY, DR. CORRIGAN--

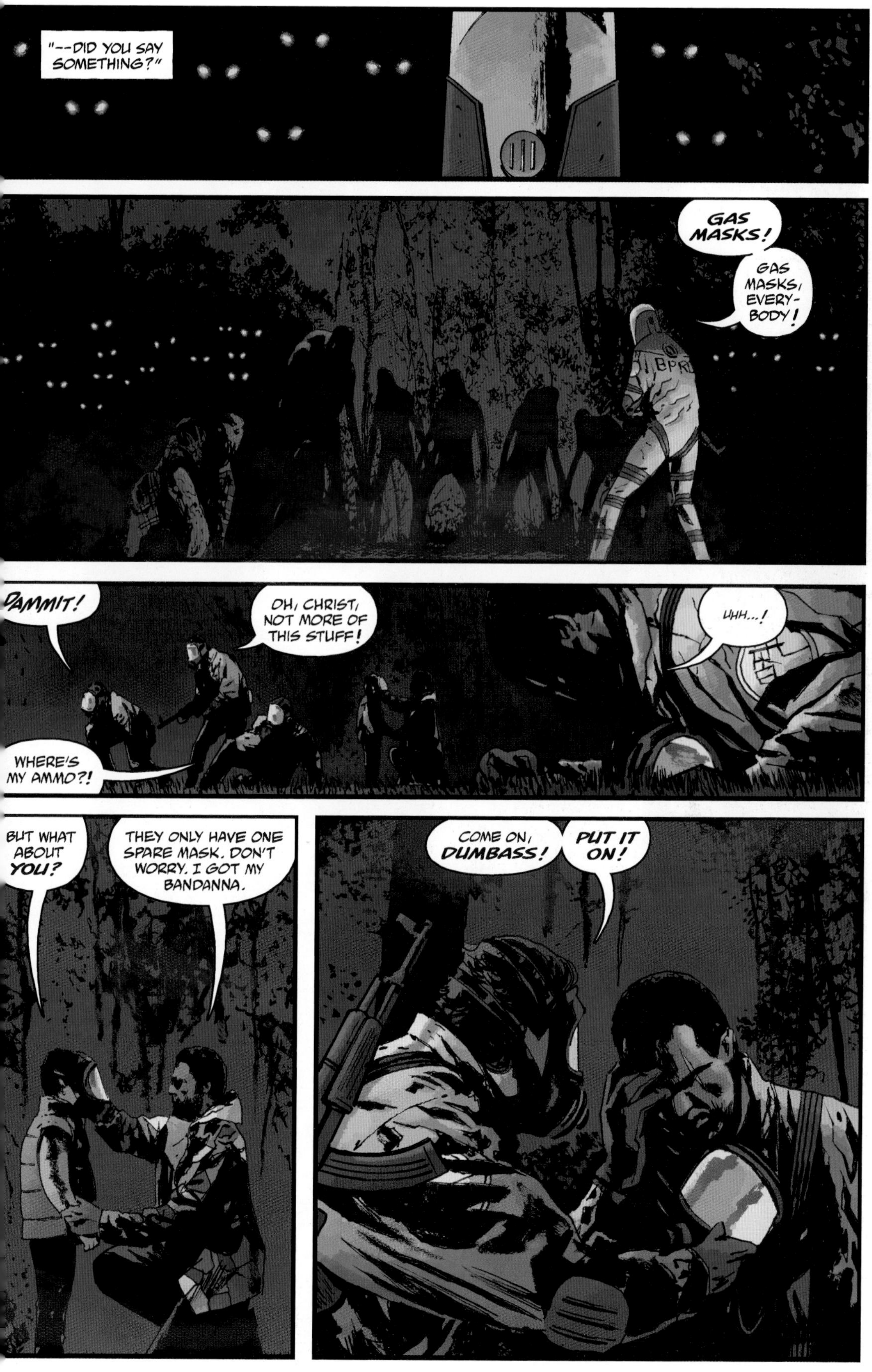
"--DID YOU SAY SOMETHING?"
GAS MASKS!
GAS MASKS, EVERY-BODY!
DAMMIT!
OH, CHRIST, NOT MORE OF THIS STUFF!
UHH...!
WHERE'S MY AMMO?!
BUT WHAT ABOUT YOU?
THEY ONLY HAVE ONE SPARE MASK. DON'T WORRY. I GOT MY BANDANNA.
COME ON, DUMBASS!
PUT IT ON!

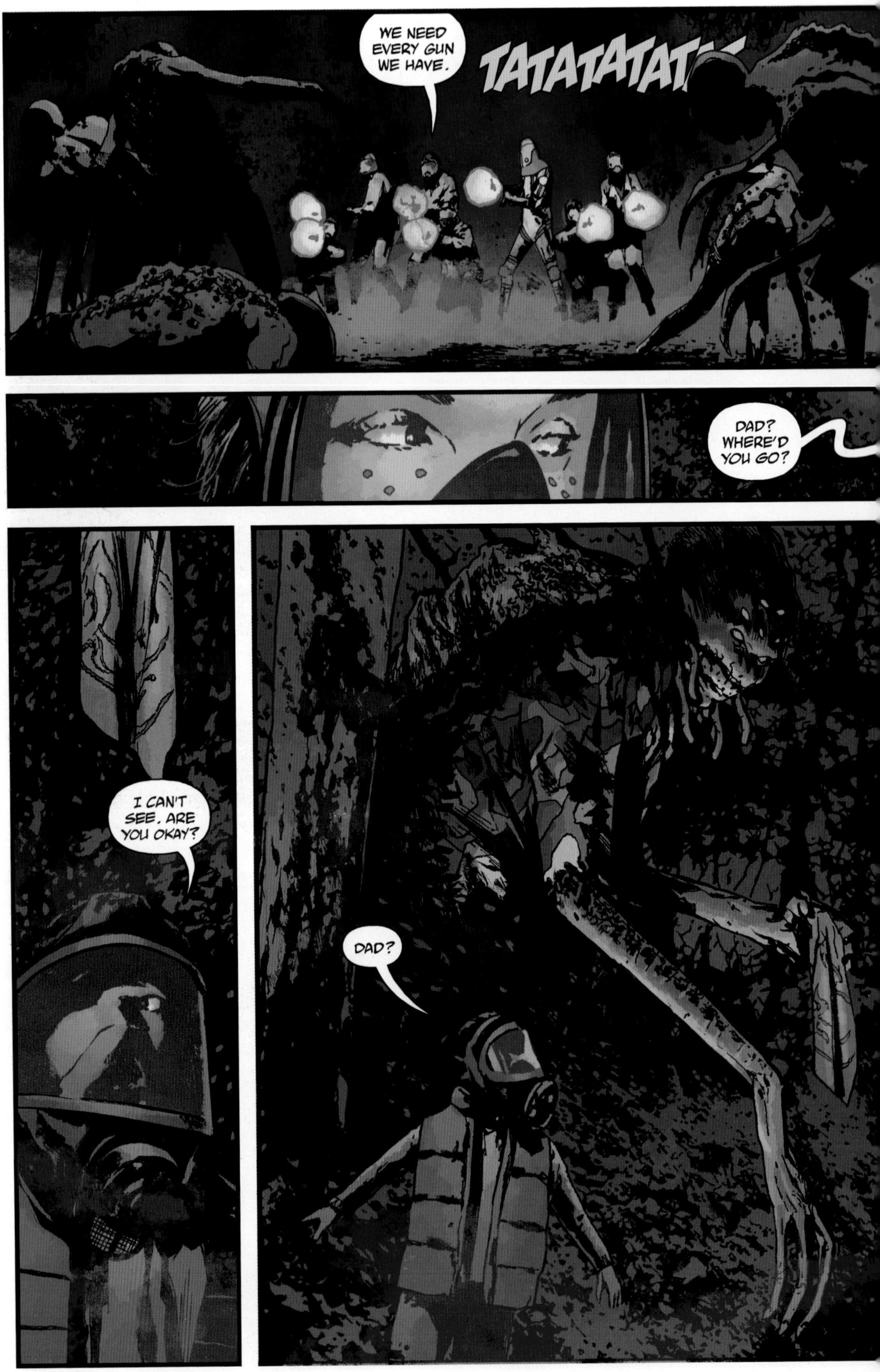
WE NEED EVERY GUN WE HAVE.
TATATATATAT
DAD? WHERE'D YOU GO?
I CAN'T SEE. ARE YOU OKAY?
DAD?

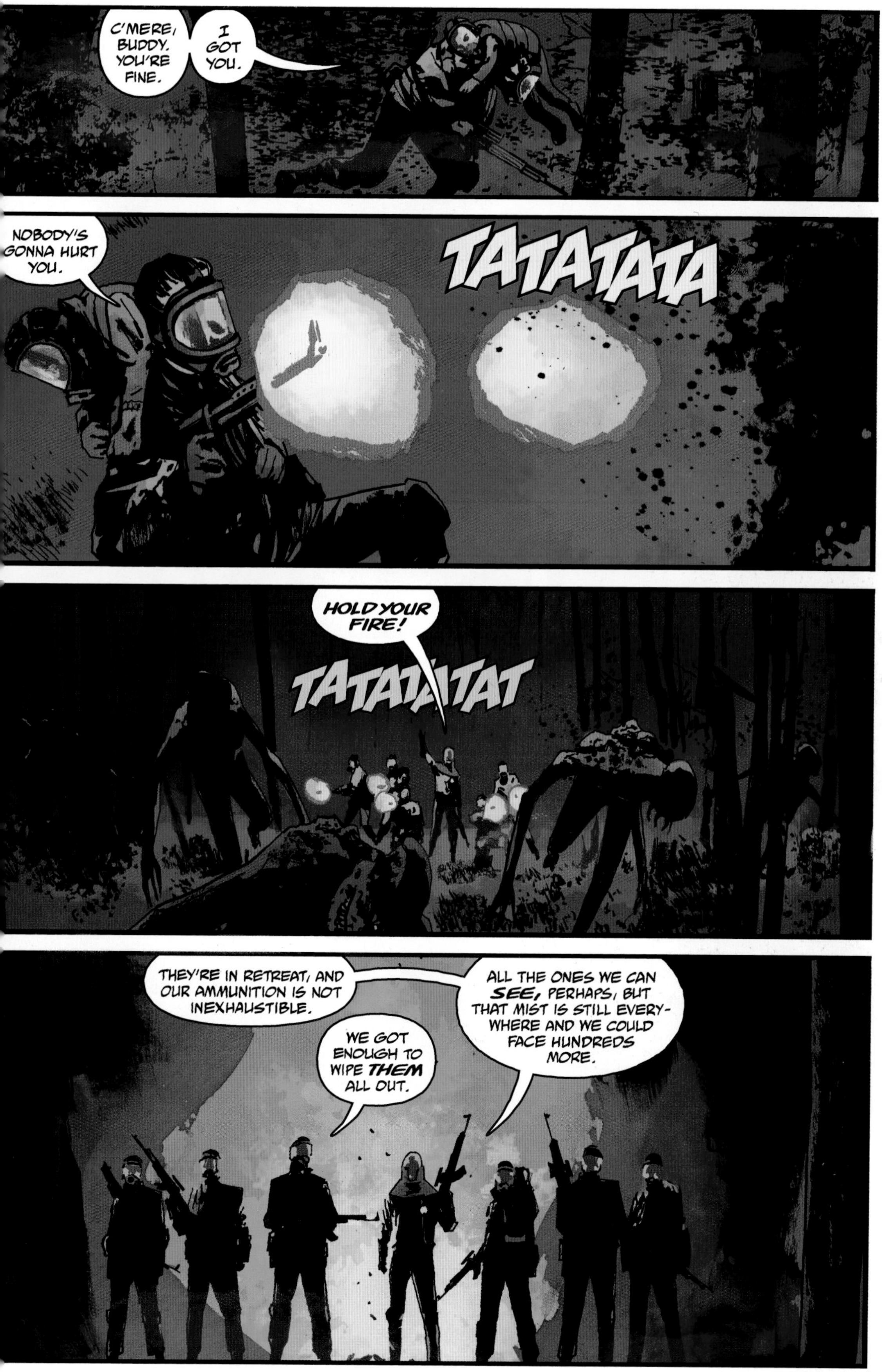
C'MERE, BUDDY. YOU'RE FINE.
I GOT YOU.
NOBODY'S GONNA HURT YOU.
TATATATA
HOLD YOUR FIRE!
TATATATAT
THEY'RE IN RETREAT, AND OUR AMMUNITION IS NOT INEXHAUSTIBLE.
WE GOT ENOUGH TO WIPE THEM ALL OUT.
ALL THE ONES WE CAN SEE, PERHAPS, BUT THAT MIST IS STILL EVERY-WHERE AND WE COULD FACE HUNDREDS MORE.

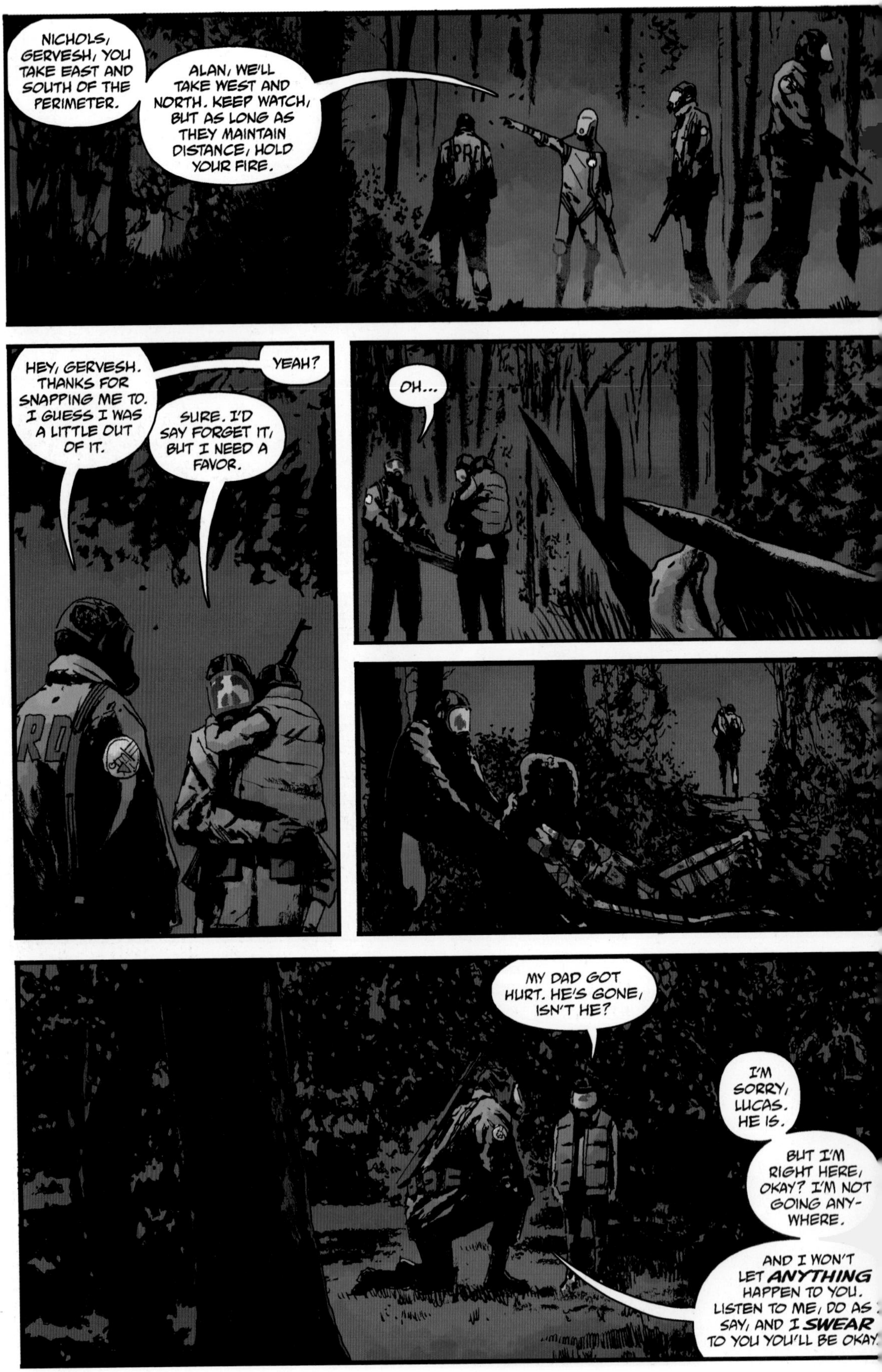
NICHOLS, GERVESH, YOU TAKE EAST AND SOUTH OF THE PERIMETER.
ALAN, WE'LL TAKE WEST AND NORTH. KEEP WATCH, BUT AS LONG AS THEY MAINTAIN DISTANCE, HOLD YOUR FIRE.
HEY, GERVESH. THANKS FOR SNAPPING ME TO. I GUESS I WAS A LITTLE OUT OF IT.
YEAH?
SURE. I'D SAY FORGET IT, BUT I NEED A FAVOR.
OH...
MY DAD GOT HURT. HE'S GONE, ISN'T HE?
I'M SORRY, LUCAS. HE IS.
BUT I'M RIGHT HERE, OKAY? I'M NOT GOING ANY-WHERE.
AND I WON'T LET ANYTHING HAPPEN TO YOU. LISTEN TO ME, DO AS I SAY, AND I SWEAR TO YOU YOU'LL BE OKAY.

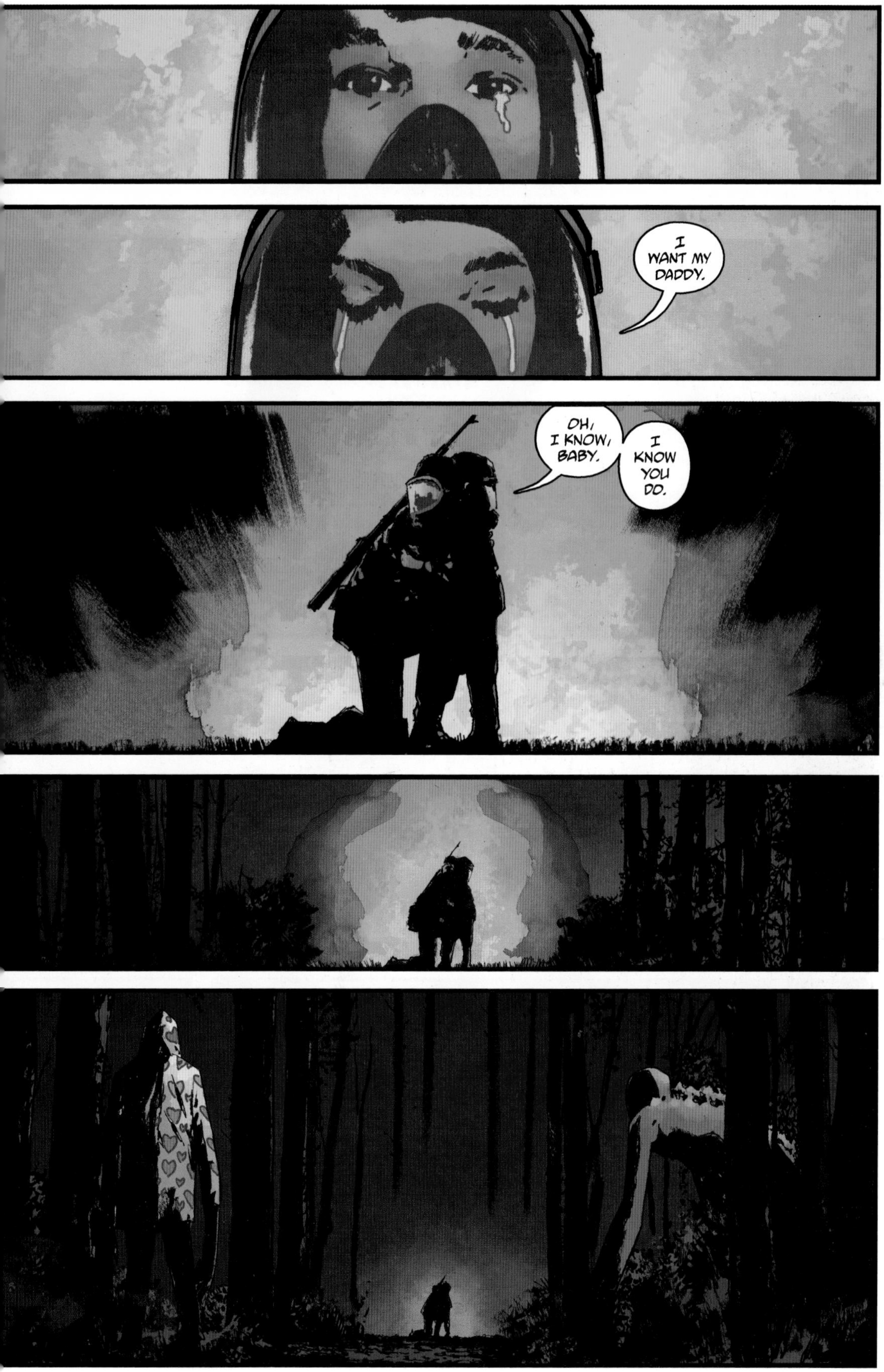
I WANT MY DADDY.
OH, I KNOW, BABY.
I KNOW YOU DO.

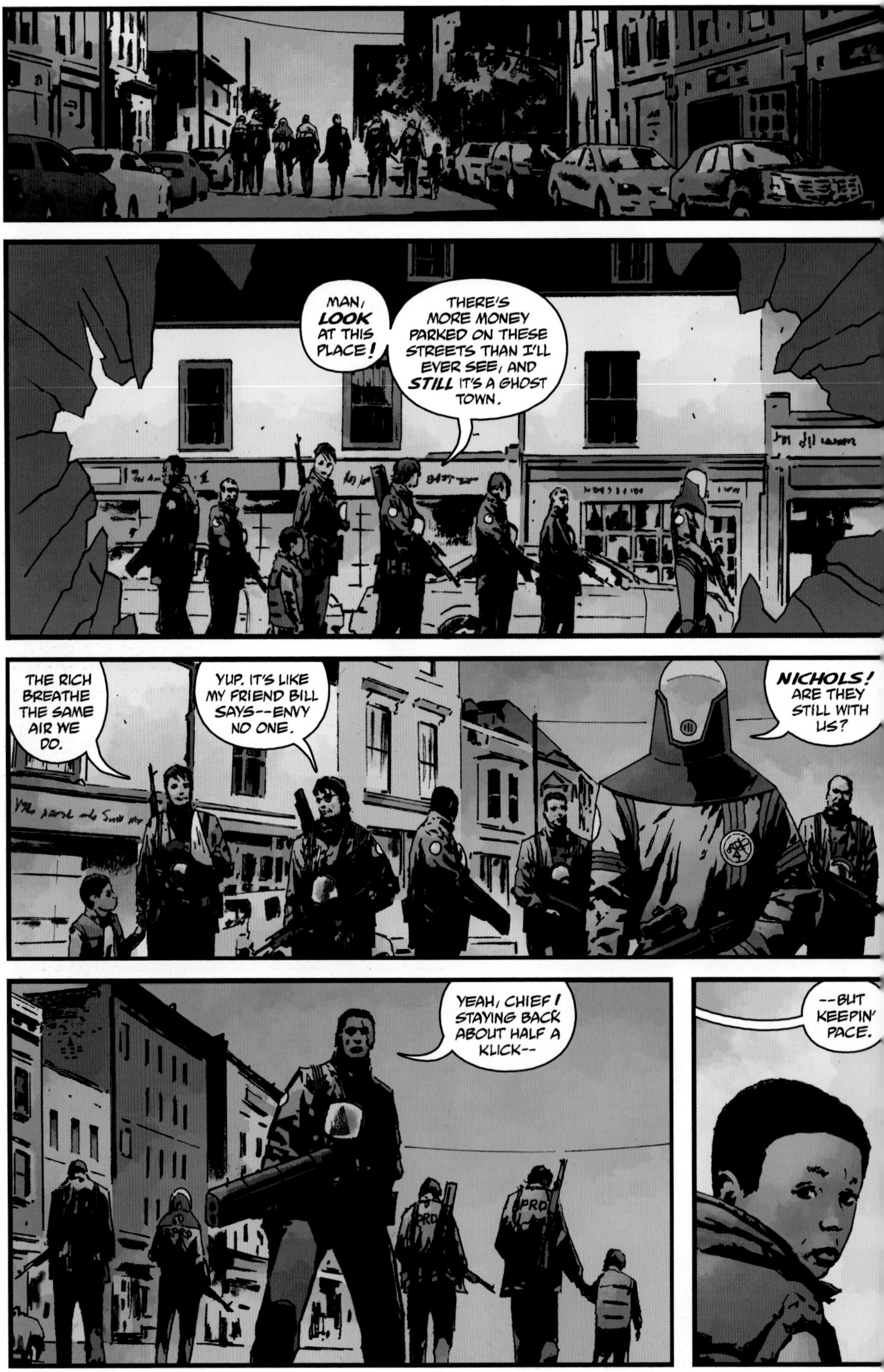
MAN, LOOK AT THIS PLACE!
THERE'S MORE MONEY PARKED ON THESE STREETS THAN I'LL EVER SEE, AND STILL IT'S A GHOST TOWN.
THE RICH BREATHE THE SAME AIR WE DO.
YUP. IT'S LIKE MY FRIEND BILL SAYS--ENVY NO ONE.
NICHOLS! ARE THEY STILL WITH US?
YEAH, CHIEF! STAYING BACK ABOUT HALF A KLICK--
--BUT KEEPIN' PACE.

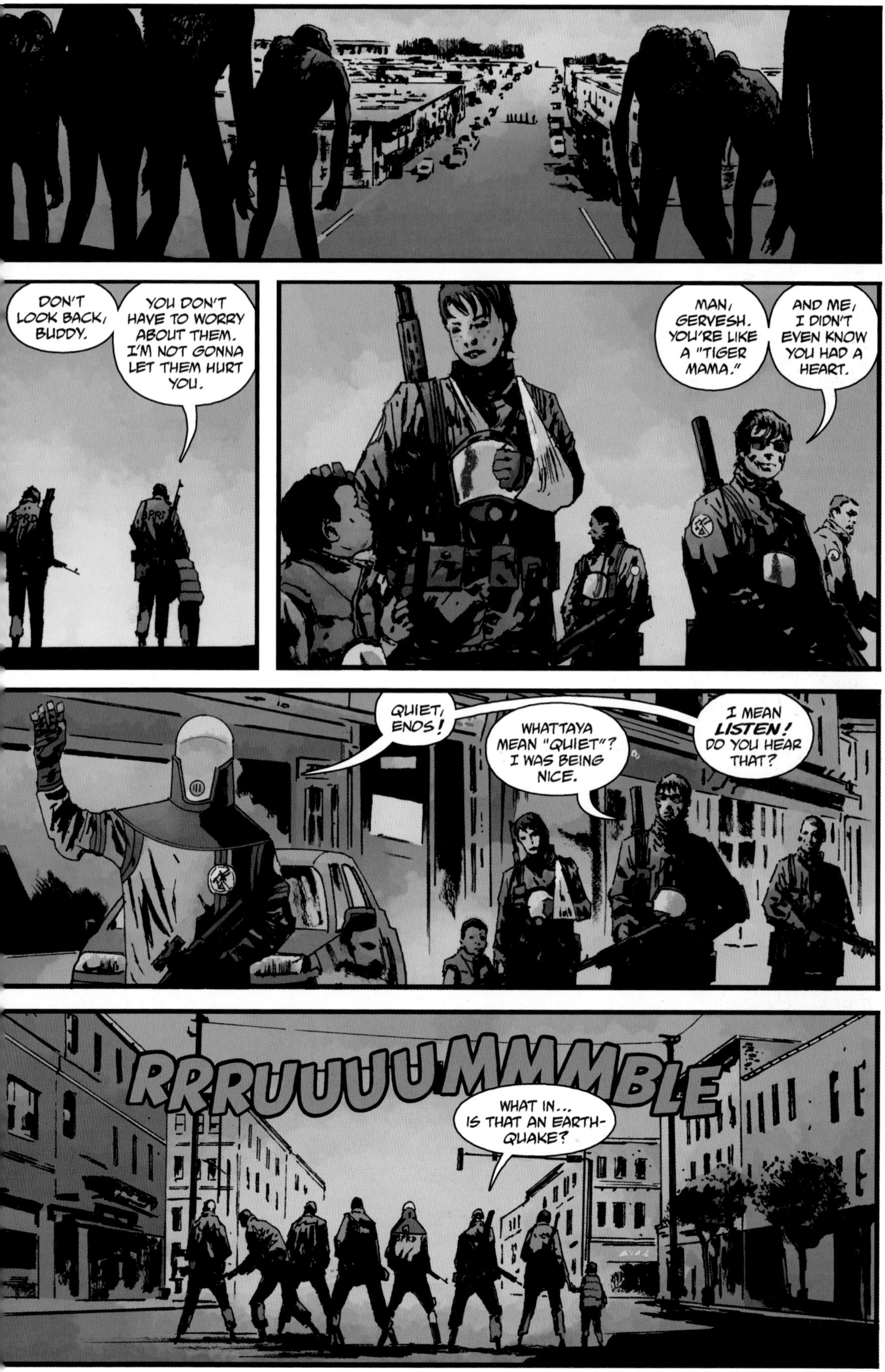
DON'T LOOK BACK, BUDDY.
YOU DON'T HAVE TO WORRY ABOUT THEM. I'M NOT GONNA LET THEM HURT YOU.
MAN, GERVESH. YOU'RE LIKE A "TIGER MAMA."
AND ME, I DIDN'T EVEN KNOW YOU HAD A HEART.
QUIET, ENOS!
WHATTAYA MEAN "QUIET"? I WAS BEING NICE.
I MEAN LISTEN! DO YOU HEAR THAT?
RRRUUUUUMMMMBLE
WHAT IN... IS THAT AN EARTH-QUAKE?

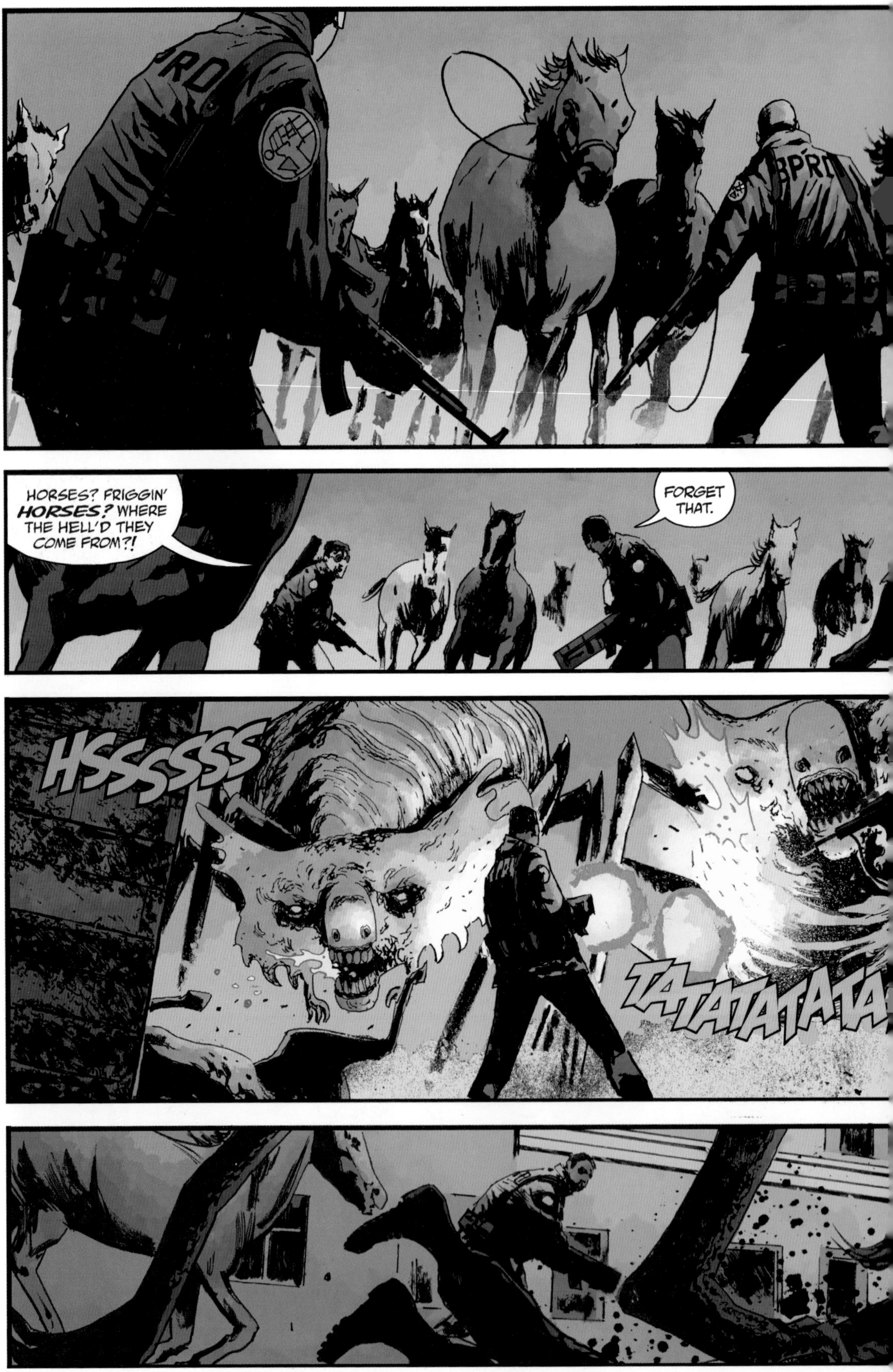
HORSES? FRIGGIN' HORSES? WHERE THE HELL'D THEY COME FROM?!
FORGET THAT.
HSSSSSS
TATATATATA

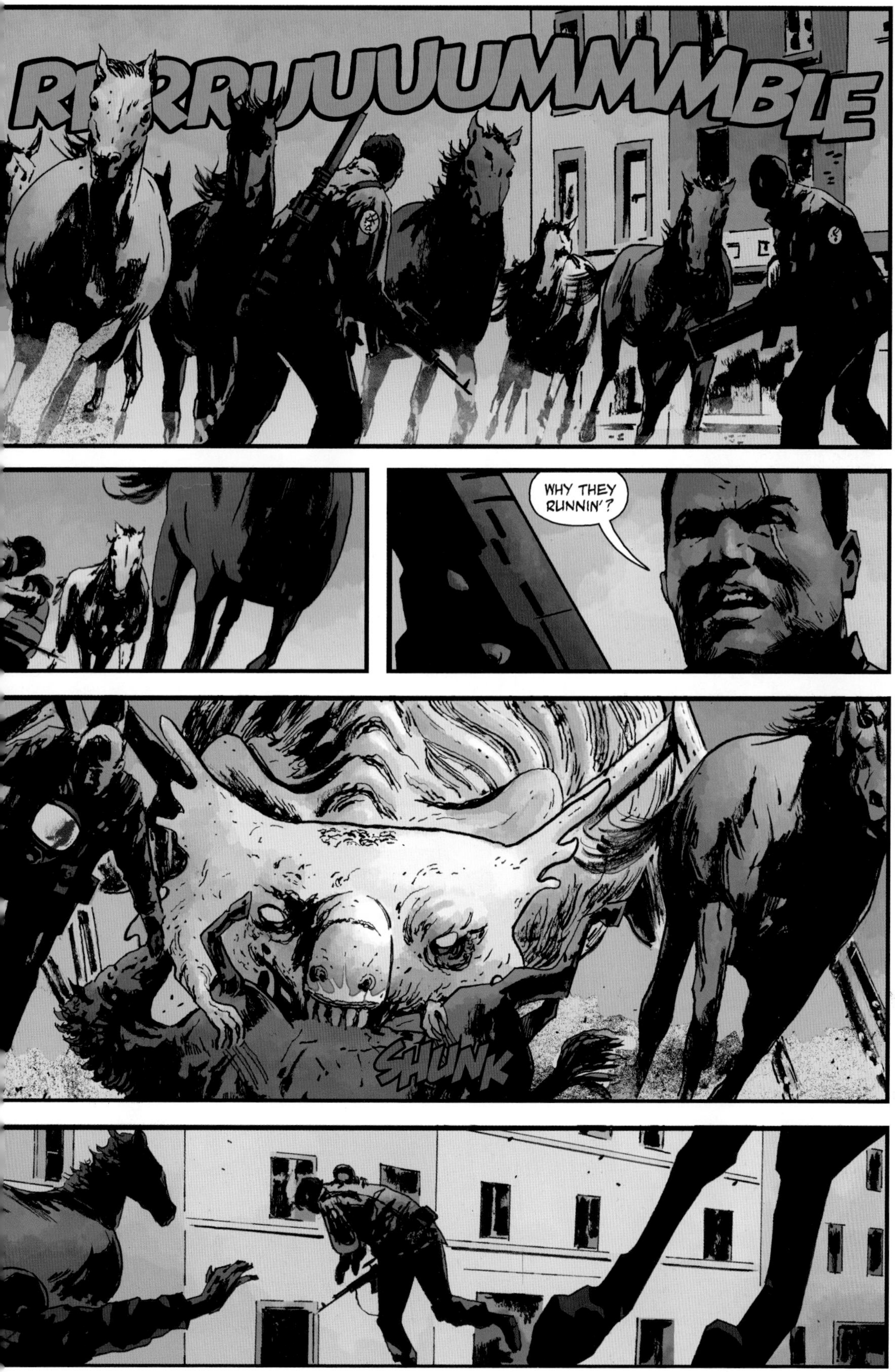
RRRRUUUUMMMMBLE
WHY THEY RUNNIN'?
SHUNK

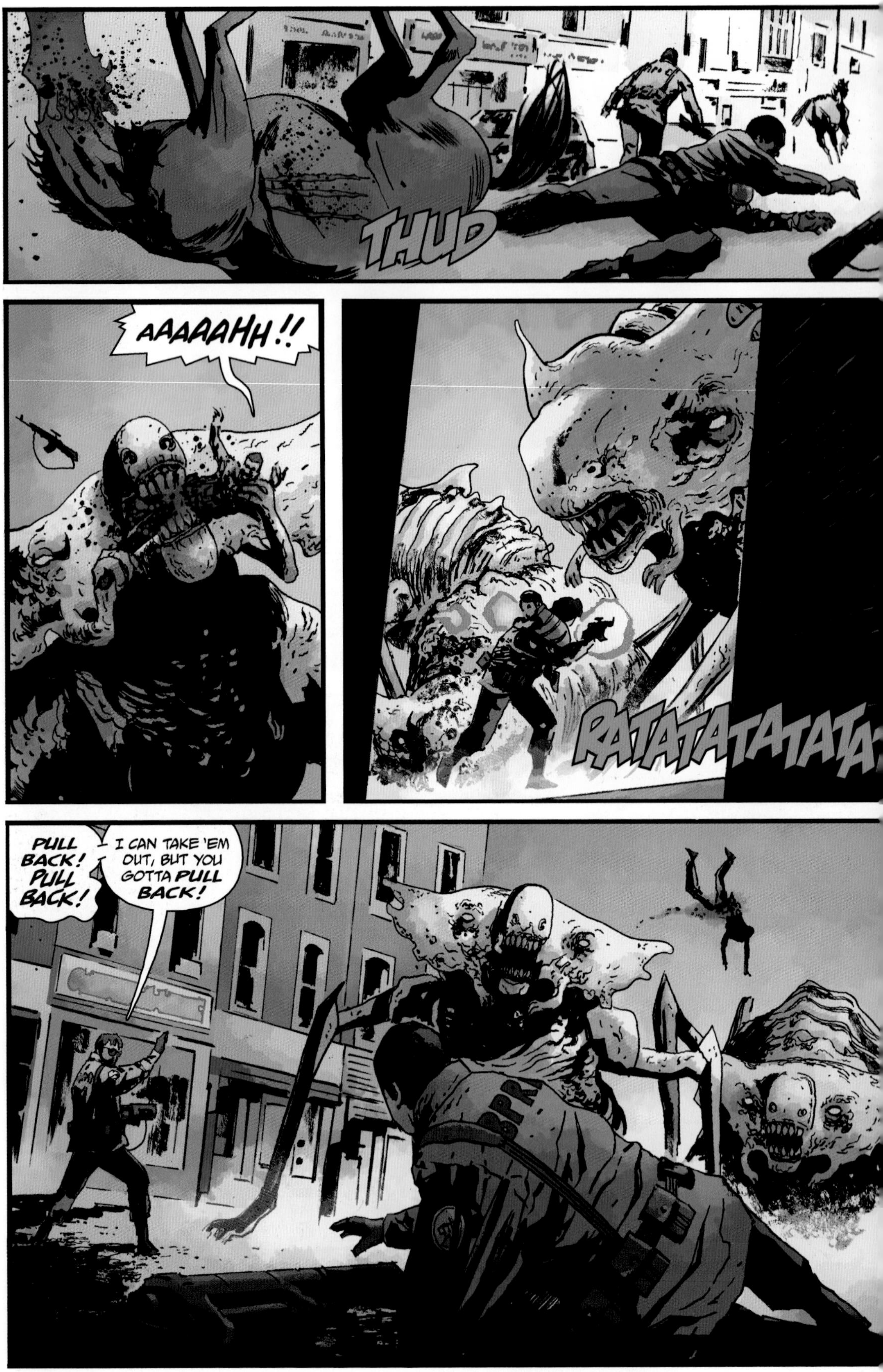
THUD
AAAAAHH!!
RATATATATATA
PULL BACK! PULL BACK!
I CAN TAKE 'EM OUT, BUT YOU GOTTA PULL BACK!

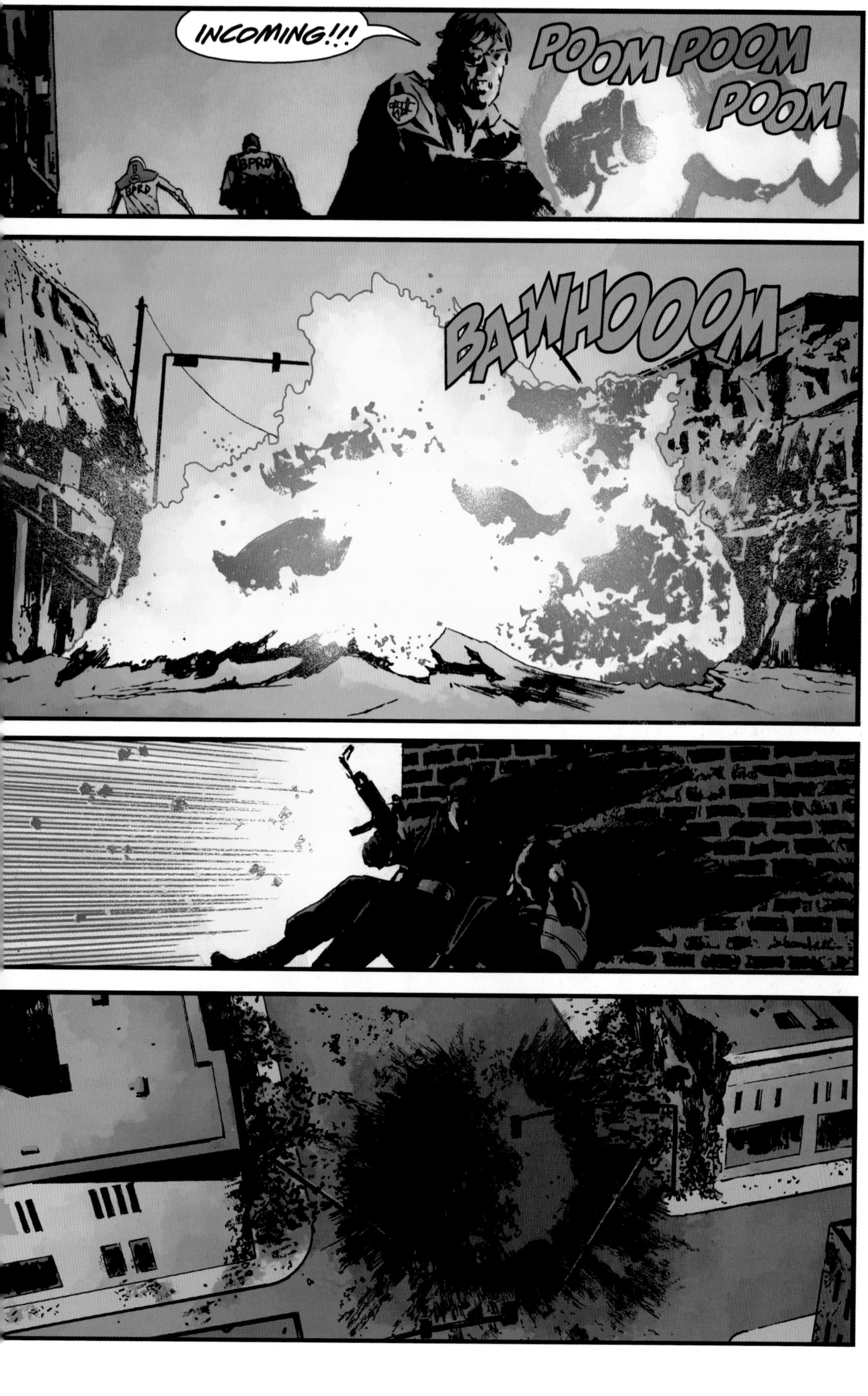
INCOMING!!!
POOM POOM
POOM
BA-WHOOOOM

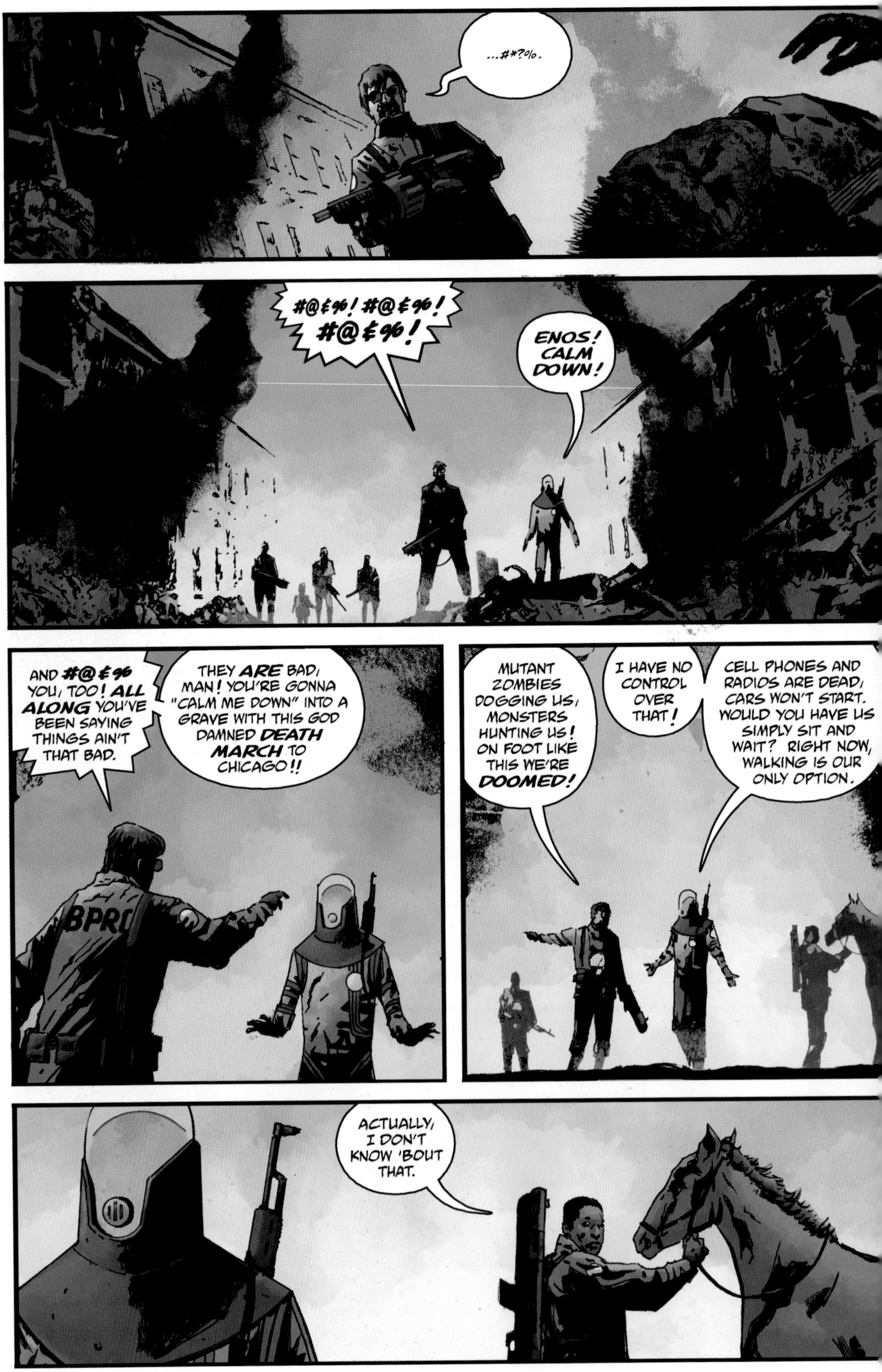
...#*?%.
#@&%! #@&%! #@&%!
ENOS! CALM DOWN!
AND #@&% YOU, TOO! ALL ALONG YOU'VE BEEN SAYING THINGS AIN'T THAT BAD.
THEY ARE BAD, MAN! YOU'RE GONNA "CALM ME DOWN" INTO A GRAVE WITH THIS GOD DAMNED DEATH MARCH TO CHICAGO!!
MUTANT ZOMBIES DOGGING US, MONSTERS HUNTING US! ON FOOT LIKE THIS WE'RE DOOMED!
I HAVE NO CONTROL OVER THAT!
CELL PHONES AND RADIOS ARE DEAD, CARS WON'T START. WOULD YOU HAVE US SIMPLY SIT AND WAIT? RIGHT NOW, WALKING IS OUR ONLY OPTION.
ACTUALLY, I DON'T KNOW 'BOUT THAT.

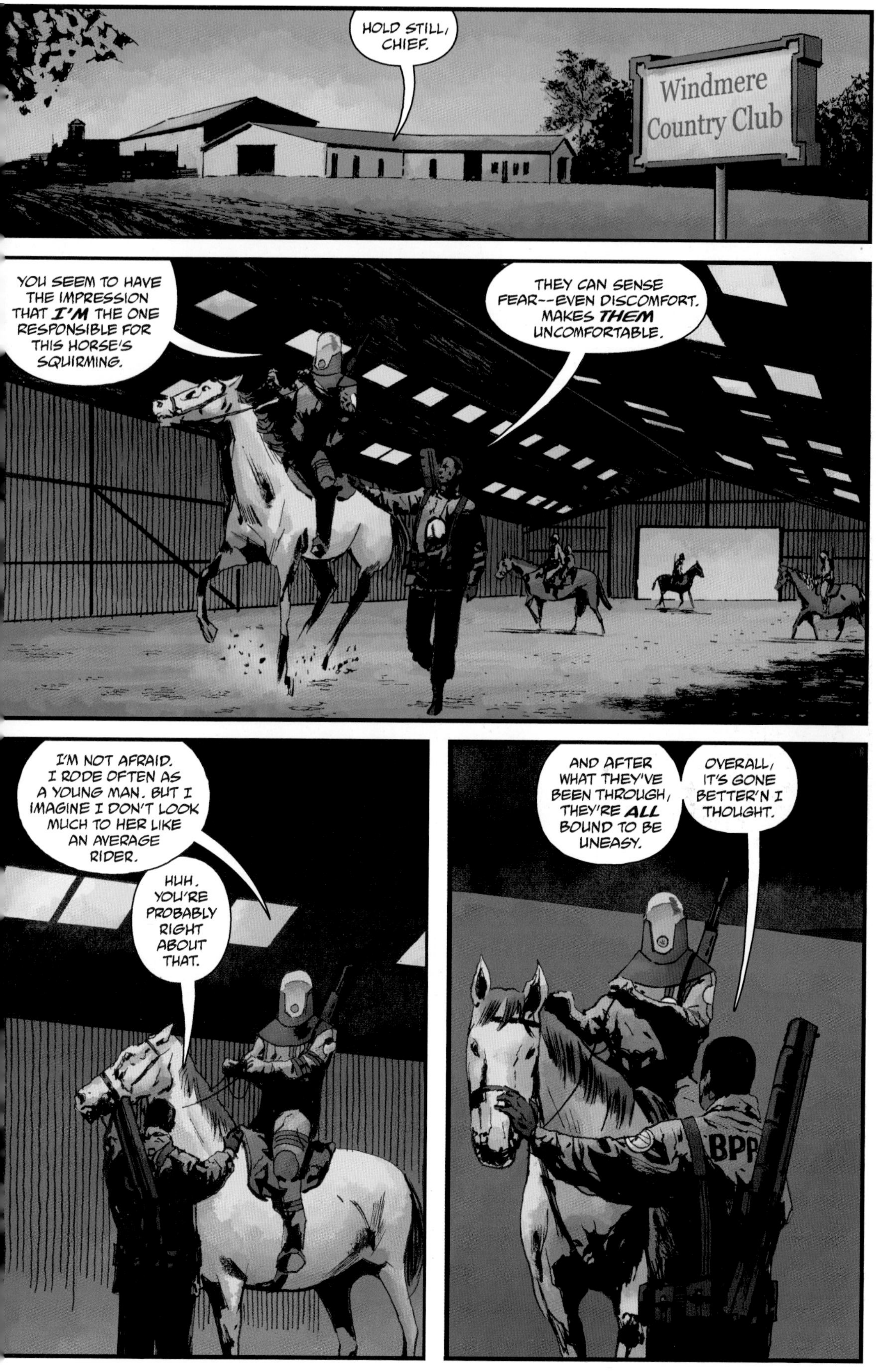

HOLD STILL, CHIEF.
Windmere Country Club
YOU SEEM TO HAVE THE IMPRESSION THAT I'M THE ONE RESPONSIBLE FOR THIS HORSE'S SQUIRMING.
THEY CAN SENSE FEAR--EVEN DISCOMFORT. MAKES THEM UNCOMFORTABLE.
I'M NOT AFRAID. I RODE OFTEN AS A YOUNG MAN. BUT I IMAGINE I DON'T LOOK MUCH TO HER LIKE AN AVERAGE RIDER.
HUH. YOU'RE PROBABLY RIGHT ABOUT THAT.
AND AFTER WHAT THEY'VE BEEN THROUGH, THEY'RE ALL BOUND TO BE UNEASY.
OVERALL, IT'S GONE BETTER'N I THOUGHT.
BPR

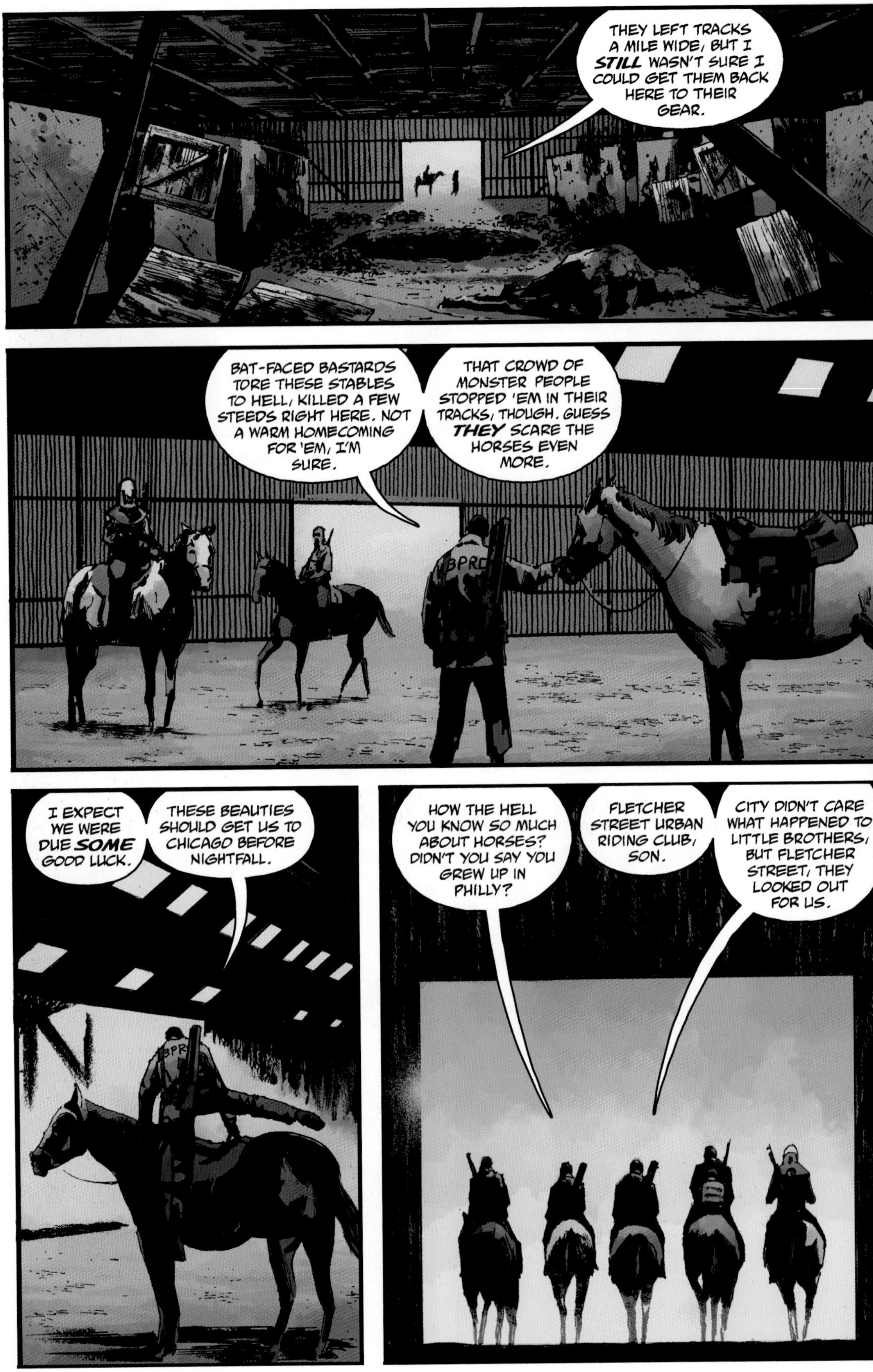
THEY LEFT TRACKS A MILE WIDE, BUT I STILL WASN'T SURE I COULD GET THEM BACK HERE TO THEIR GEAR.
BAT-FACED BASTARDS TORE THESE STABLES TO HELL, KILLED A FEW STEEDS RIGHT HERE. NOT A WARM HOMECOMING FOR 'EM, I'M SURE.
THAT CROWD OF MONSTER PEOPLE STOPPED 'EM IN THEIR TRACKS, THOUGH. GUESS THEY SCARE THE HORSES EVEN MORE.
BPRD
I EXPECT WE WERE DUE SOME GOOD LUCK.
THESE BEAUTIES SHOULD GET US TO CHICAGO BEFORE NIGHTFALL.
HOW THE HELL YOU KNOW SO MUCH ABOUT HORSES? DIDN'T YOU SAY YOU GREW UP IN PHILLY?
FLETCHER STREET URBAN RIDING CLUB, SON.
CITY DIDN'T CARE WHAT HAPPENED TO LITTLE BROTHERS, BUT FLETCHER STREET, THEY LOOKED OUT FOR US.

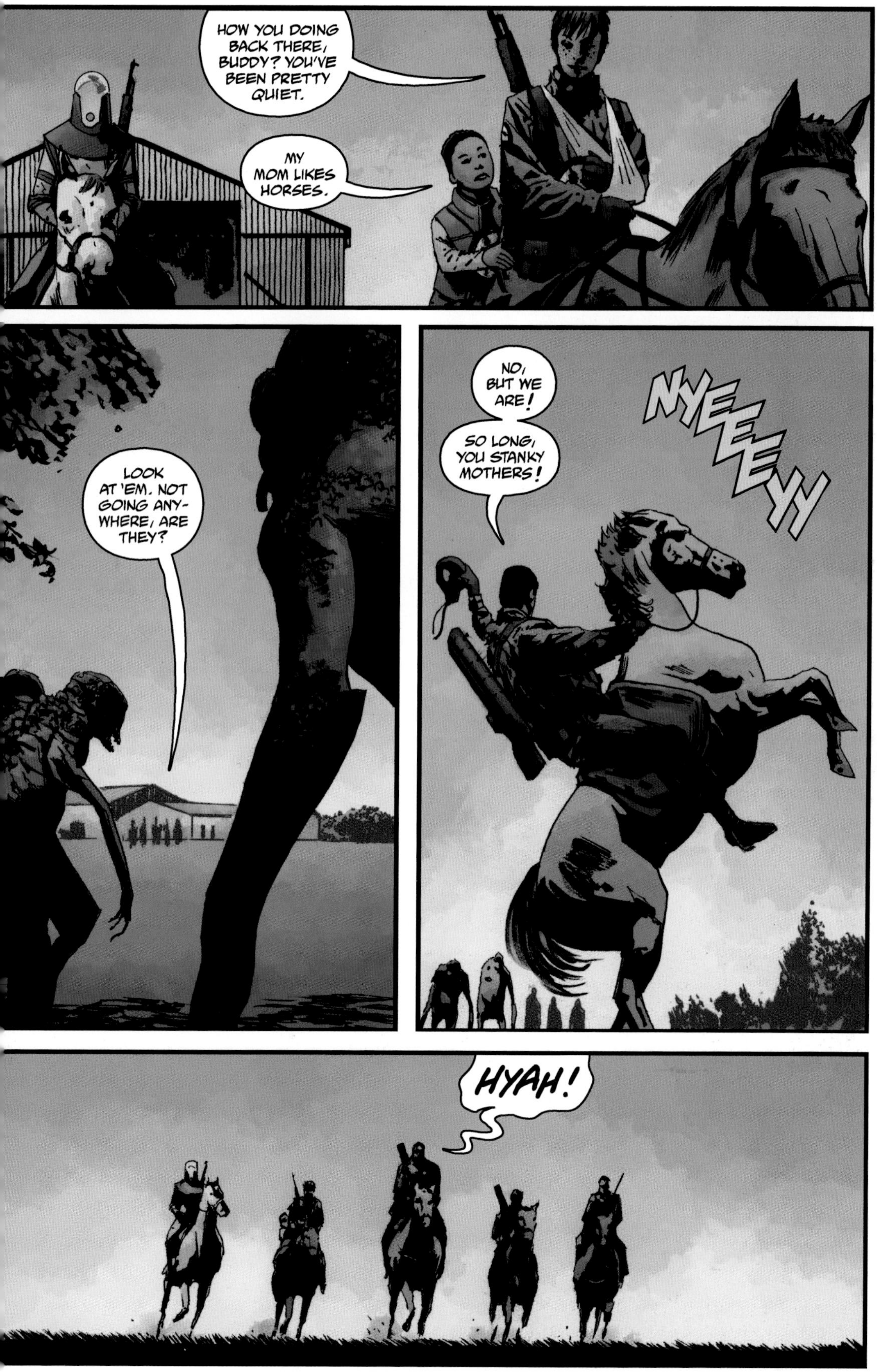
HOW YOU DOING BACK THERE, BUDDY? YOU'VE BEEN PRETTY QUIET.
MY MOM LIKES HORSES.
LOOK AT 'EM. NOT GOING ANY-WHERE, ARE THEY?
NO, BUT WE ARE!
SO LONG, YOU STANKY MOTHERS!
NYEEEEYY
HYAH!

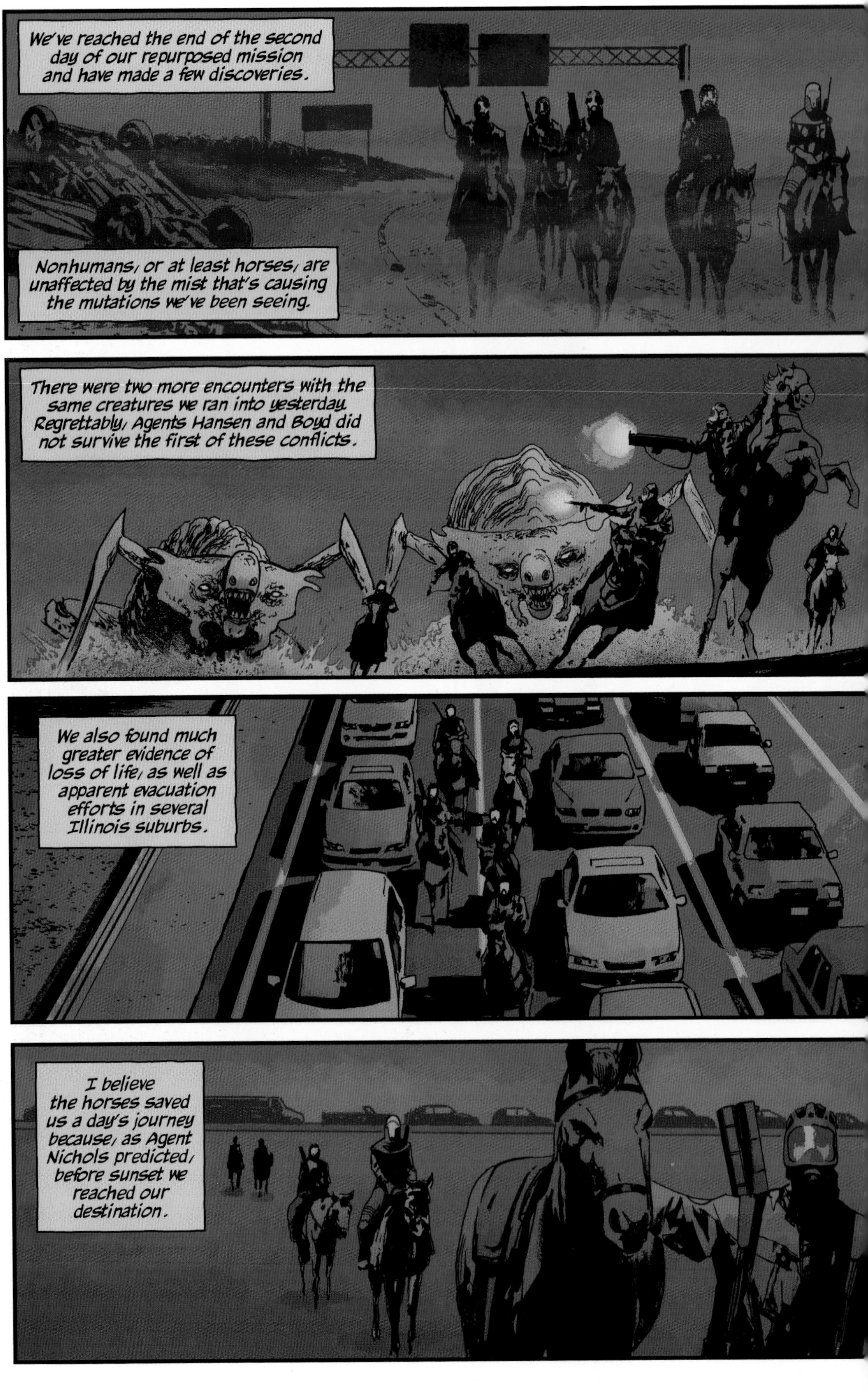
We've reached the end of the second day of our repurposed mission and have made a few discoveries.
Nonhumans, or at least horses, are unaffected by the mist that's causing the mutations we've been seeing.
There were two more encounters with the same creatures we ran into yesterday. Regrettably, Agents Hansen and Boyd did not survive the first of these conflicts.
We also found much greater evidence of loss of life, as well as apparent evacuation efforts in several Illinois suburbs.
I believe the horses saved us a day's journey because, as Agent Nichols predicted, before sunset we reached our destination.

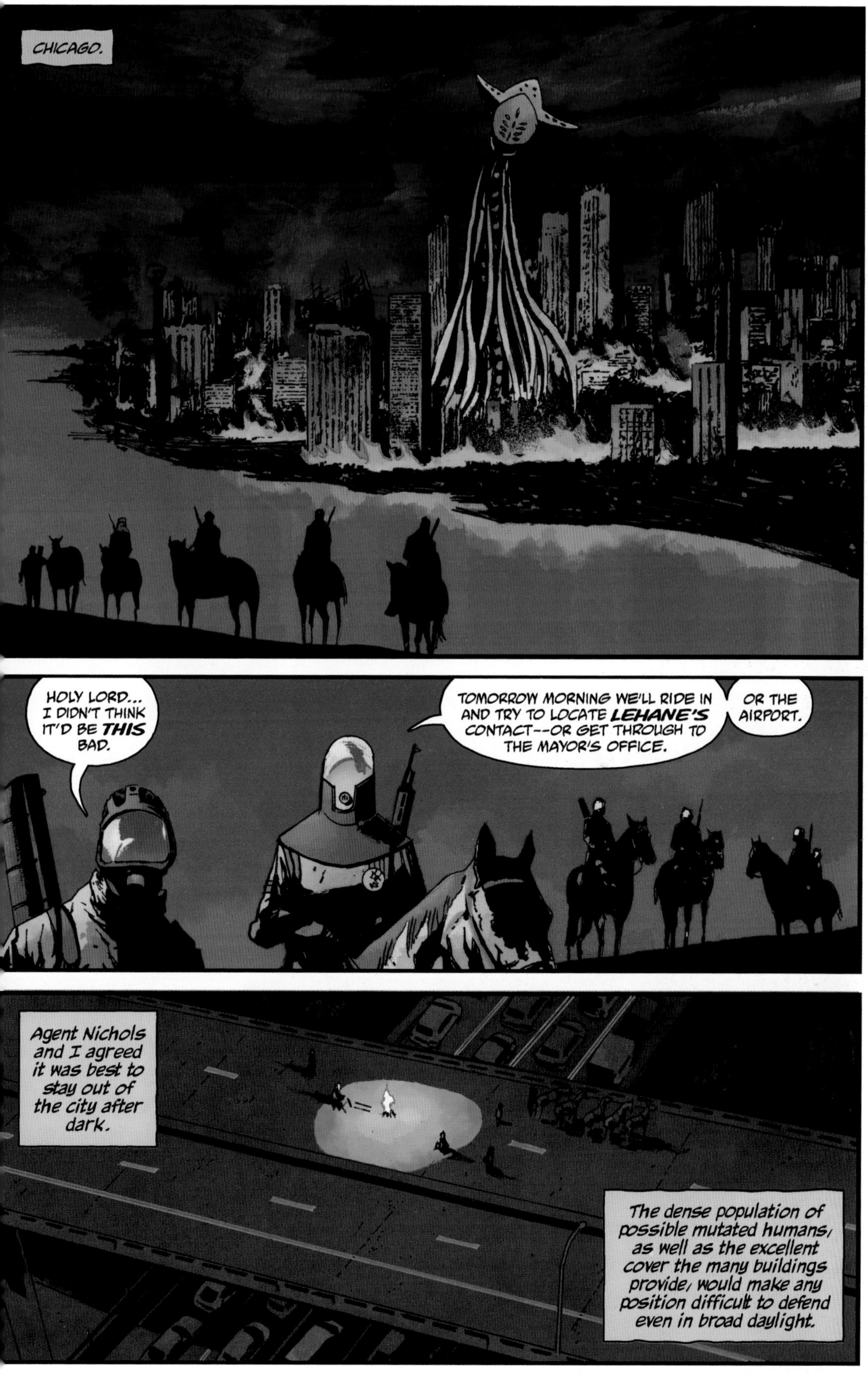
CHICAGO.
HOLY LORD... I DIDN'T THINK IT'D BE **THIS** BAD.
TOMORROW MORNING WE'LL RIDE IN AND TRY TO LOCATE **LEHANE'S** CONTACT--OR GET THROUGH TO THE MAYOR'S OFFICE.
OR THE AIRPORT.
Agent Nichols and I agreed it was best to stay out of the city after dark.
The dense population of possible mutated humans, as well as the excellent cover the many buildings provide, would make any position difficult to defend even in broad daylight.

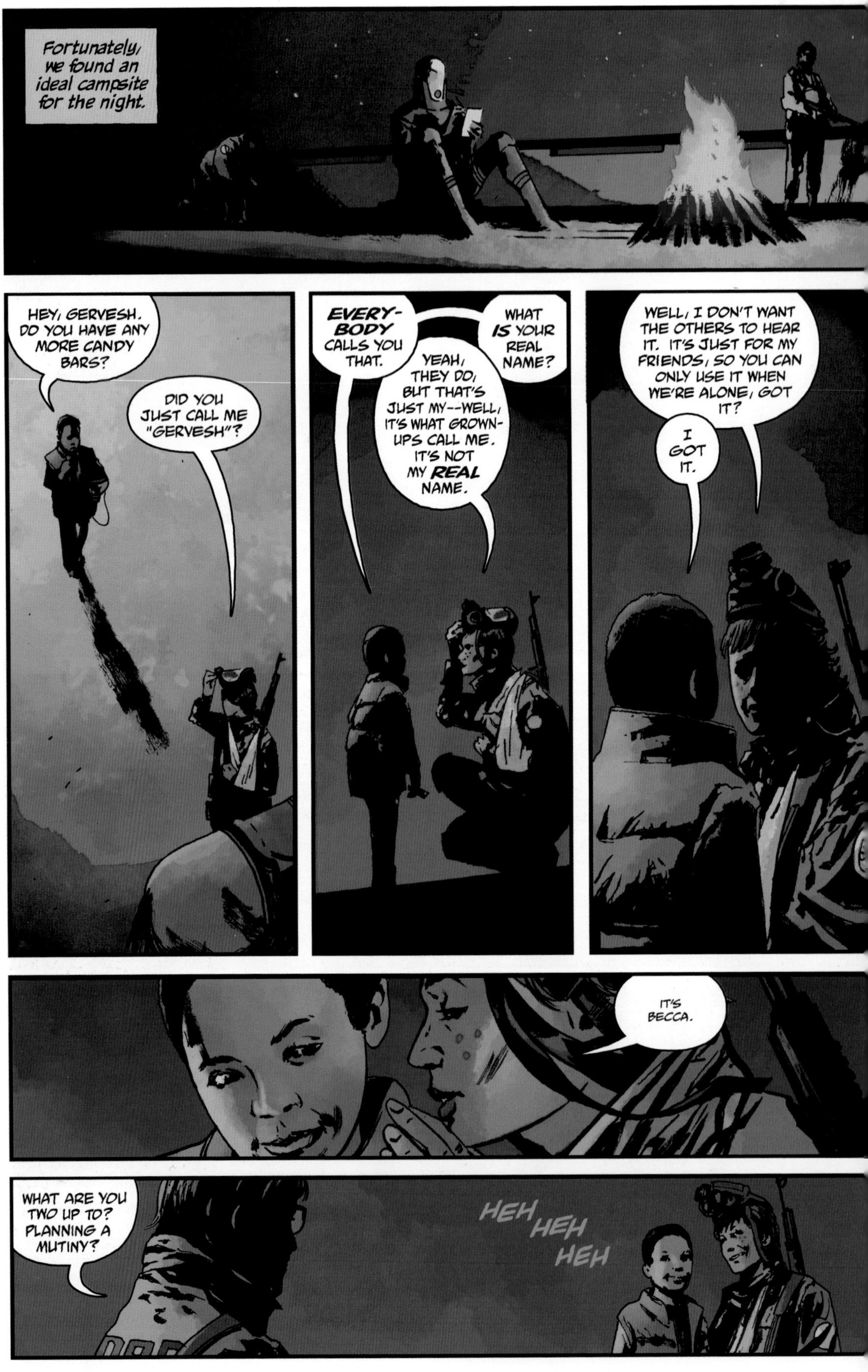
Fortunately, we found an ideal campsite for the night.
HEY, GERVESH. DO YOU HAVE ANY MORE CANDY BARS?
DID YOU JUST CALL ME "GERVESH"?
EVERY-BODY CALLS YOU THAT.
YEAH, THEY DO, BUT THAT'S JUST MY--WELL, IT'S WHAT GROWN-UPS CALL ME. IT'S NOT MY REAL NAME.
WHAT IS YOUR REAL NAME?
WELL, I DON'T WANT THE OTHERS TO HEAR IT. IT'S JUST FOR MY FRIENDS, SO YOU CAN ONLY USE IT WHEN WE'RE ALONE, GOT IT?
I GOT IT.
IT'S BECCA.
WHAT ARE YOU TWO UP TO? PLANNING A MUTINY?
HEH HEH HEH

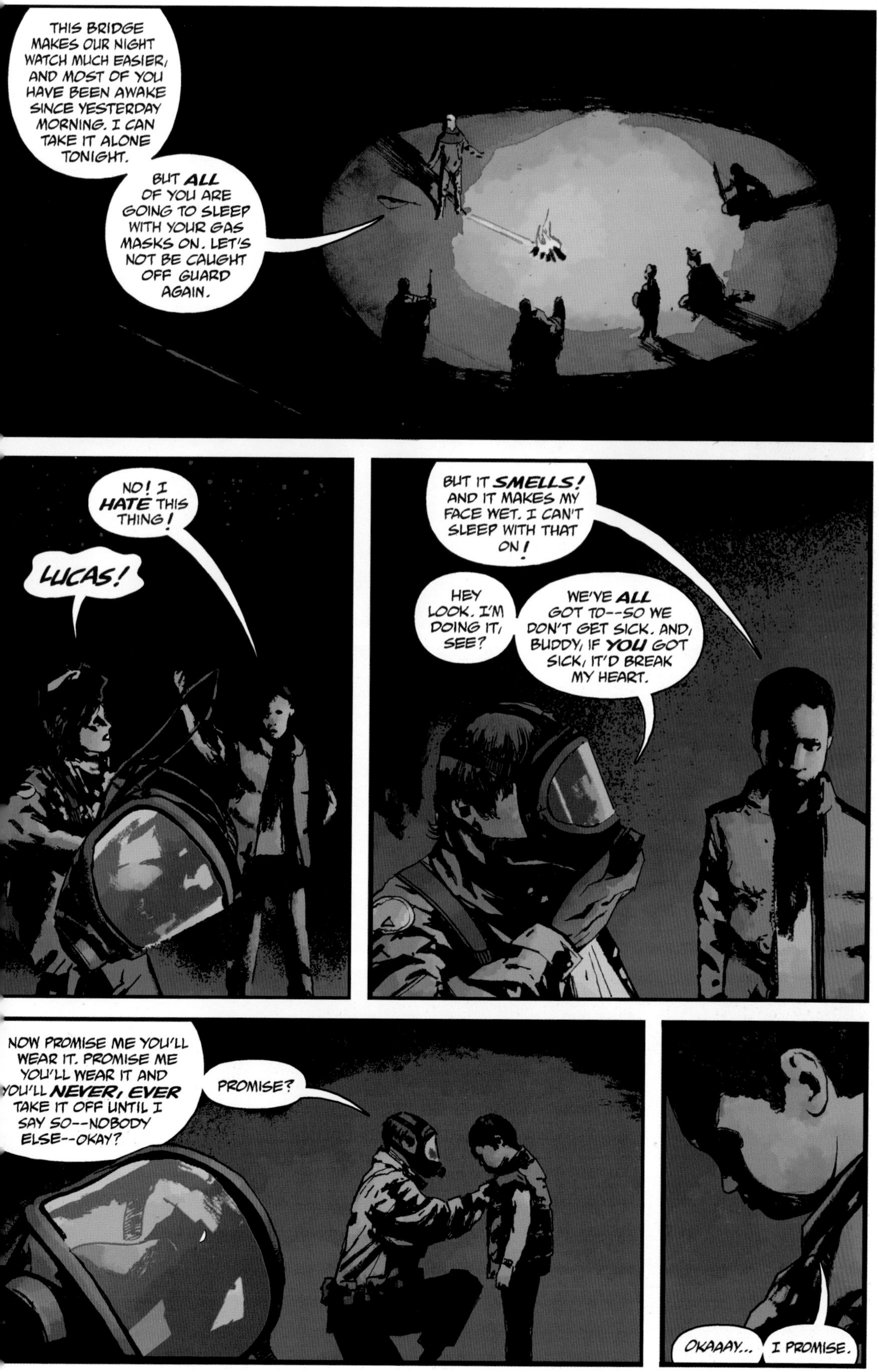
THIS BRIDGE MAKES OUR NIGHT WATCH MUCH EASIER, AND MOST OF YOU HAVE BEEN AWAKE SINCE YESTERDAY MORNING. I CAN TAKE IT ALONE TONIGHT.
BUT **ALL** OF YOU ARE GOING TO SLEEP WITH YOUR GAS MASKS ON. LET'S NOT BE CAUGHT OFF GUARD AGAIN.
NO! I **HATE** THIS THING!
LUCAS!
BUT IT **SMELLS!** AND IT MAKES MY FACE WET. I CAN'T SLEEP WITH THAT ON!
HEY LOOK. I'M DOING IT, SEE?
WE'VE **ALL** GOT TO--SO WE DON'T GET SICK. AND, BUDDY, IF **YOU** GOT SICK, IT'D BREAK MY HEART.
NOW PROMISE ME YOU'LL WEAR IT. PROMISE ME YOU'LL WEAR IT AND YOU'LL **NEVER, EVER** TAKE IT OFF UNTIL I SAY SO--NOBODY ELSE--OKAY?
PROMISE?
OKAAAY...
I PROMISE.

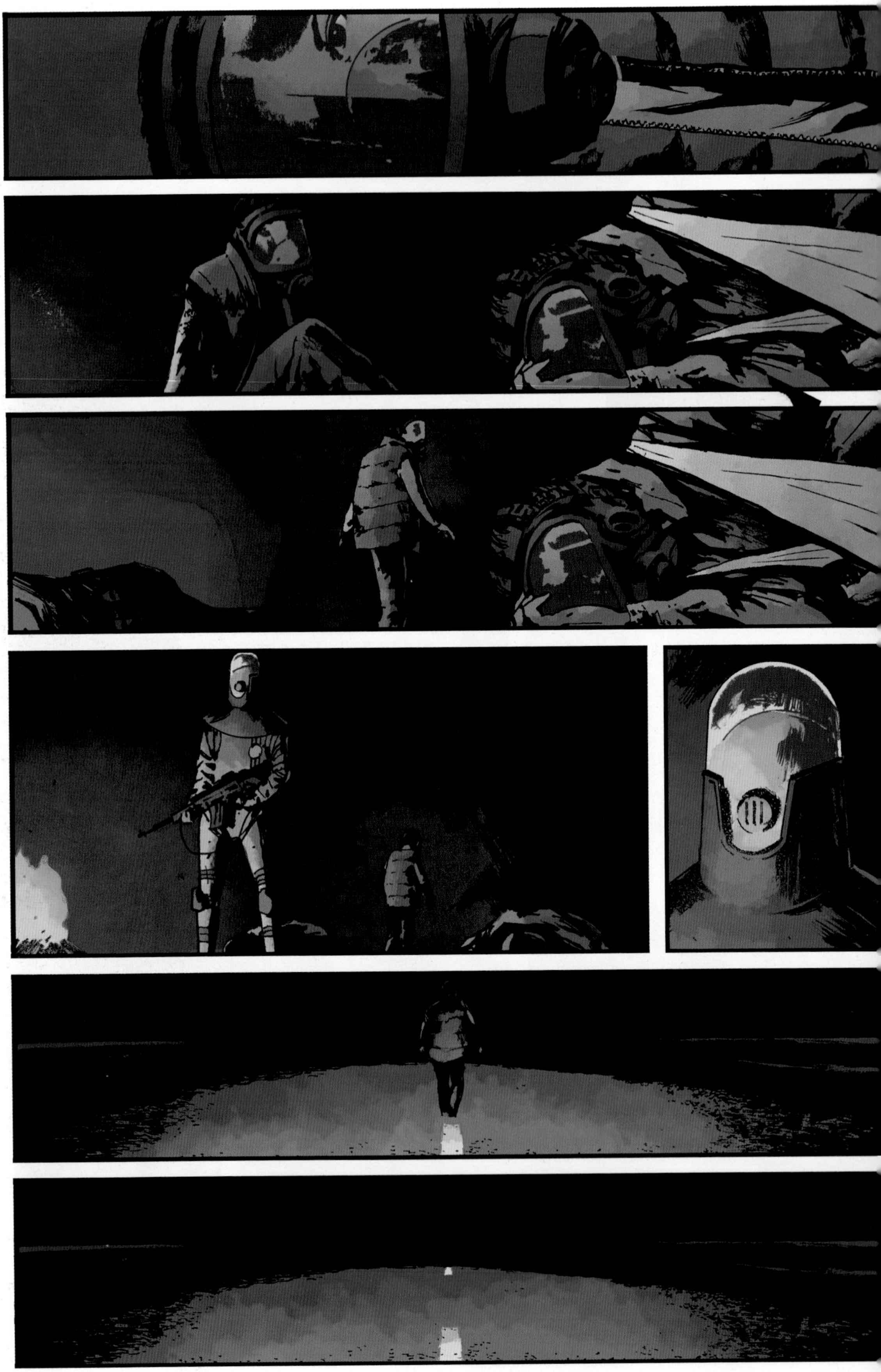

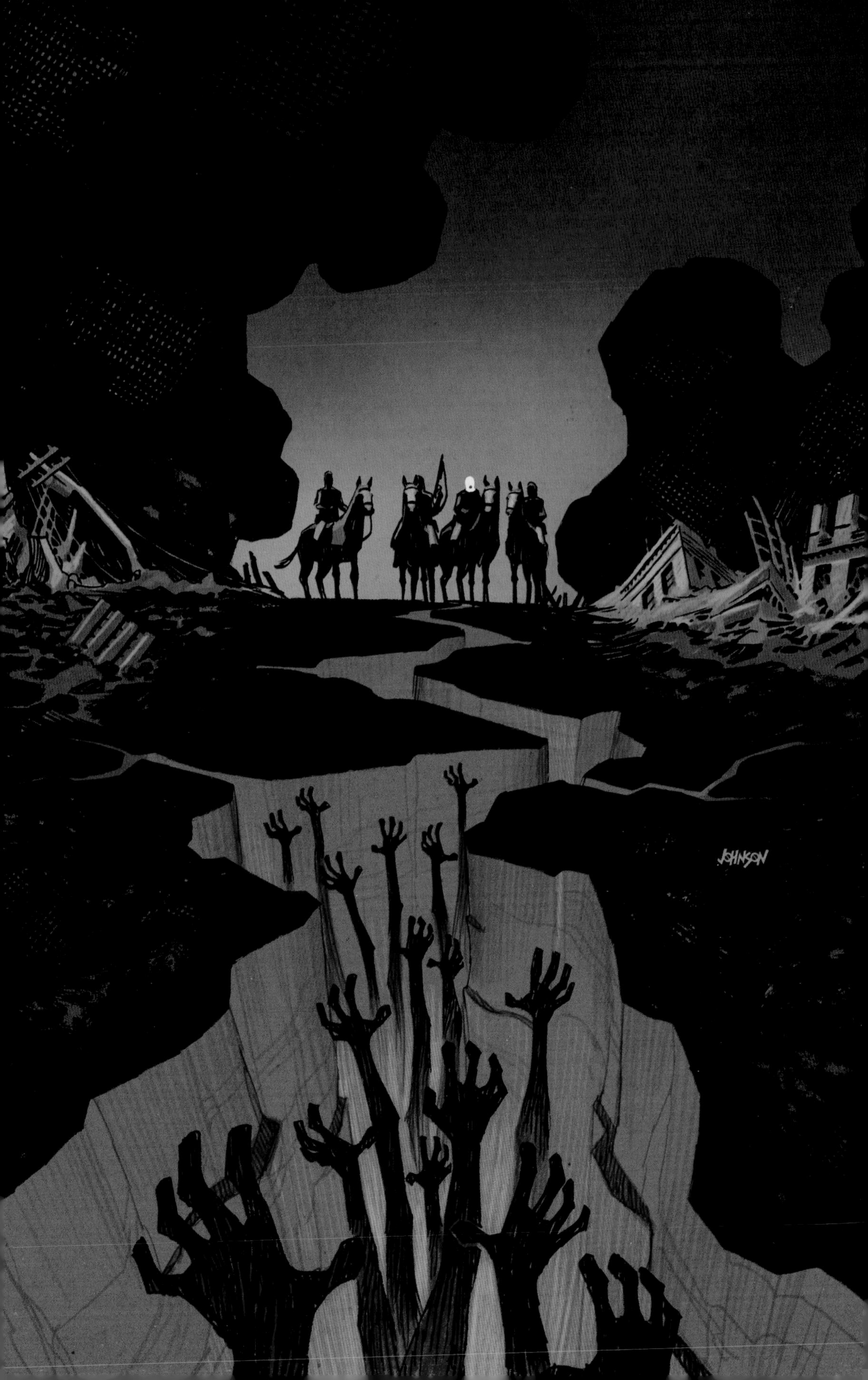
JOHNSON

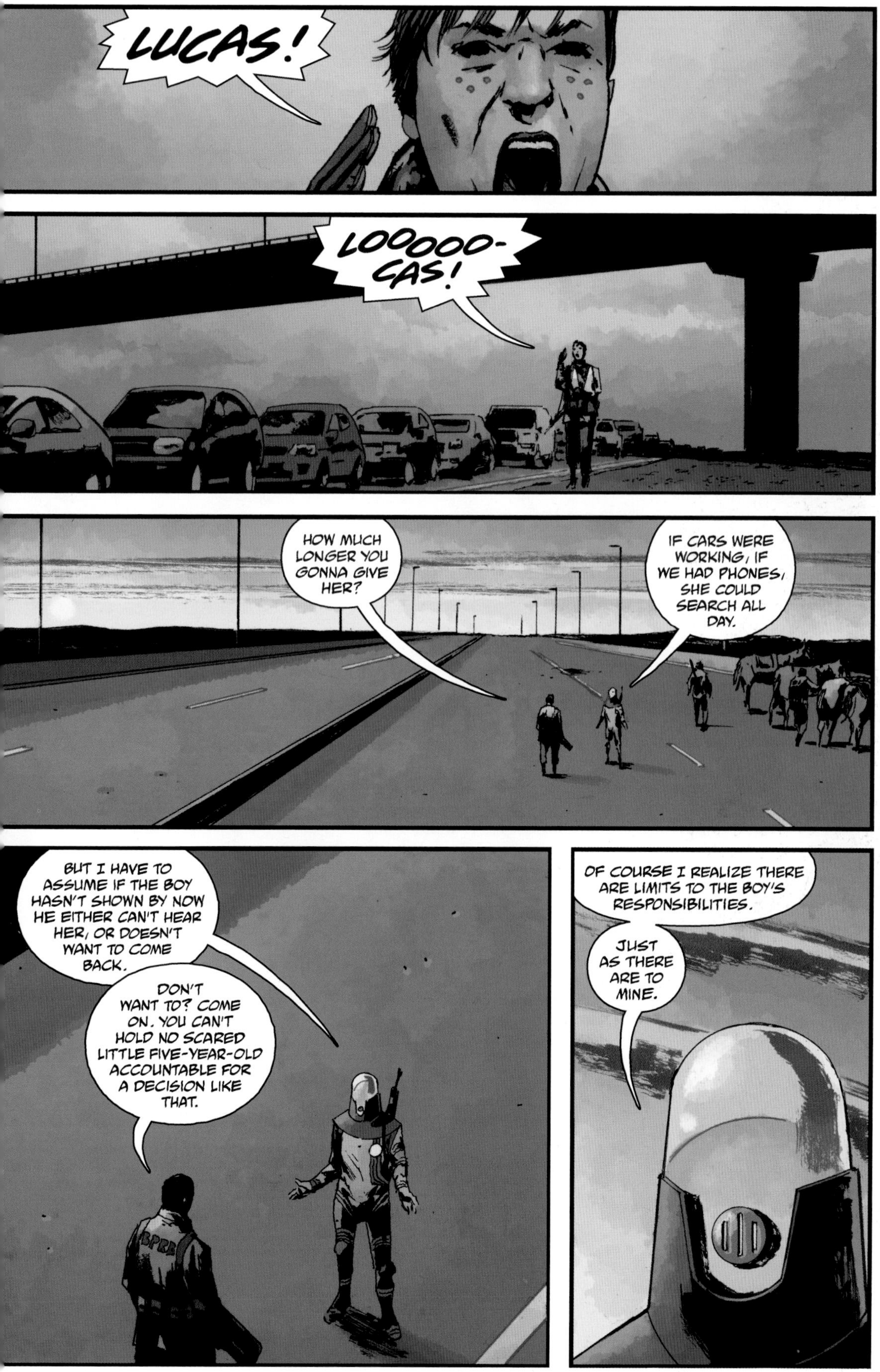
LUCAS!
LOOOOOO-CAS!
HOW MUCH LONGER YOU GONNA GIVE HER?
IF CARS WERE WORKING, IF WE HAD PHONES, SHE COULD SEARCH ALL DAY.
BUT I HAVE TO ASSUME IF THE BOY HASN'T SHOWN BY NOW HE EITHER CAN'T HEAR HER, OR DOESN'T WANT TO COME BACK.
DON'T WANT TO? COME ON. YOU CAN'T HOLD NO SCARED LITTLE FIVE-YEAR-OLD ACCOUNTABLE FOR A DECISION LIKE THAT.
BPRD
OF COURSE I REALIZE THERE ARE LIMITS TO THE BOY'S RESPONSIBILITIES.
JUST AS THERE ARE TO MINE.

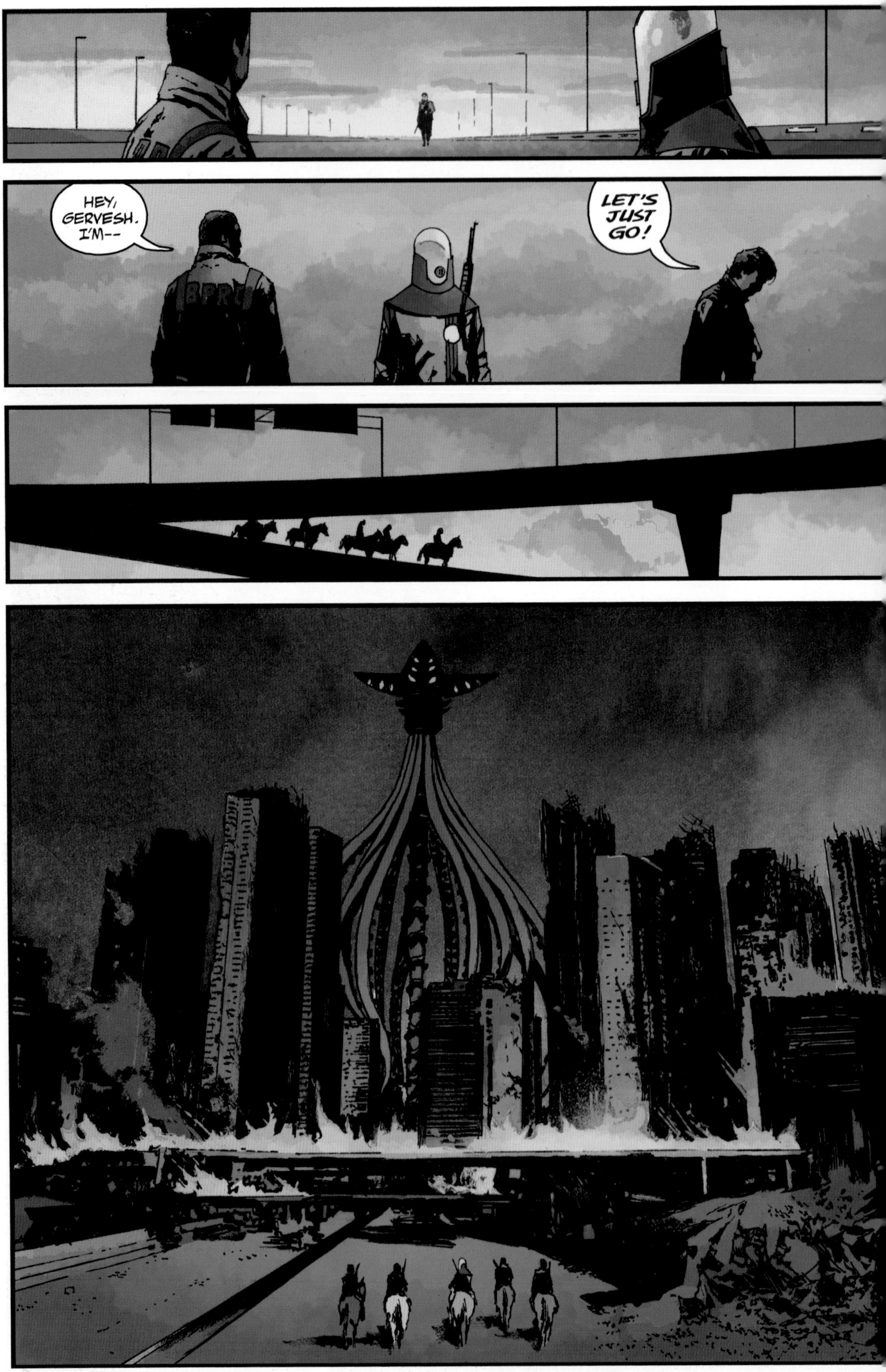
HEY, GERVESH. I'M--
LET'S JUST GO!

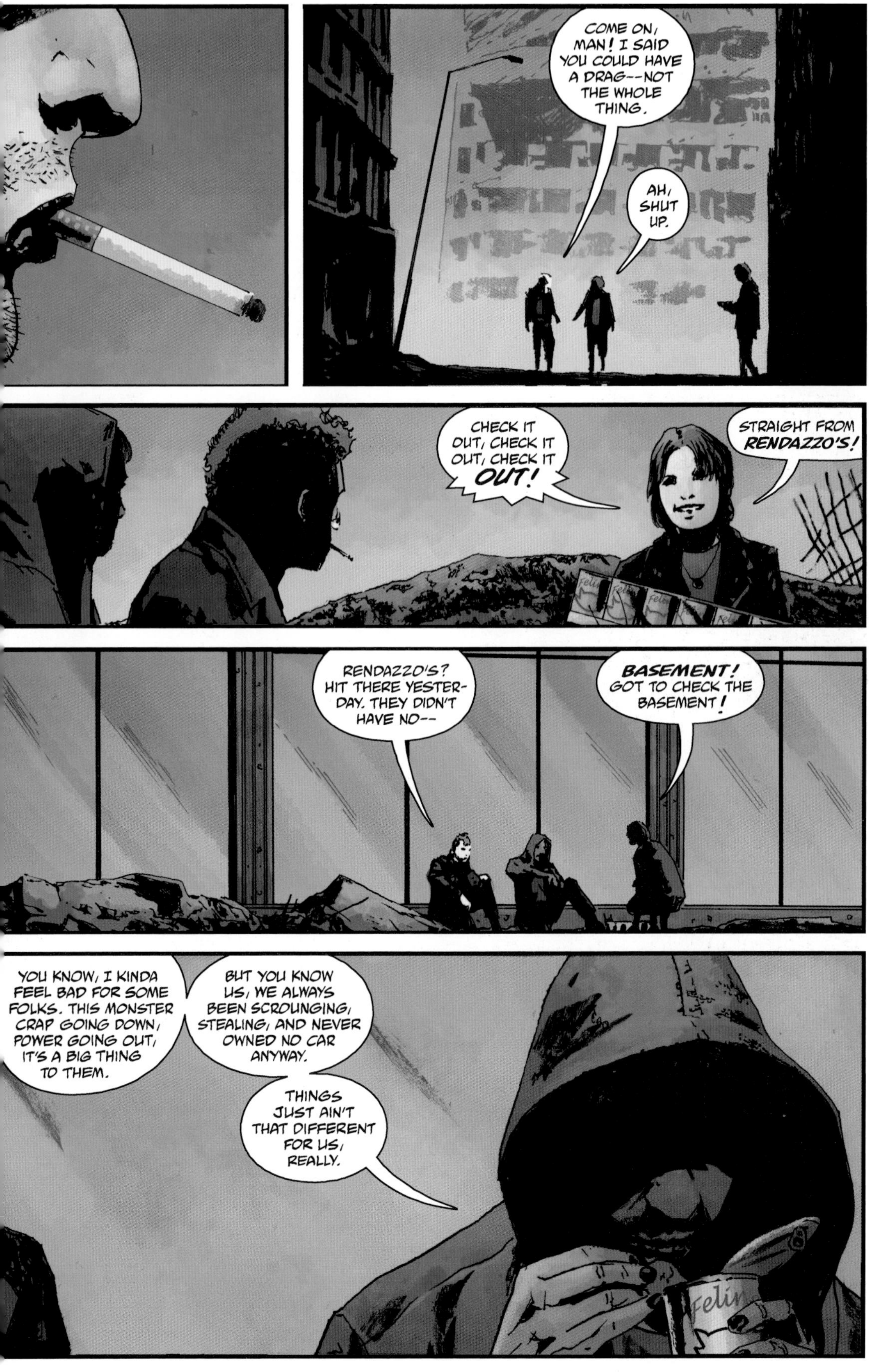
COME ON, MAN! I SAID YOU COULD HAVE A DRAG--NOT THE WHOLE THING.
AH, SHUT UP.
CHECK IT OUT, CHECK IT OUT, CHECK IT OUT!
STRAIGHT FROM RENDAZZO'S!
RENDAZZO'S? HIT THERE YESTER-DAY. THEY DIDN'T HAVE NO--
BASEMENT! GOT TO CHECK THE BASEMENT!
YOU KNOW, I KINDA FEEL BAD FOR SOME FOLKS. THIS MONSTER CRAP GOING DOWN, POWER GOING OUT, IT'S A BIG THING TO THEM.
BUT YOU KNOW US, WE ALWAYS BEEN SCROUNGING, STEALING, AND NEVER OWNED NO CAR ANYWAY.
THINGS JUST AIN'T THAT DIFFERENT FOR US, REALLY.

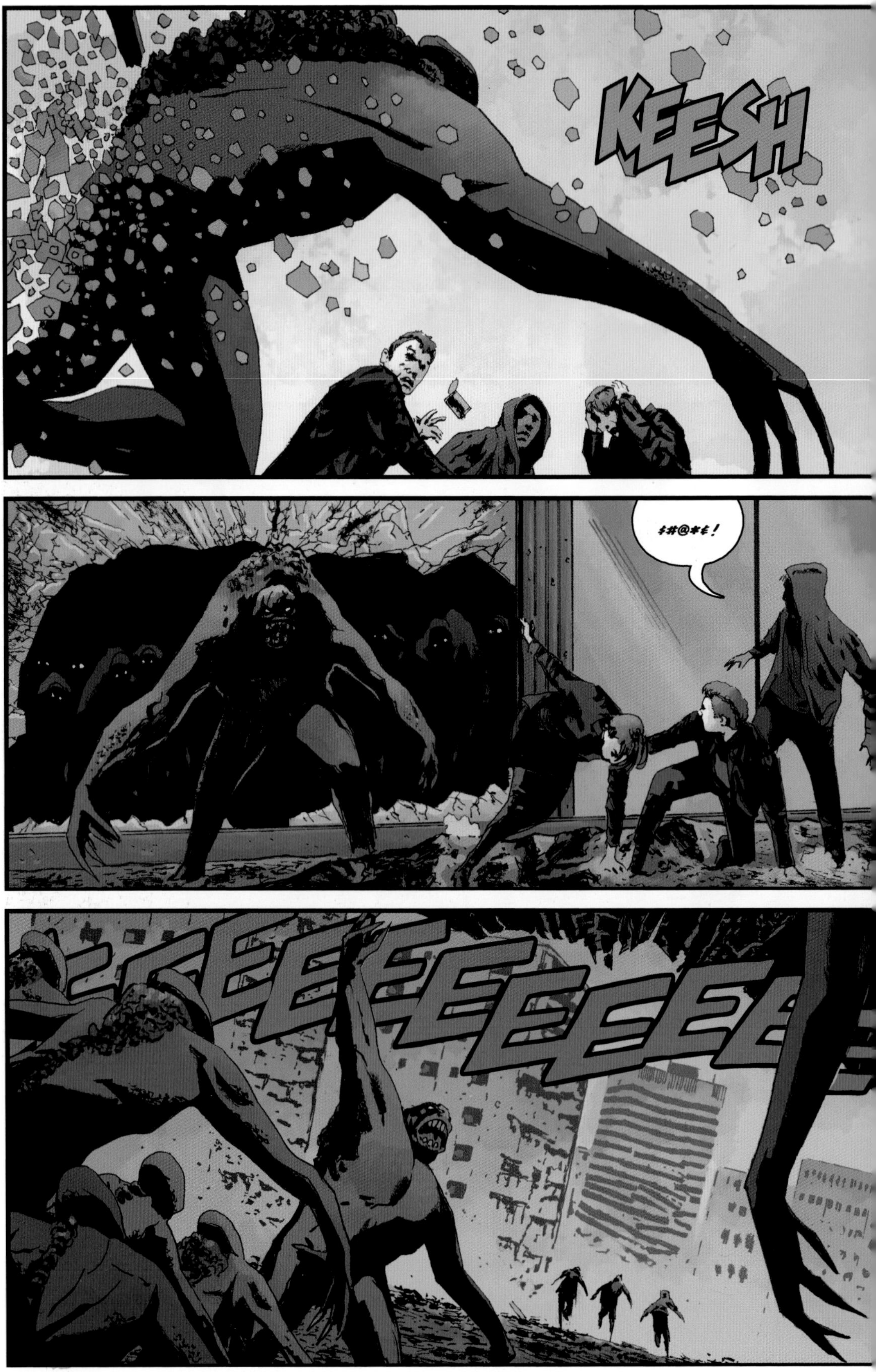
KEESH
$#@*€!
EEEEEEEEEE

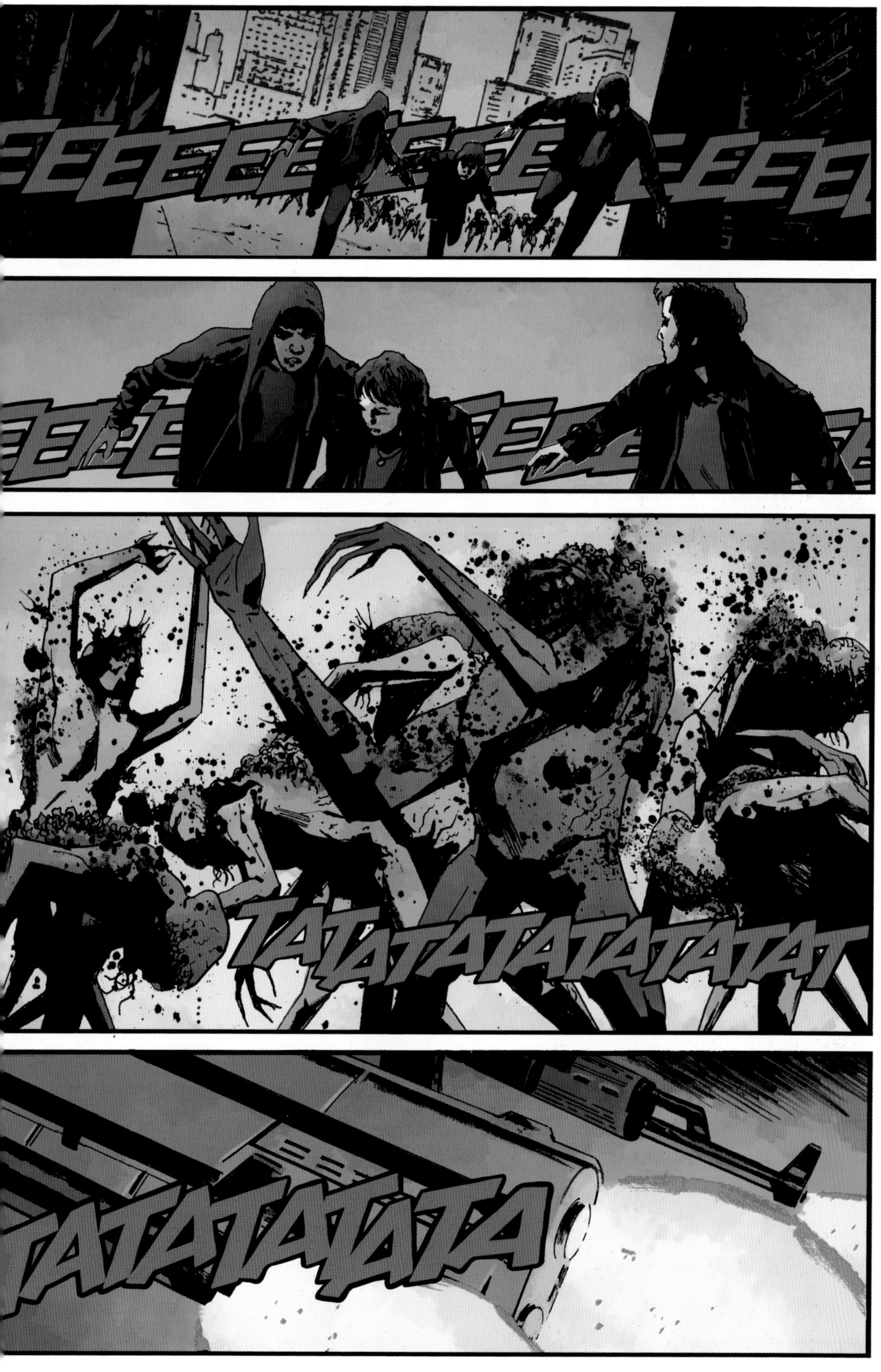
EEEEEEEEEEEEEEEEE
EEEEEEEEEEEEE
TATATATATATATAT
TATATATATATA

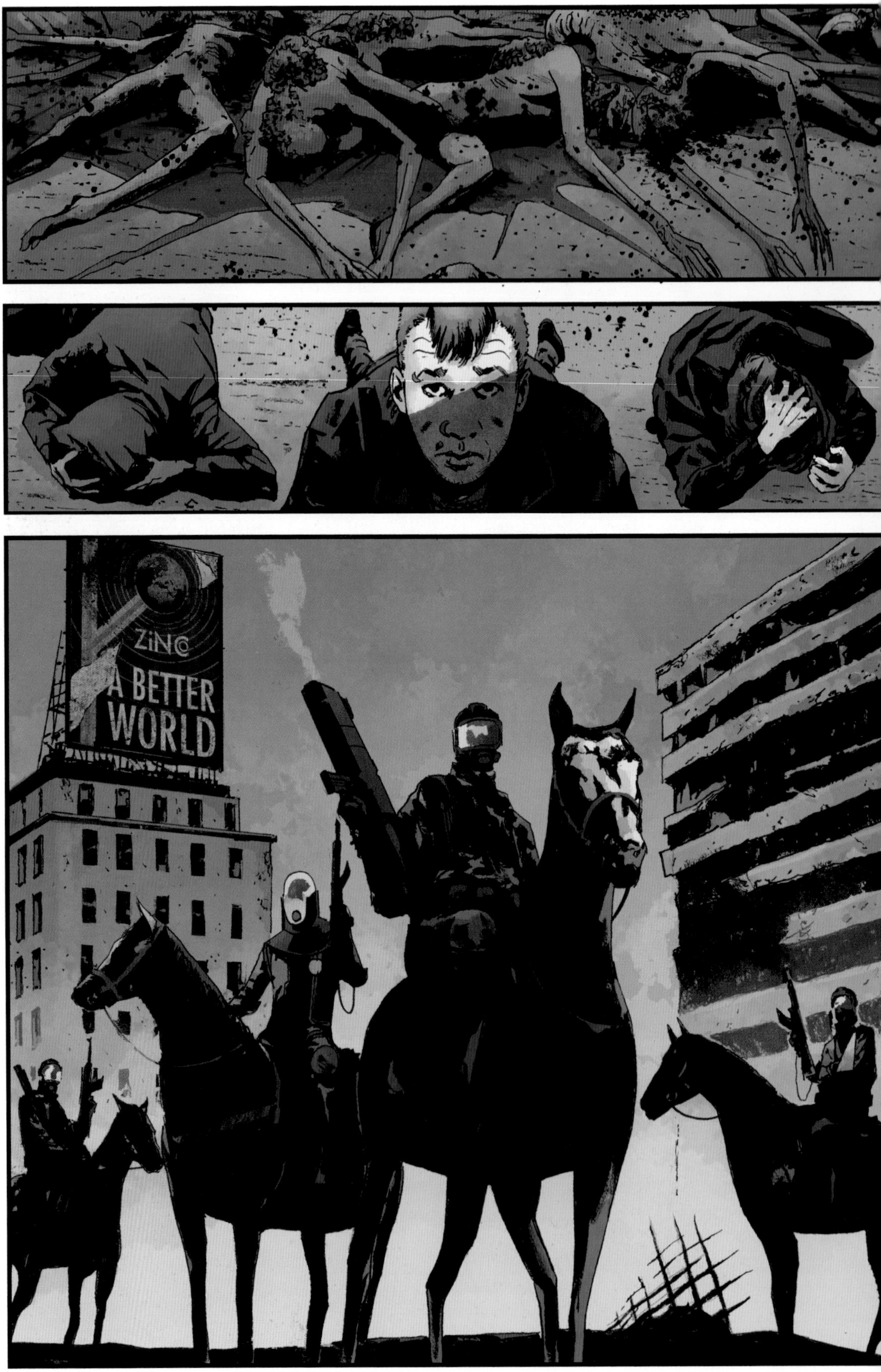
ZiNC
A BETTER WORLD

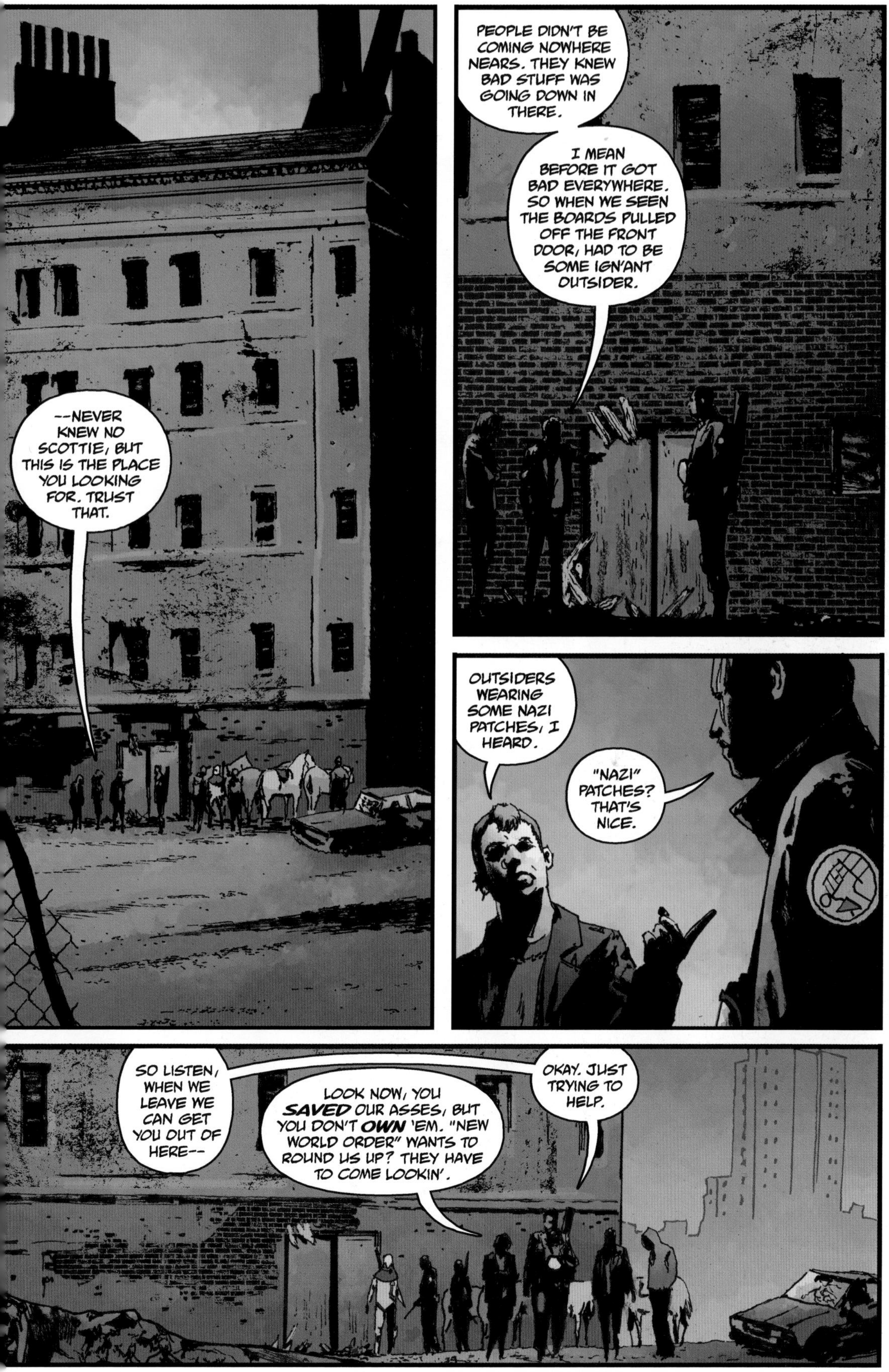
--NEVER KNEW NO SCOTTIE, BUT THIS IS THE PLACE YOU LOOKING FOR. TRUST THAT.
PEOPLE DIDN'T BE COMING NOWHERE NEARS. THEY KNEW BAD STUFF WAS GOING DOWN IN THERE.
I MEAN BEFORE IT GOT BAD EVERYWHERE. SO WHEN WE SEEN THE BOARDS PULLED OFF THE FRONT DOOR, HAD TO BE SOME IGN'ANT OUTSIDER.
OUTSIDERS WEARING SOME NAZI PATCHES, I HEARD.
"NAZI" PATCHES? THAT'S NICE.
SO LISTEN, WHEN WE LEAVE WE CAN GET YOU OUT OF HERE--
LOOK NOW, YOU SAVED OUR ASSES, BUT YOU DON'T OWN 'EM. "NEW WORLD ORDER" WANTS TO ROUND US UP? THEY HAVE TO COME LOOKIN'.
OKAY. JUST TRYING TO HELP.

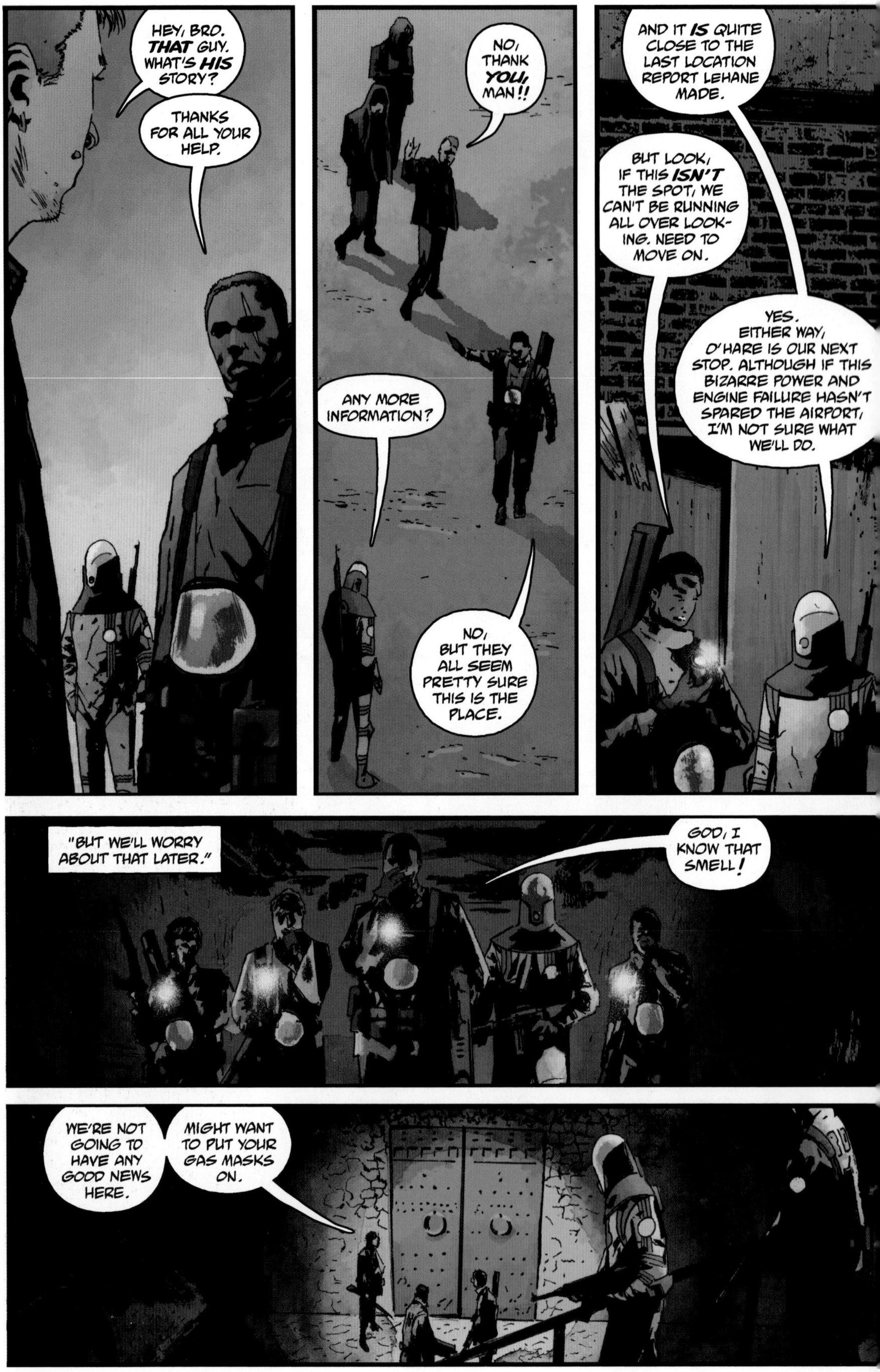
HEY, BRO. THAT GUY. WHAT'S HIS STORY?
THANKS FOR ALL YOUR HELP.
NO, THANK YOU, MAN!!
ANY MORE INFORMATION?
NO, BUT THEY ALL SEEM PRETTY SURE THIS IS THE PLACE.
AND IT IS QUITE CLOSE TO THE LAST LOCATION REPORT LEHANE MADE.
BUT LOOK, IF THIS ISN'T THE SPOT, WE CAN'T BE RUNNING ALL OVER LOOK-ING. NEED TO MOVE ON.
YES. EITHER WAY, O'HARE IS OUR NEXT STOP. ALTHOUGH IF THIS BIZARRE POWER AND ENGINE FAILURE HASN'T SPARED THE AIRPORT, I'M NOT SURE WHAT WE'LL DO.
"BUT WE'LL WORRY ABOUT THAT LATER."
GOD, I KNOW THAT SMELL!
WE'RE NOT GOING TO HAVE ANY GOOD NEWS HERE.
MIGHT WANT TO PUT YOUR GAS MASKS ON.

BZZZZZZZ

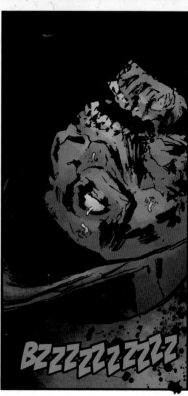

BZZZZZZZZZZ

BZZZZZZZZZZ

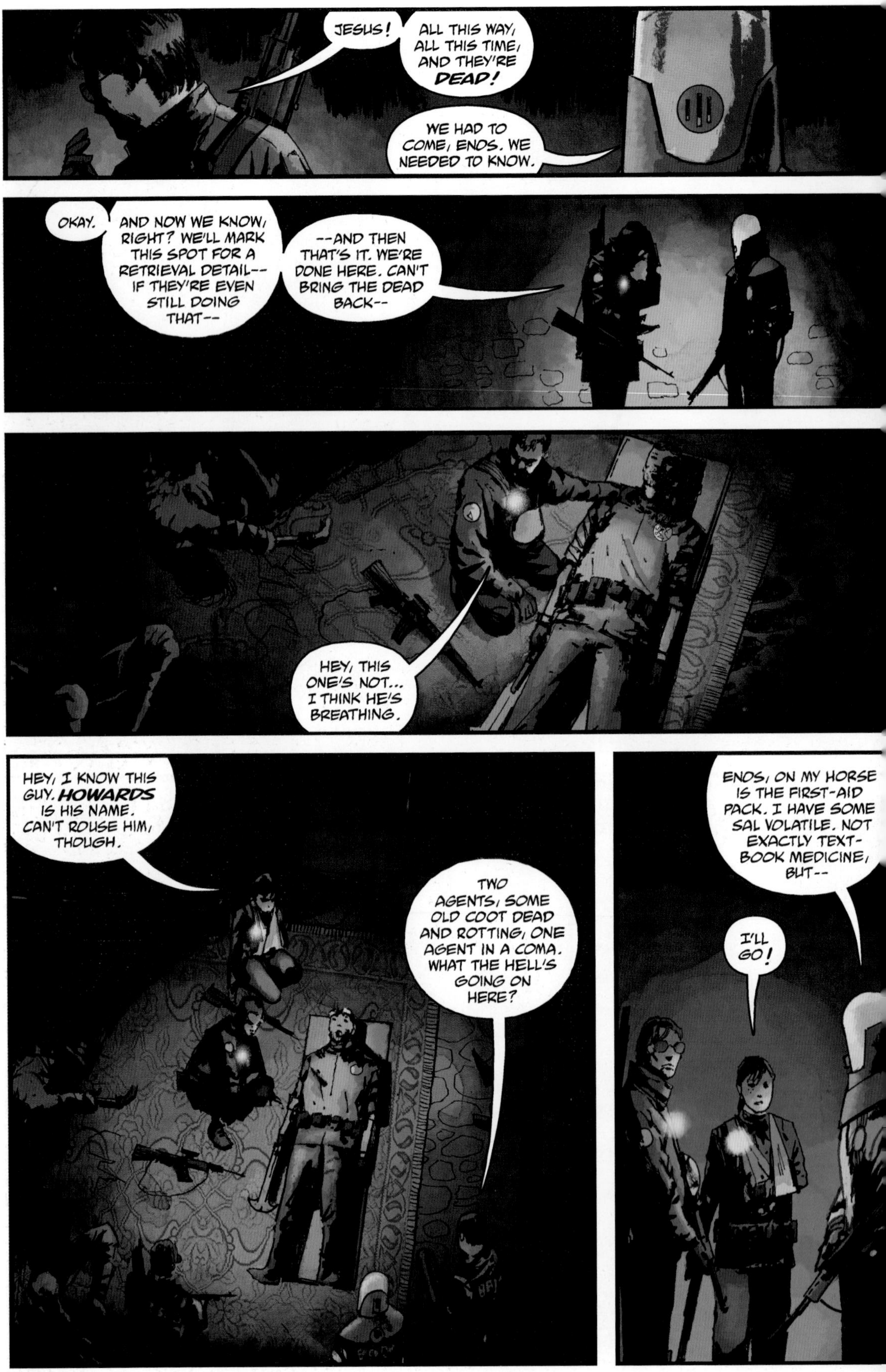

JESUS!
ALL THIS WAY, ALL THIS TIME, AND THEY'RE **DEAD!**
WE HAD TO COME, ENOS. WE NEEDED TO KNOW.
OKAY.
AND NOW WE KNOW, RIGHT? WE'LL MARK THIS SPOT FOR A RETRIEVAL DETAIL-- IF THEY'RE EVEN STILL DOING THAT--
--AND THEN THAT'S IT. WE'RE DONE HERE. CAN'T BRING THE DEAD BACK--
HEY, THIS ONE'S NOT... I THINK HE'S BREATHING.
HEY, I KNOW THIS GUY. **HOWARDS** IS HIS NAME. CAN'T ROUSE HIM, THOUGH.
TWO AGENTS, SOME OLD COOT DEAD AND ROTTING, ONE AGENT IN A COMA. WHAT THE HELL'S GOING ON HERE?
ENOS, ON MY HORSE IS THE FIRST-AID PACK. I HAVE SOME SAL VOLATILE. NOT EXACTLY TEXT-BOOK MEDICINE, BUT--
I'LL GO!

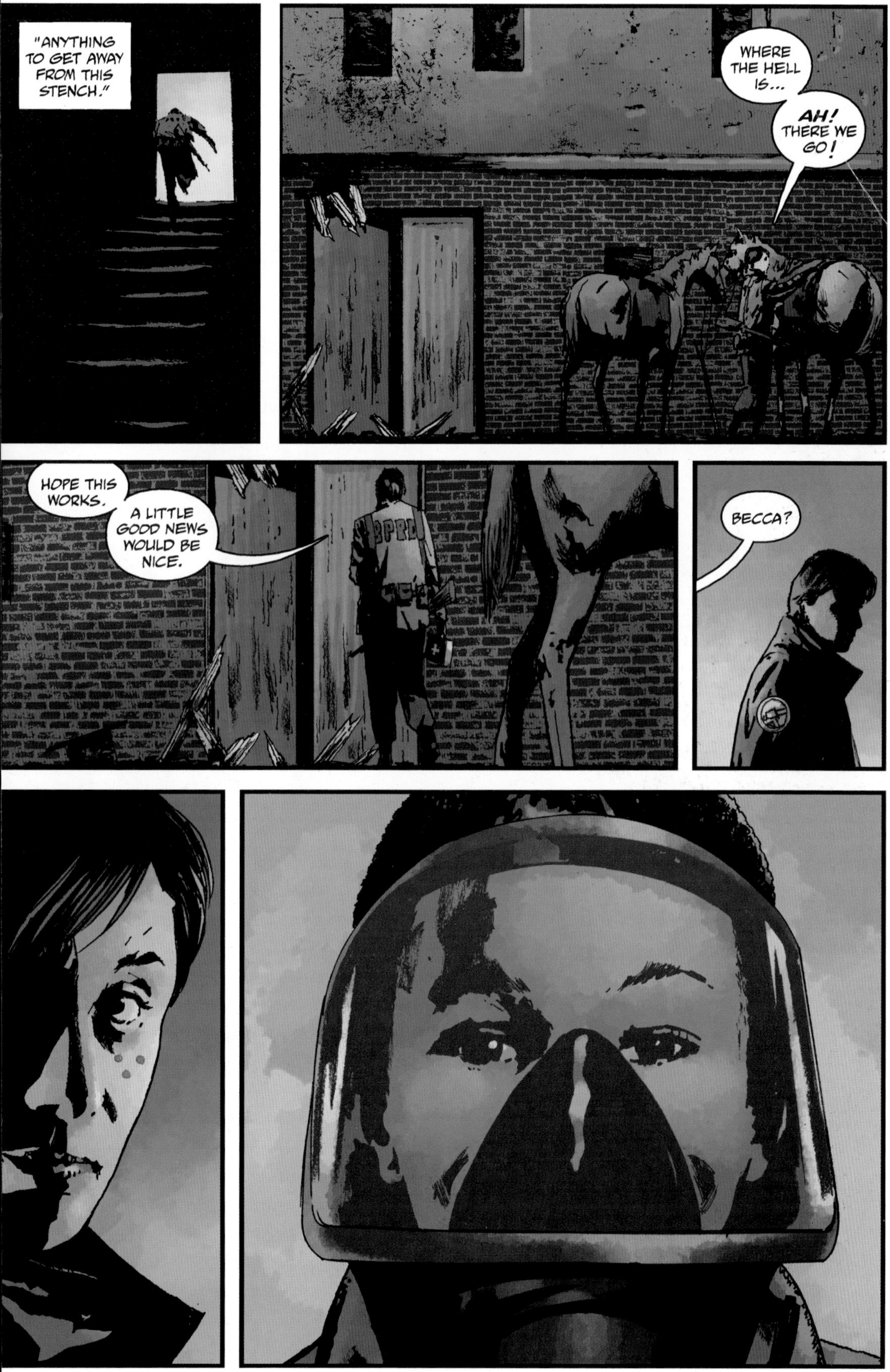
"ANYTHING TO GET AWAY FROM THIS STENCH."
WHERE THE HELL IS...
AH! THERE WE GO!
HOPE THIS WORKS.
A LITTLE GOOD NEWS WOULD BE NICE.
BECCA?

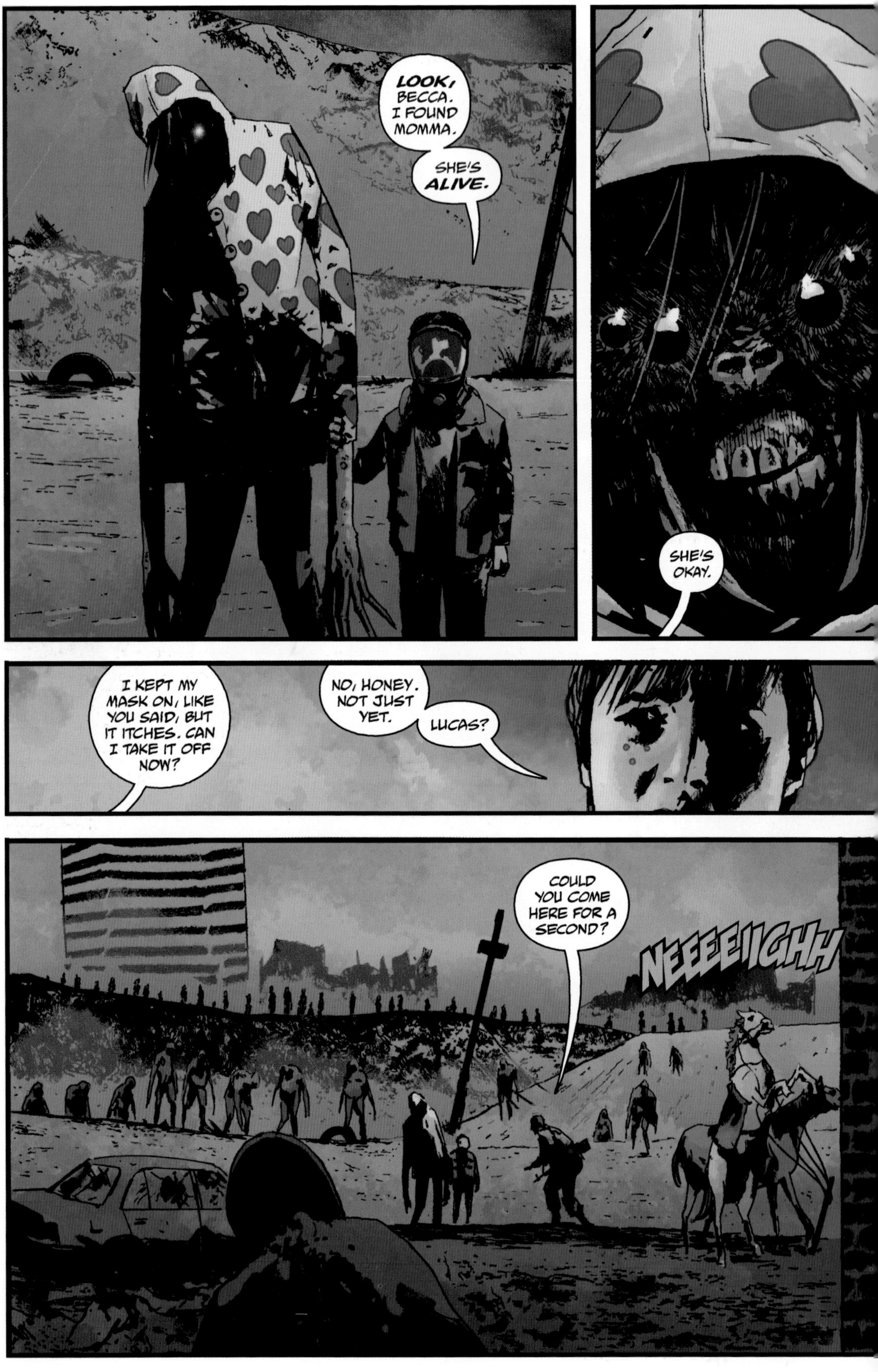
LOOK, BECCA. I FOUND MOMMA.
SHE'S ALIVE.
SHE'S OKAY.
I KEPT MY MASK ON, LIKE YOU SAID, BUT IT ITCHES. CAN I TAKE IT OFF NOW?
NO, HONEY. NOT JUST YET.
LUCAS?
COULD YOU COME HERE FOR A SECOND?
NEEEEIIGHH

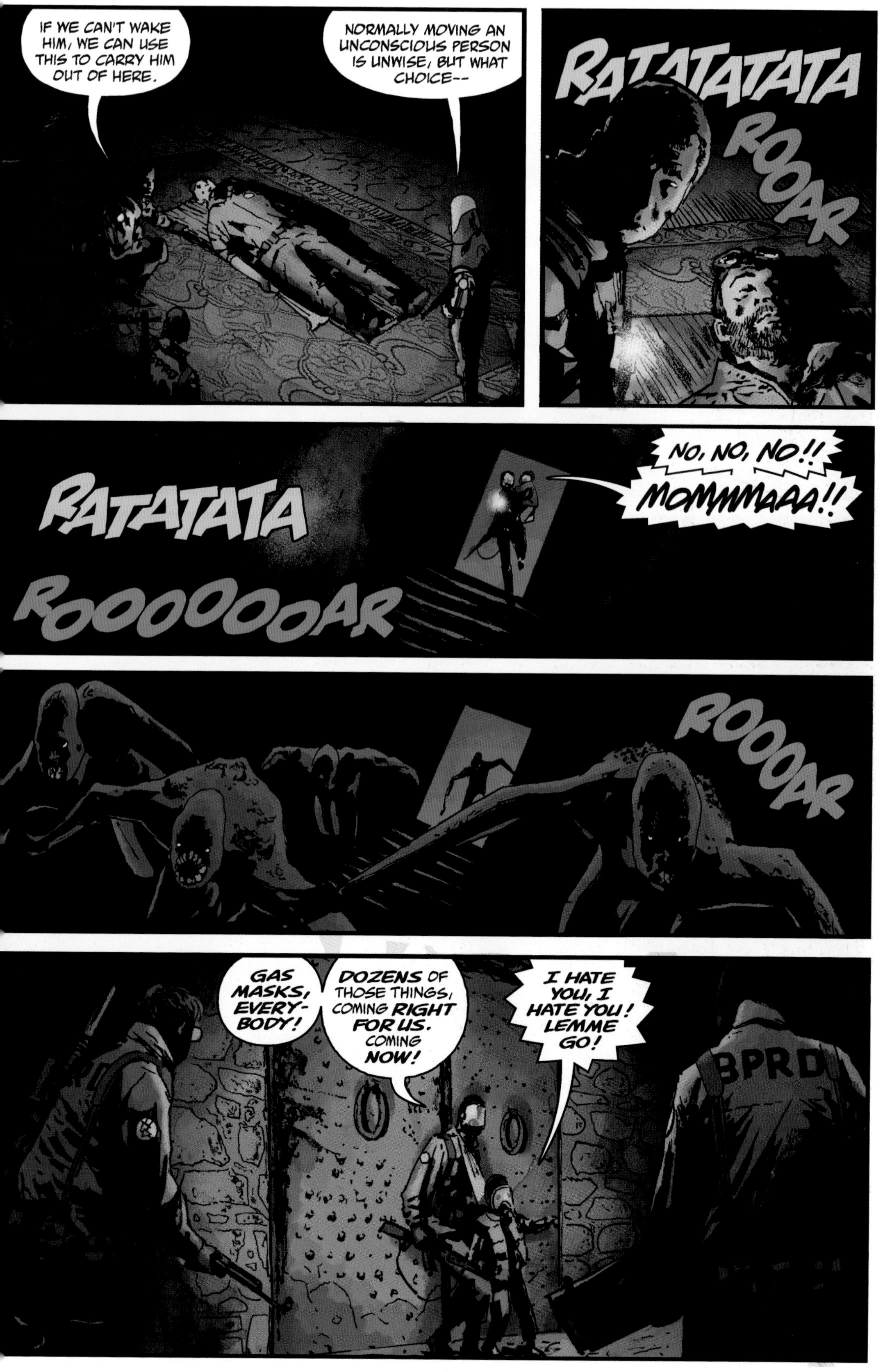
IF WE CAN'T WAKE HIM, WE CAN USE THIS TO CARRY HIM OUT OF HERE.
NORMALLY MOVING AN UNCONSCIOUS PERSON IS UNWISE, BUT WHAT CHOICE--
RATATATATA
ROOOAR
RATATATA
ROOOOOOOAR
NO, NO, NO!! MOMMMAAA!!
ROOOAR
GAS MASKS, EVERY-BODY!
DOZENS OF THOSE THINGS, COMING RIGHT FOR US. COMING NOW!
I HATE YOU, I HATE YOU! LEMME GO!
BPRD

HERE. WE NEED TO BAR THE DOOR.
LET ME GO! LET ME--
BOY!
THAT'S ENOUGH FROM YOU!
BUMP
THOK
THOK
BUMP
ROARR
BAM
BAM
THOK
KNOCK
BANG
BAM

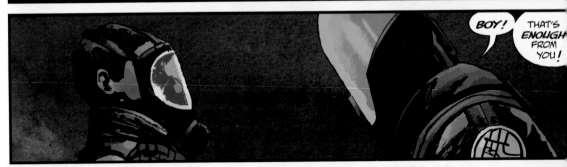

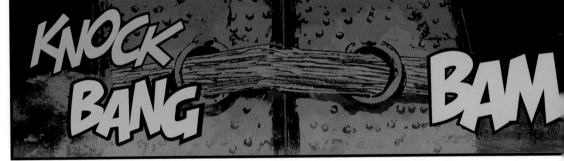

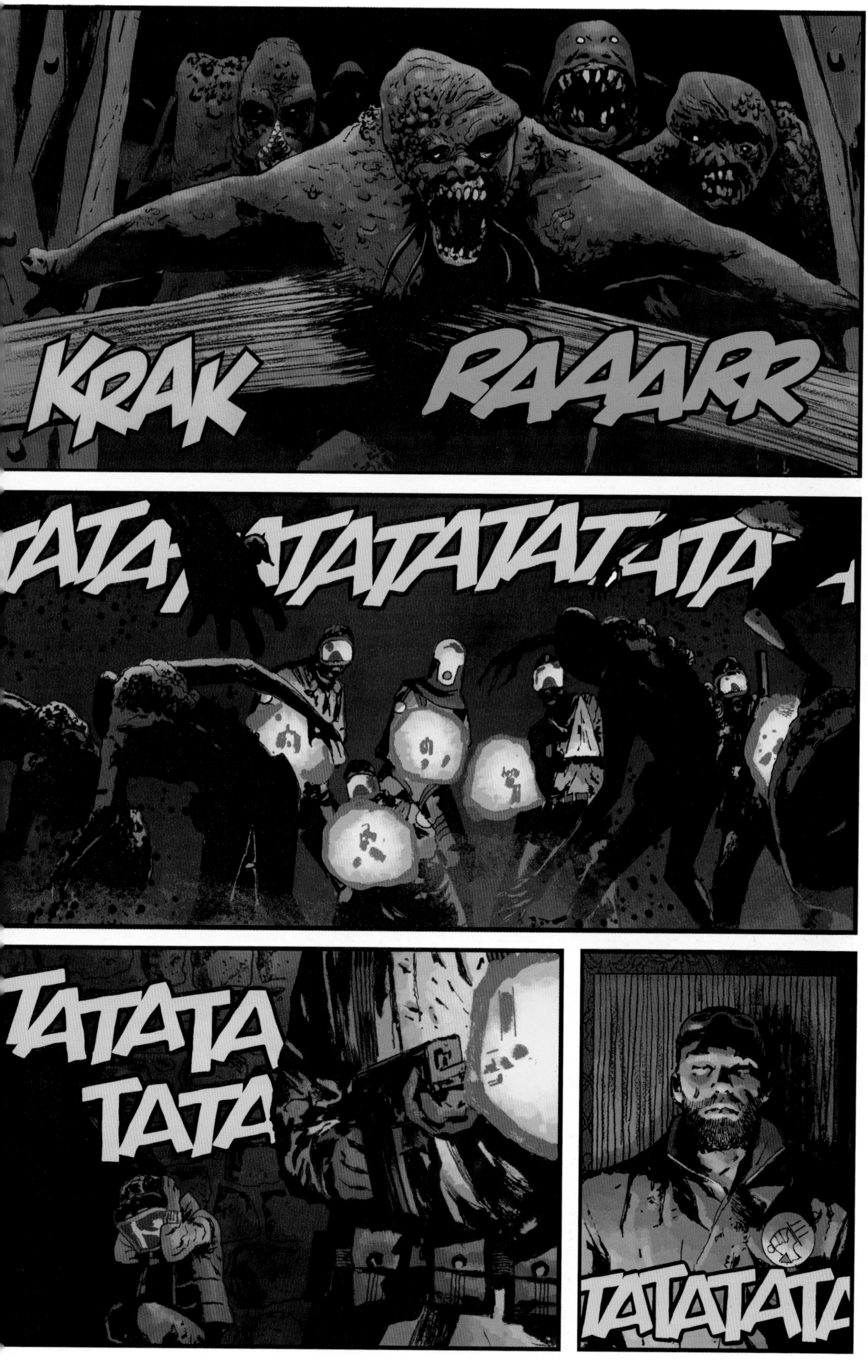
KRAK
RAAARR
TATA
TATATATATATA
TATATA
TATA
TATATATA

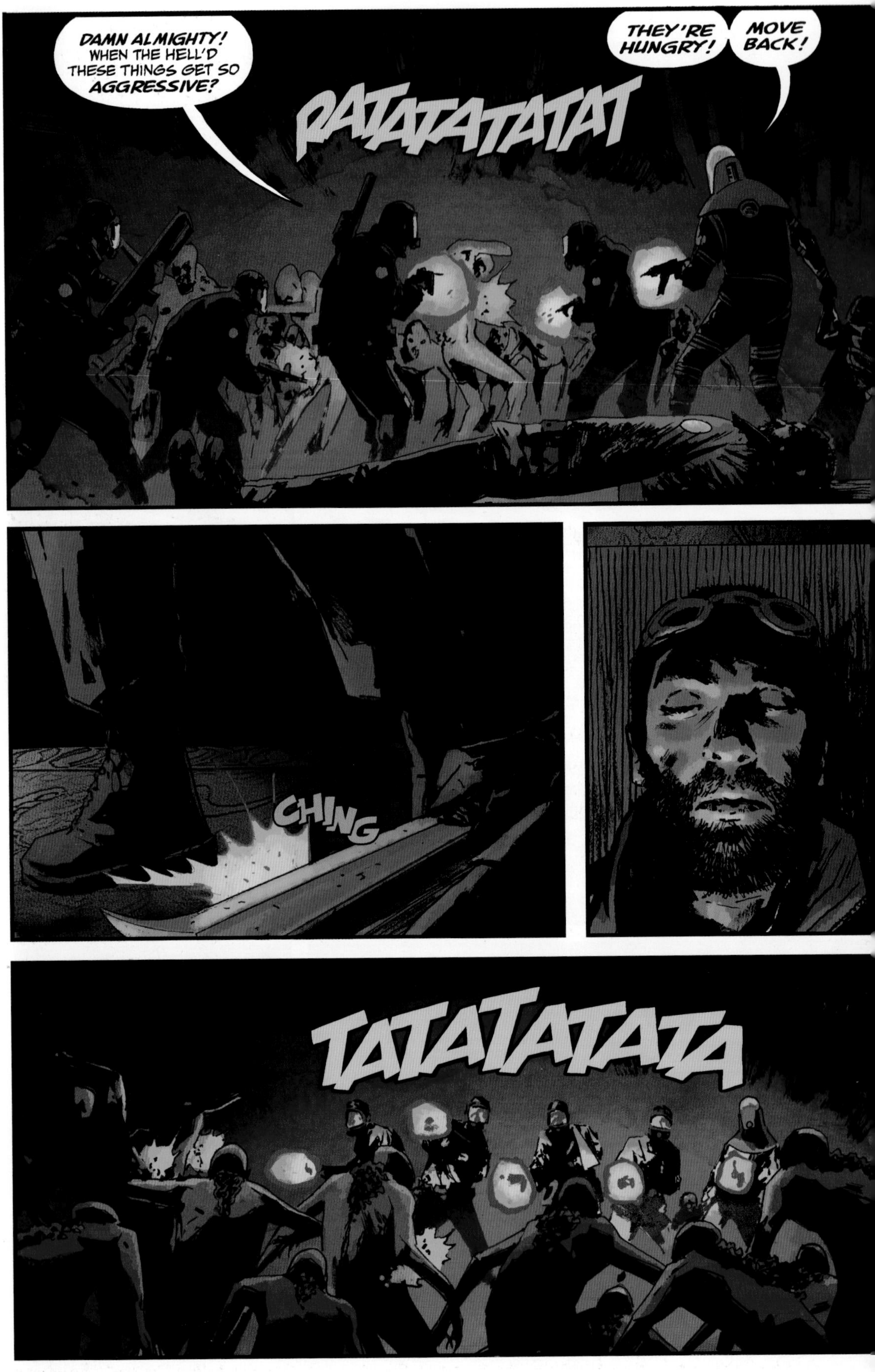
DAMN ALMIGHTY! WHEN THE HELL'D THESE THINGS GET SO AGGRESSIVE?
RATATATATATAT
THEY'RE HUNGRY!
MOVE BACK!
CHING
TATATATATA

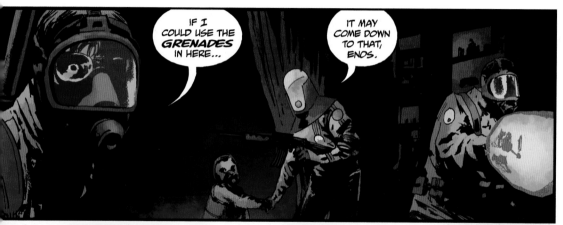

IF I COULD USE THE **GRENADES** IN HERE...

IT MAY COME DOWN TO THAT, ENOS.

**WHAT?** WHAT THE HELL DOES **THAT** MEAN?

IF WE'RE OVERTAKEN, THE GRENADES ARE OUR LAST OPTION.

YOU MEAN **OUR** LAST OPTION! YOU, YOU'LL JUST FLIT YOUR **GHOST ASS** RIGHT ON OUTTA HERE, **WON'T** YOU?

NOT NOW, ENDS! IS **EVERYTHING** A FIGHT TO--

**GHH!**

**RRRRRR--!**

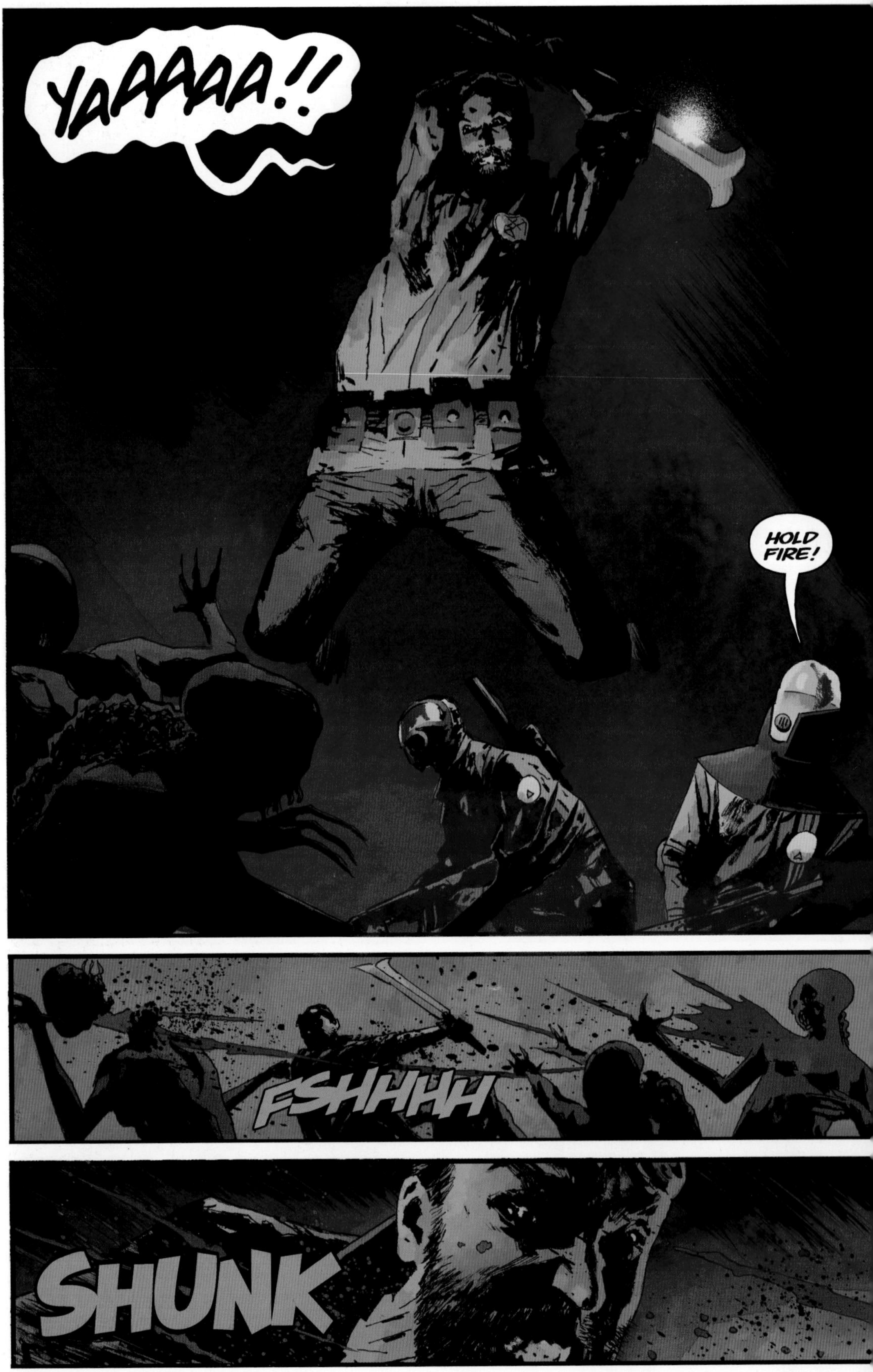
YAAAAA!!
HOLD FIRE!
FSHHHH
SHUNK

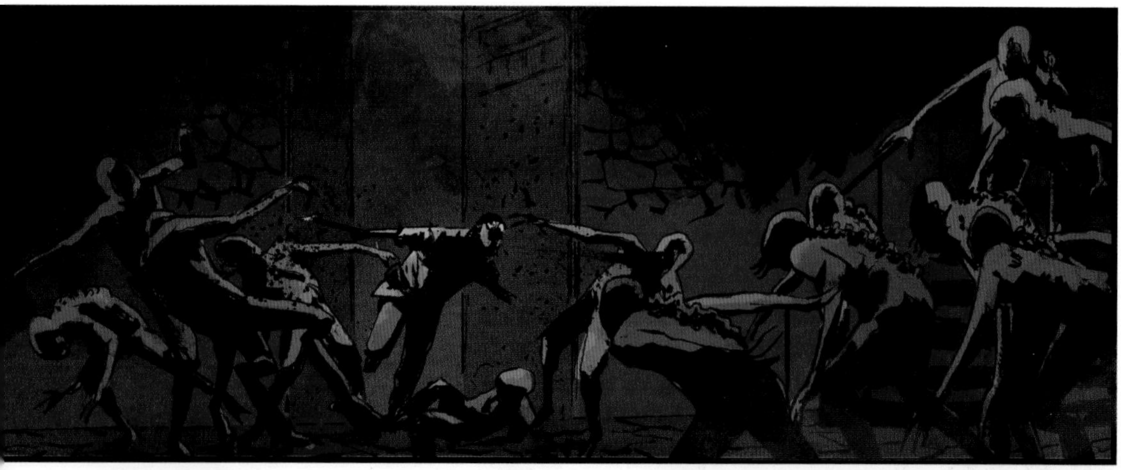

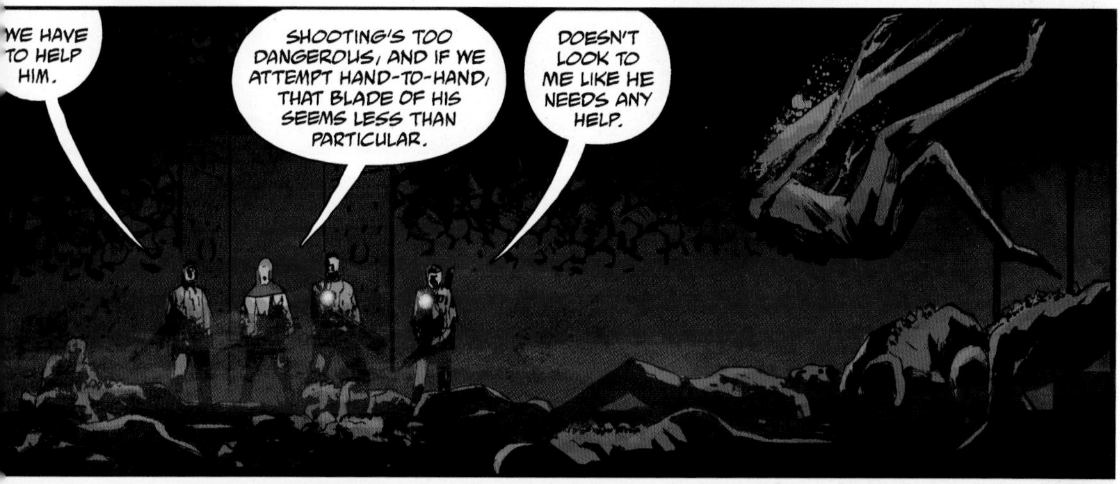

WE HAVE TO HELP HIM.
SHOOTING'S TOO DANGEROUS, AND IF WE ATTEMPT HAND-TO-HAND, THAT BLADE OF HIS SEEMS LESS THAN PARTICULAR.
DOESN'T LOOK TO ME LIKE HE NEEDS ANY HELP.


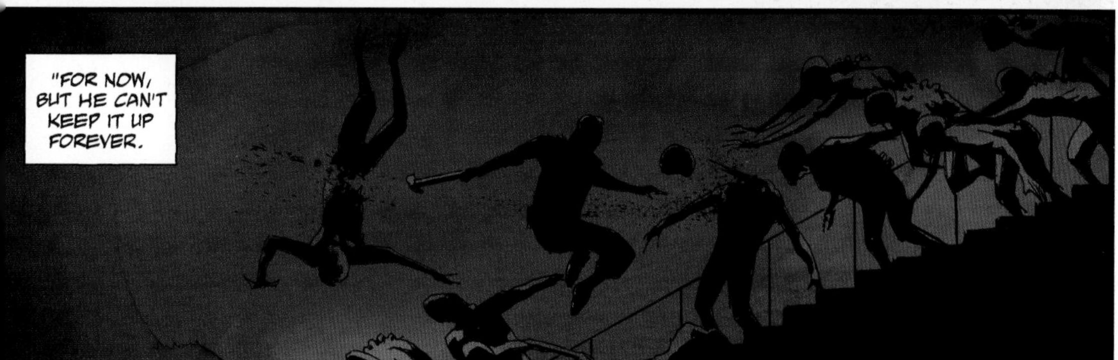

"FOR NOW, BUT HE CAN'T KEEP IT UP FOREVER.


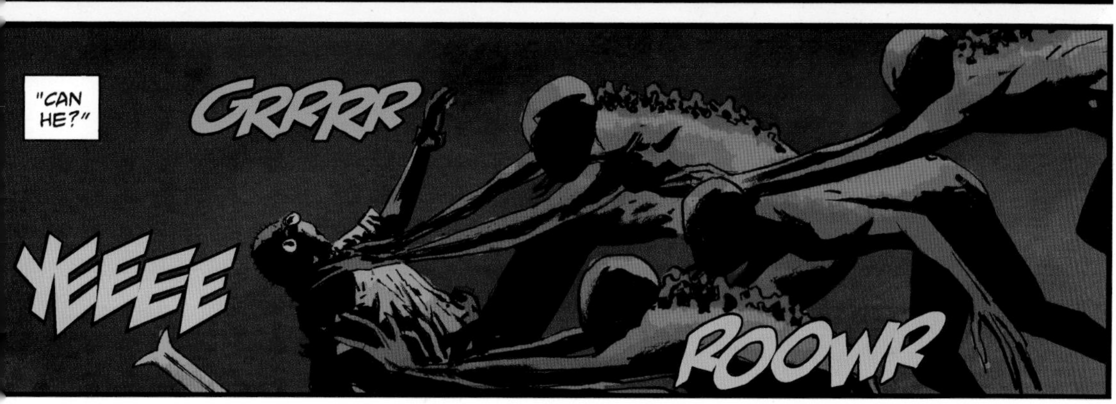

"CAN HE?"
GRRRR
YEEEE
ROOWR

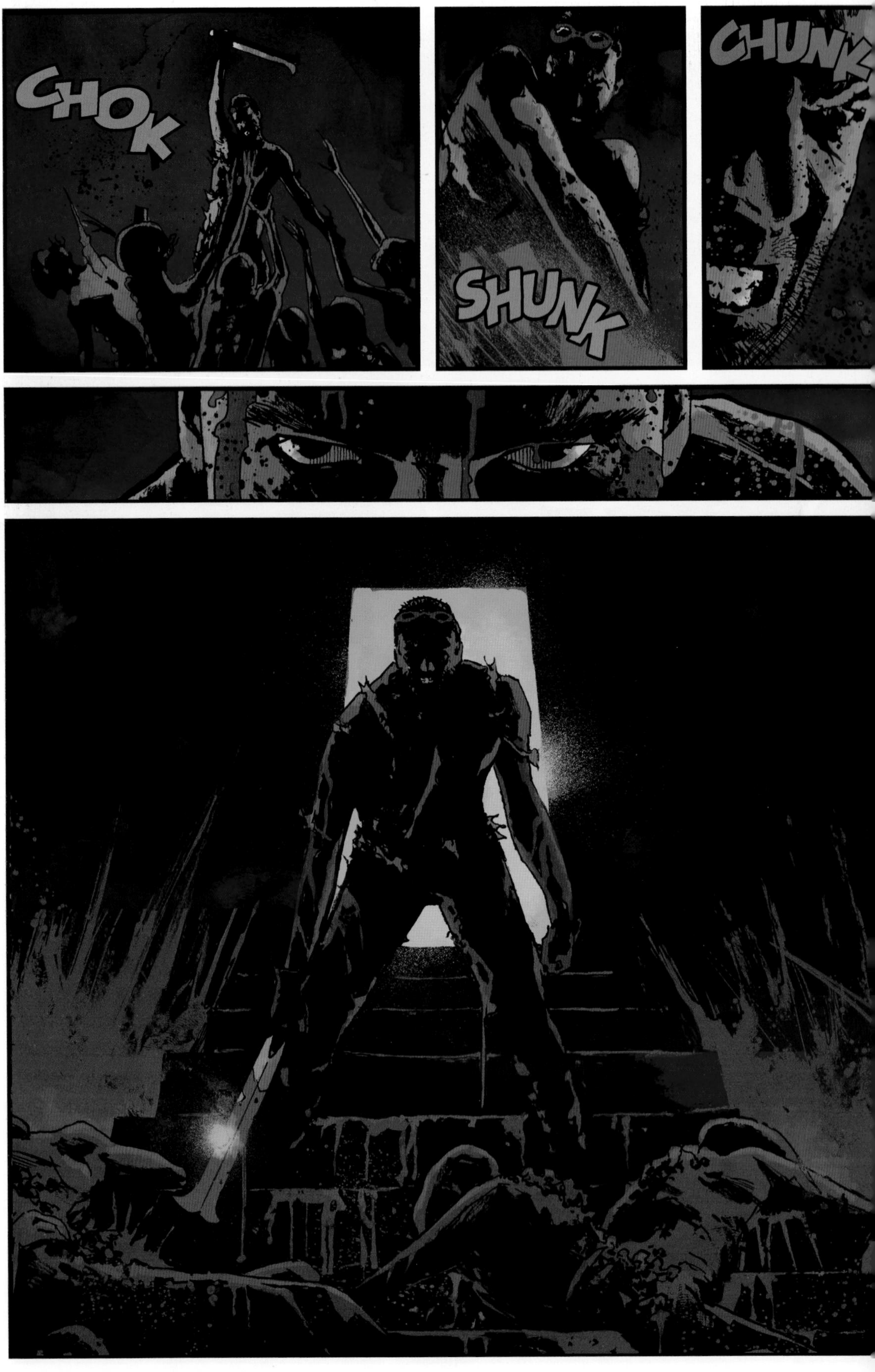
CHOK
SHUNK
CHUNK

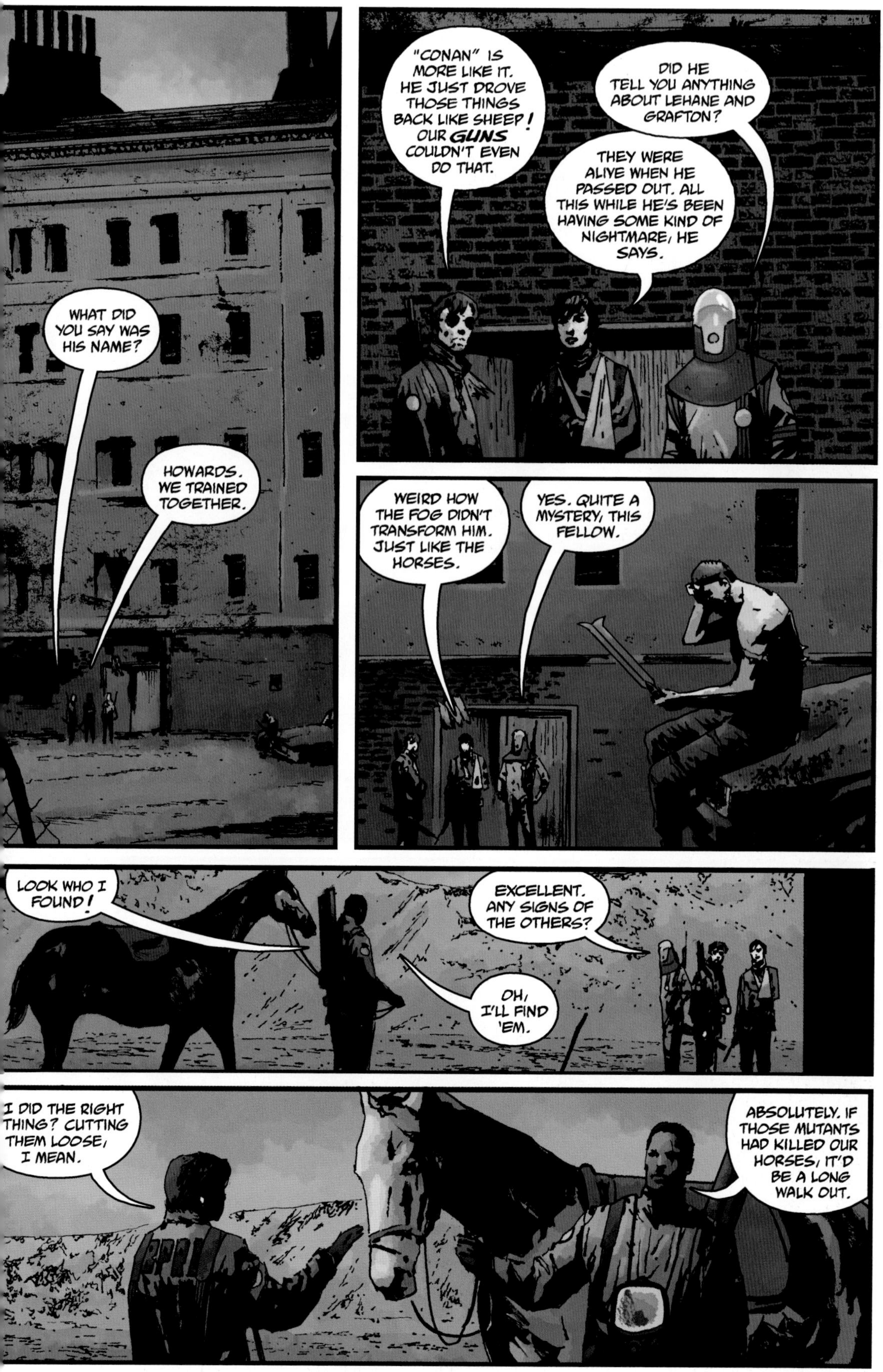

WHAT DID YOU SAY WAS HIS NAME?
HOWARDS. WE TRAINED TOGETHER.
"CONAN" IS MORE LIKE IT. HE JUST DROVE THOSE THINGS BACK LIKE SHEEP! OUR GUNS COULDN'T EVEN DO THAT.
DID HE TELL YOU ANYTHING ABOUT LEHANE AND GRAFTON?
THEY WERE ALIVE WHEN HE PASSED OUT. ALL THIS WHILE HE'S BEEN HAVING SOME KIND OF NIGHTMARE, HE SAYS.
WEIRD HOW THE FOG DIDN'T TRANSFORM HIM. JUST LIKE THE HORSES.
YES. QUITE A MYSTERY, THIS FELLOW.
LOOK WHO I FOUND!
EXCELLENT. ANY SIGNS OF THE OTHERS?
OH, I'LL FIND 'EM.
I DID THE RIGHT THING? CUTTING THEM LOOSE, I MEAN.
ABSOLUTELY. IF THOSE MUTANTS HAD KILLED OUR HORSES, IT'D BE A LONG WALK OUT.

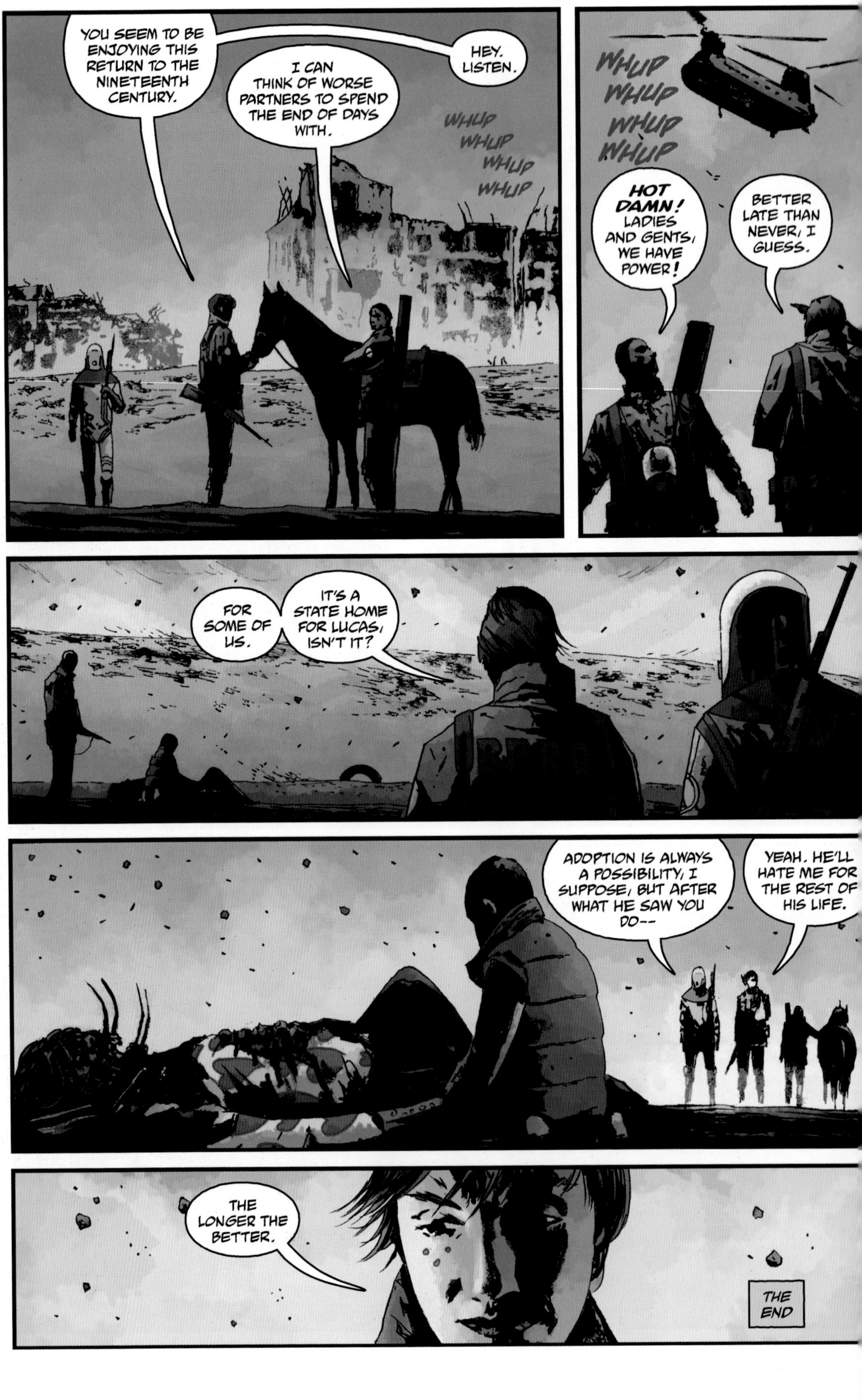

YOU SEEM TO BE ENJOYING THIS RETURN TO THE NINETEENTH CENTURY.
HEY. LISTEN.
I CAN THINK OF WORSE PARTNERS TO SPEND THE END OF DAYS WITH.
WHUP WHUP WHUP WHUP
WHUP WHUP WHUP WHUP
HOT DAMN! LADIES AND GENTS, WE HAVE POWER!
BETTER LATE THAN NEVER, I GUESS.
FOR SOME OF US.
IT'S A STATE HOME FOR LUCAS, ISN'T IT?
ADOPTION IS ALWAYS A POSSIBILITY, I SUPPOSE, BUT AFTER WHAT HE SAW YOU DO--
YEAH. HE'LL HATE ME FOR THE REST OF HIS LIFE.
THE LONGER THE BETTER.
THE END

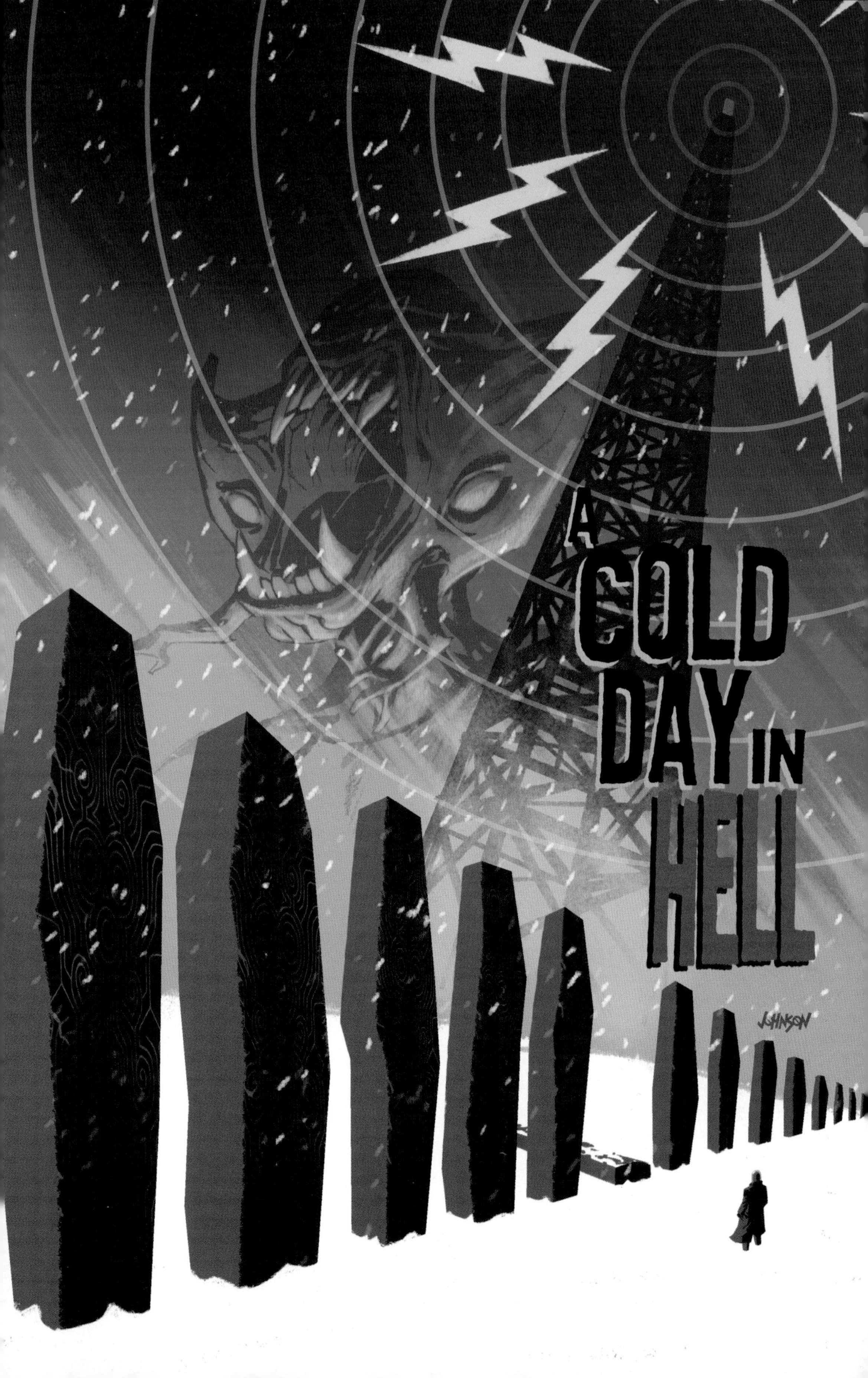
A COLD DAY IN HELL
JOHNSON

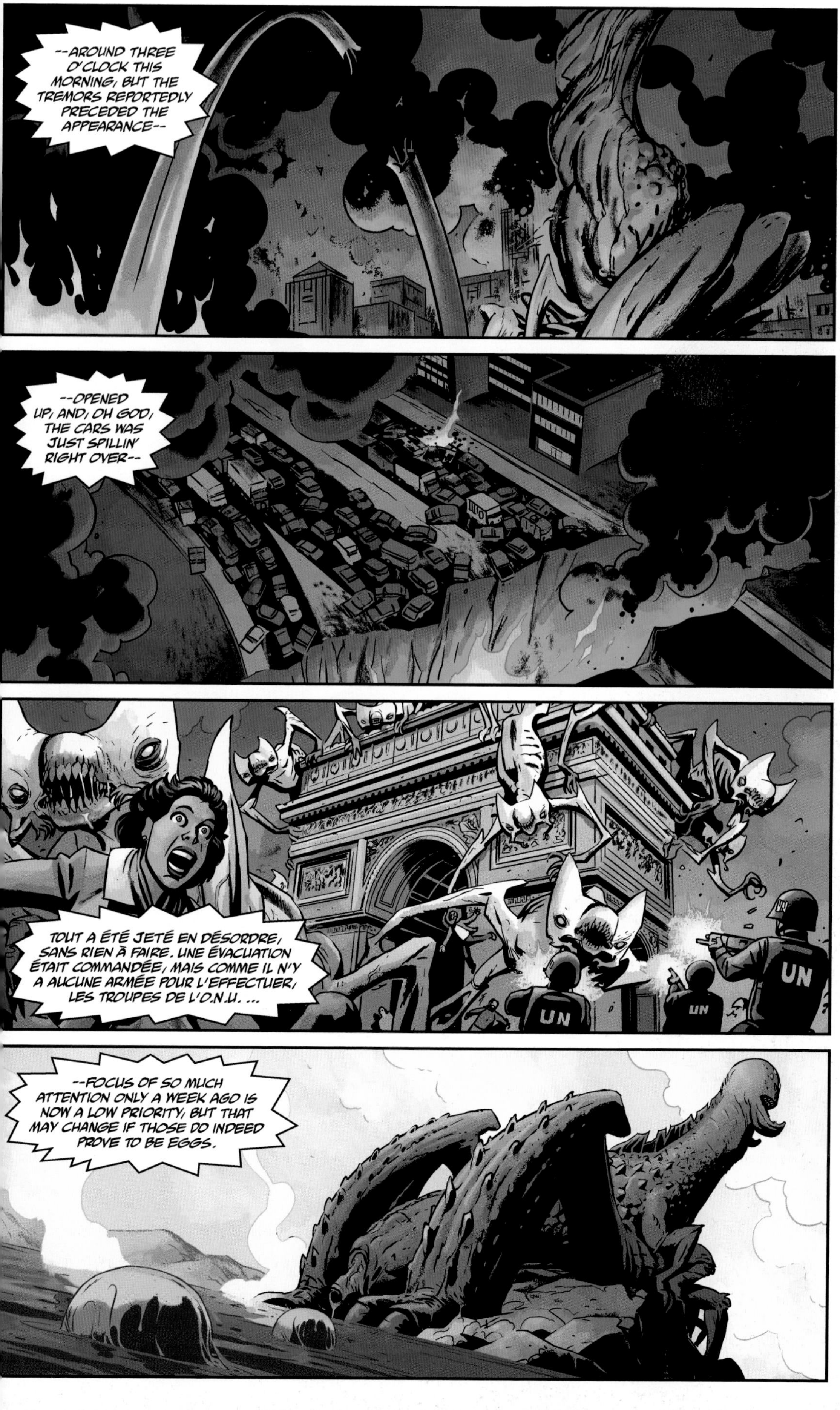
--AROUND THREE O'CLOCK THIS MORNING, BUT THE TREMORS REPORTEDLY PRECEDED THE APPEARANCE--
--OPENED UP, AND, OH GOD, THE CARS WAS JUST SPILLIN' RIGHT OVER--
TOUT A ÉTÉ JETÉ EN DÉSORDRE, SANS RIEN À FAIRE. UNE ÉVACUATION ÉTAIT COMMANDÉE, MAIS COMME IL N'Y A AUCUNE ARMÉE POUR L'EFFECTUER, LES TROUPES DE L'O.N.U. ...
UN
UN
UN
--FOCUS OF SO MUCH ATTENTION ONLY A WEEK AGO IS NOW A LOW PRIORITY, BUT THAT MAY CHANGE IF THOSE DO INDEED PROVE TO BE EGGS.

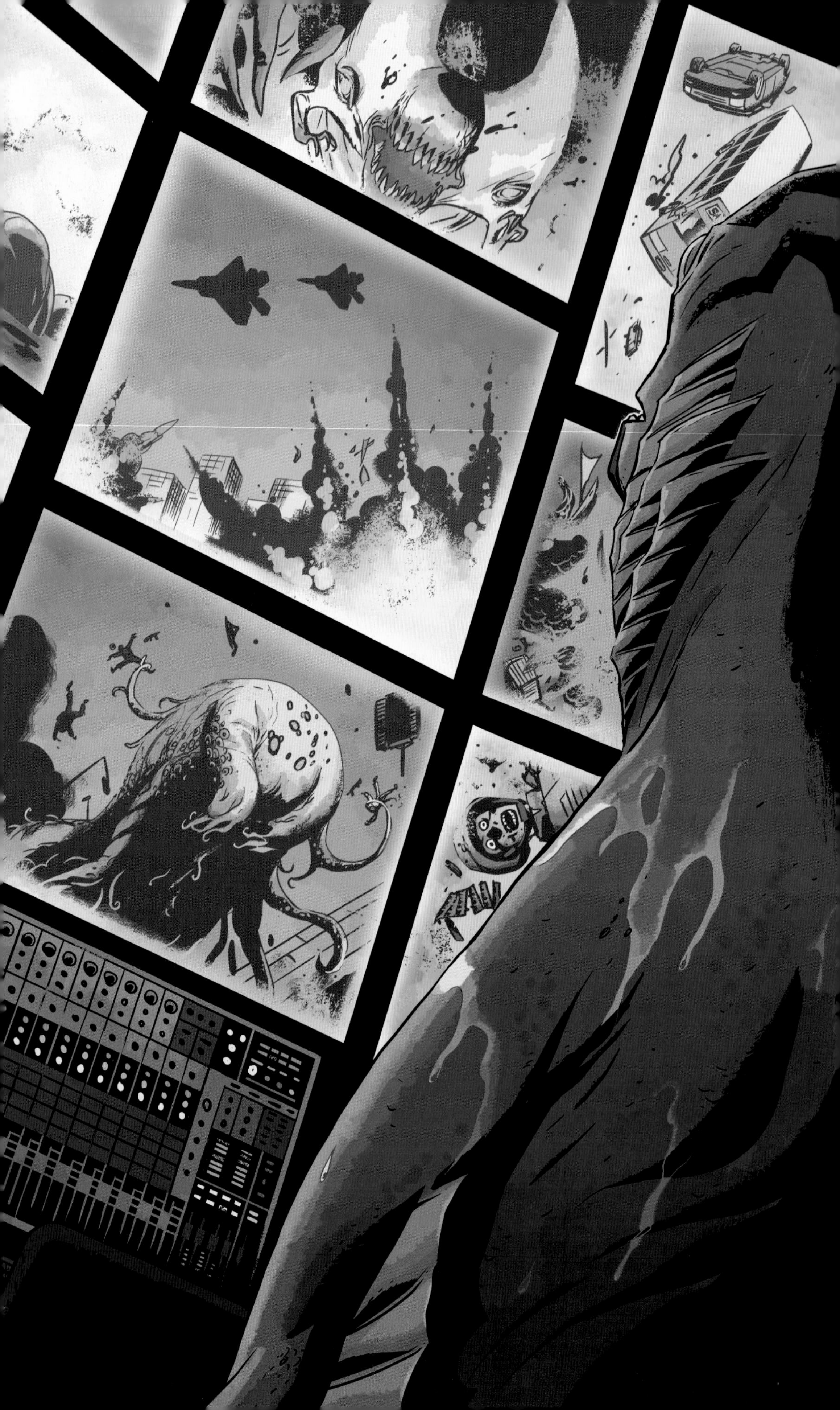

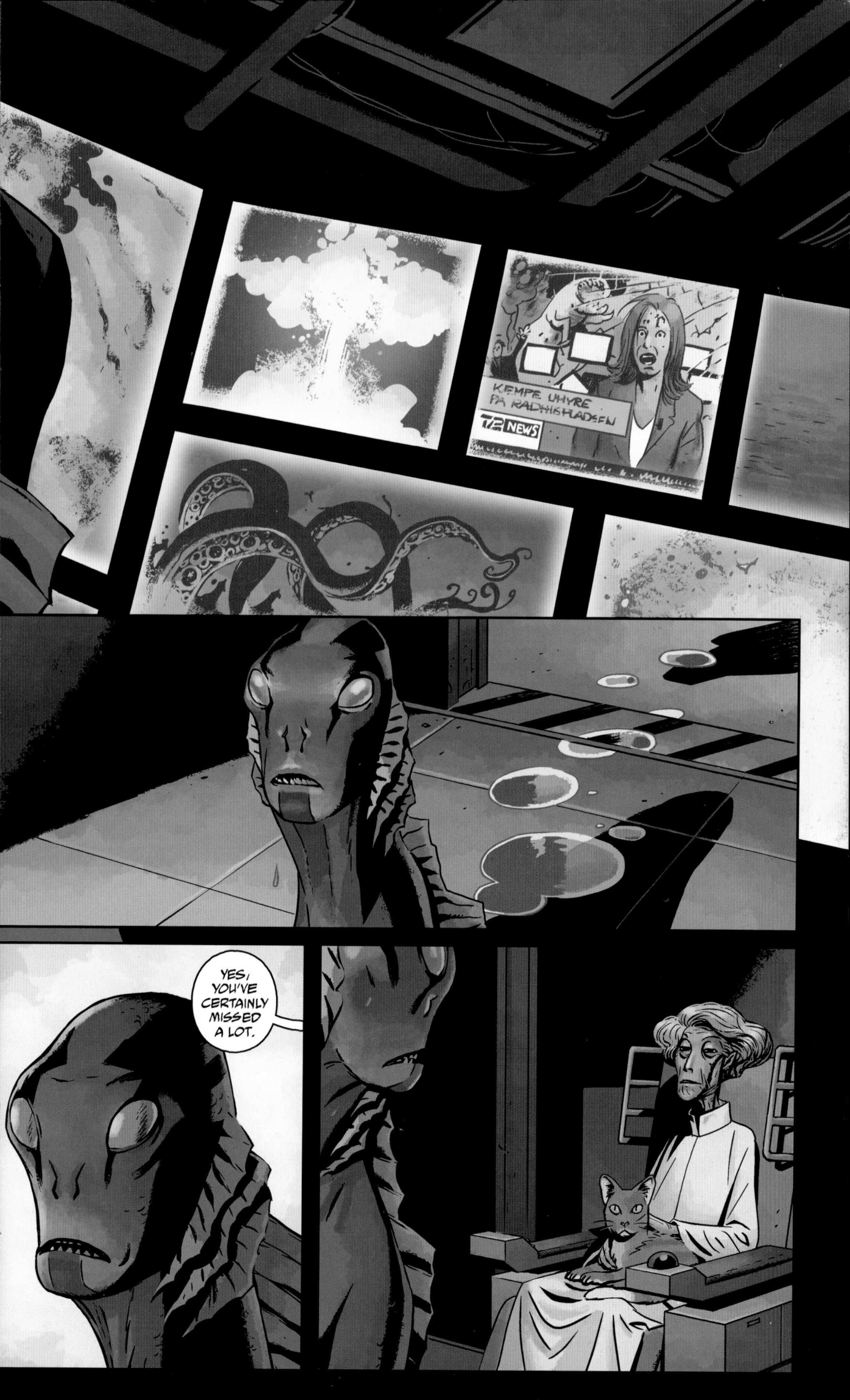
KEMPE UHYRE
PÅ RÅDHUSPLADSEN
T2 NEWS
YES, YOU'VE CERTAINLY MISSED A LOT.

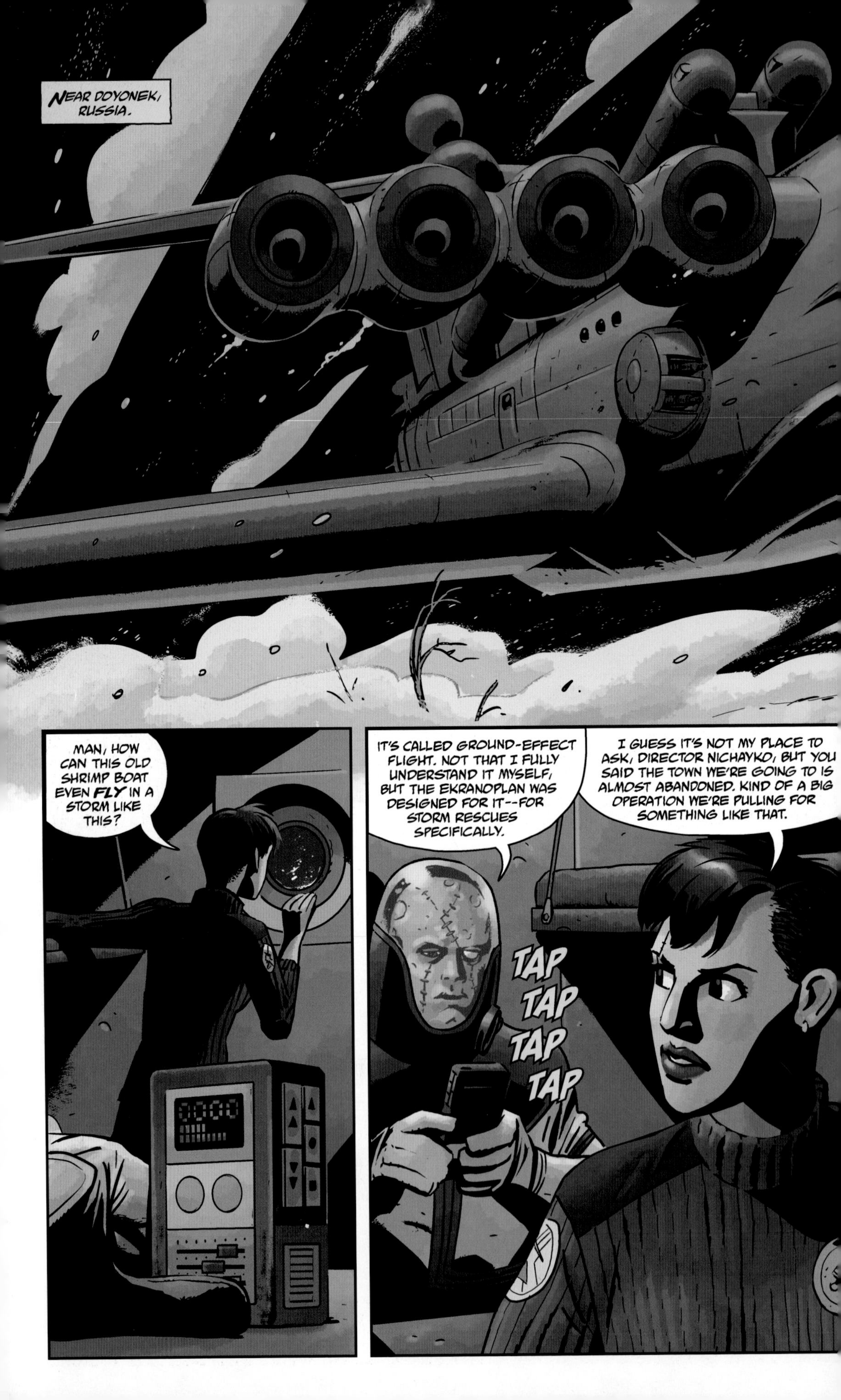
NEAR DOYONEK, RUSSIA.
MAN, HOW CAN THIS OLD SHRIMP BOAT EVEN FLY IN A STORM LIKE THIS?
IT'S CALLED GROUND-EFFECT FLIGHT. NOT THAT I FULLY UNDERSTAND IT MYSELF, BUT THE EKRANOPLAN WAS DESIGNED FOR IT--FOR STORM RESCUES SPECIFICALLY.
I GUESS IT'S NOT MY PLACE TO ASK, DIRECTOR NICHAYKO, BUT YOU SAID THE TOWN WE'RE GOING TO IS ALMOST ABANDONED. KIND OF A BIG OPERATION WE'RE PULLING FOR SOMETHING LIKE THAT.
TAP TAP TAP TAP

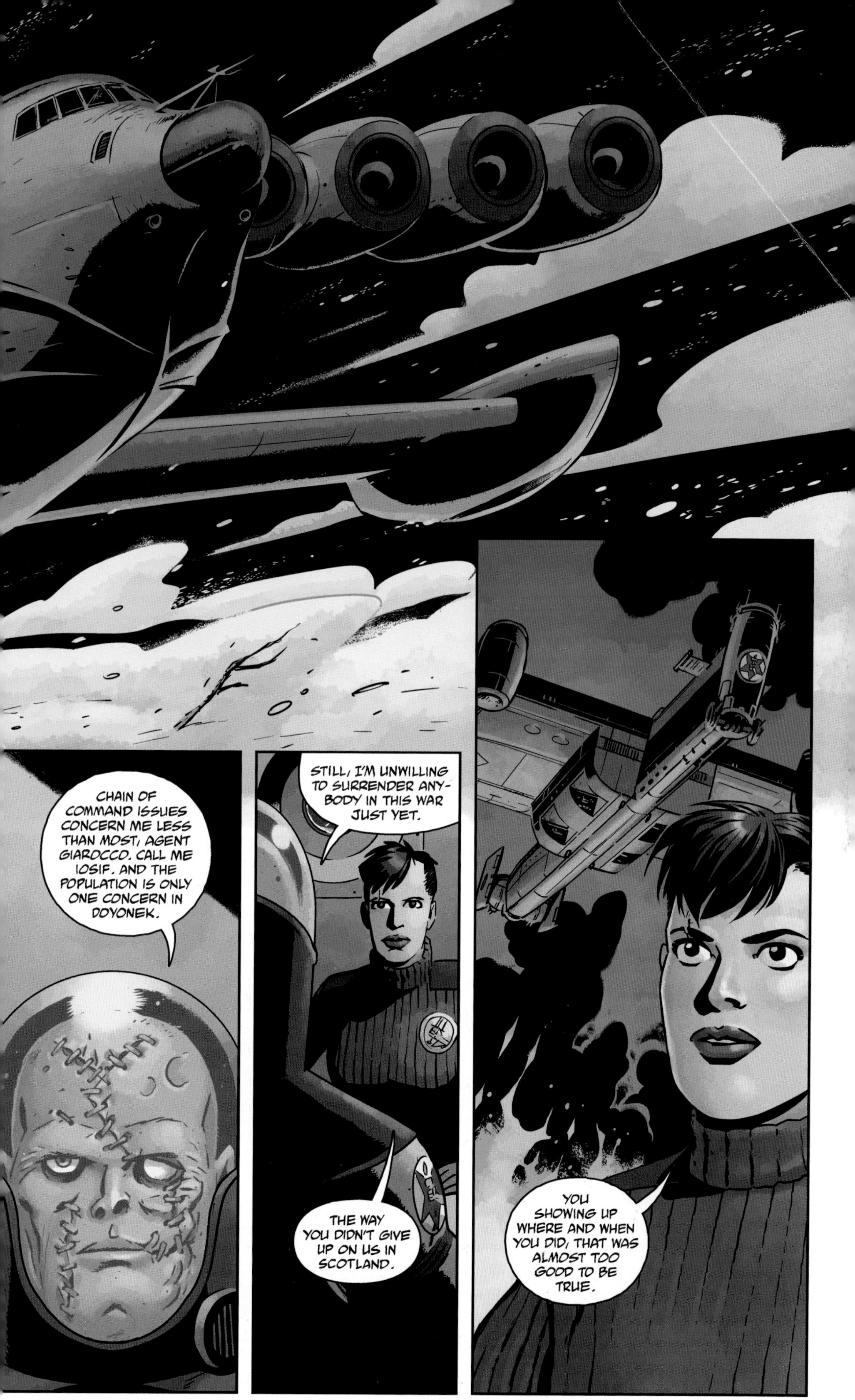
CHAIN OF COMMAND ISSUES CONCERN ME LESS THAN MOST, AGENT GIAROCCO. CALL ME IOSIF. AND THE POPULATION IS ONLY ONE CONCERN IN DOYONEK.
STILL, I'M UNWILLING TO SURRENDER ANY-BODY IN THIS WAR JUST YET.
THE WAY YOU DIDN'T GIVE UP ON US IN SCOTLAND.
YOU SHOWING UP WHERE AND WHEN YOU DID, THAT WAS ALMOST TOO GOOD TO BE TRUE.

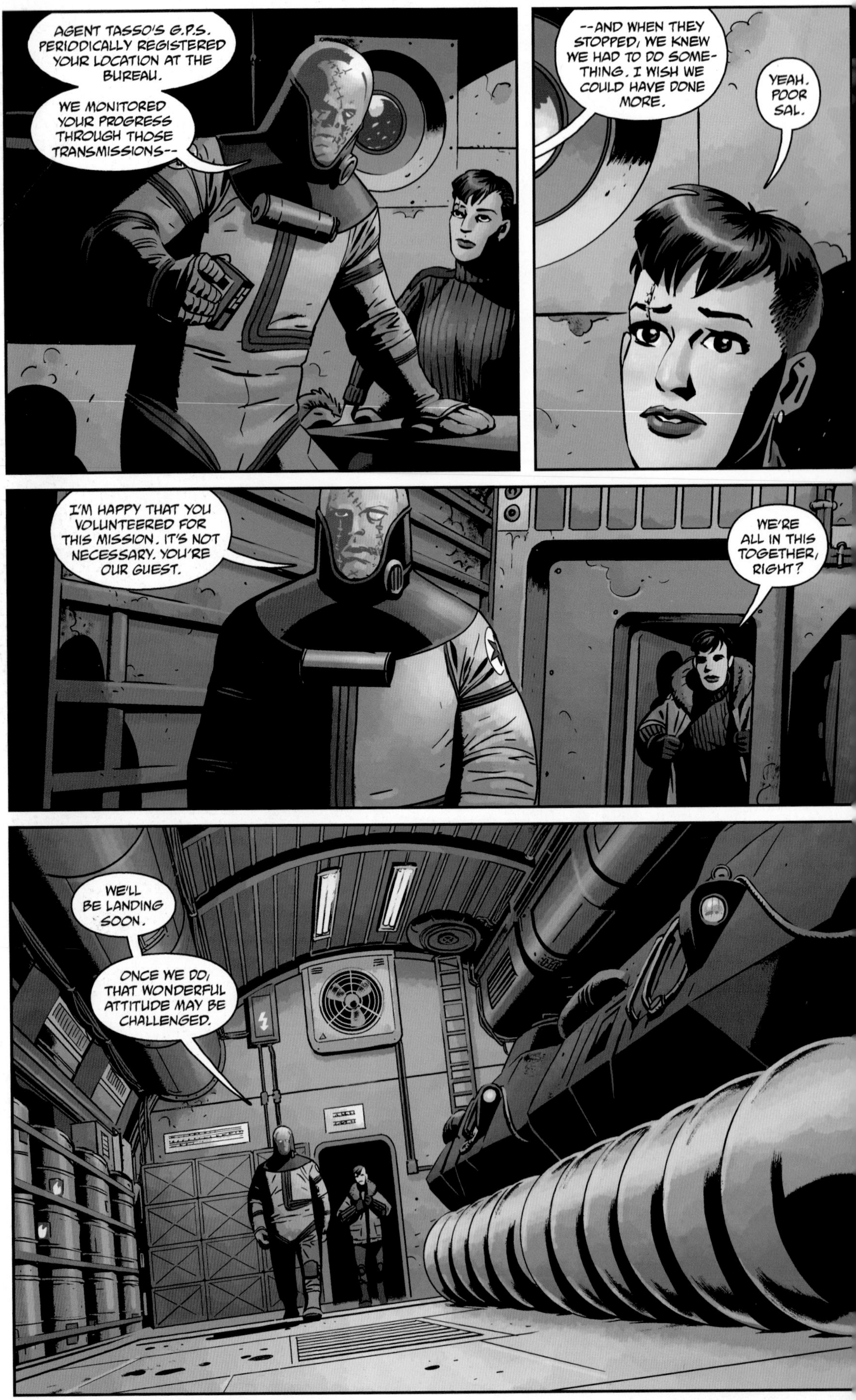
AGENT TASSO'S G.P.S. PERIODICALLY REGISTERED YOUR LOCATION AT THE BUREAU.
WE MONITORED YOUR PROGRESS THROUGH THOSE TRANSMISSIONS--
--AND WHEN THEY STOPPED, WE KNEW WE HAD TO DO SOMETHING. I WISH WE COULD HAVE DONE MORE.
YEAH. POOR SAL.
I'M HAPPY THAT YOU VOLUNTEERED FOR THIS MISSION. IT'S NOT NECESSARY. YOU'RE OUR GUEST.
WE'RE ALL IN THIS TOGETHER, RIGHT?
WE'LL BE LANDING SOON.
ONCE WE DO, THAT WONDERFUL ATTITUDE MAY BE CHALLENGED.

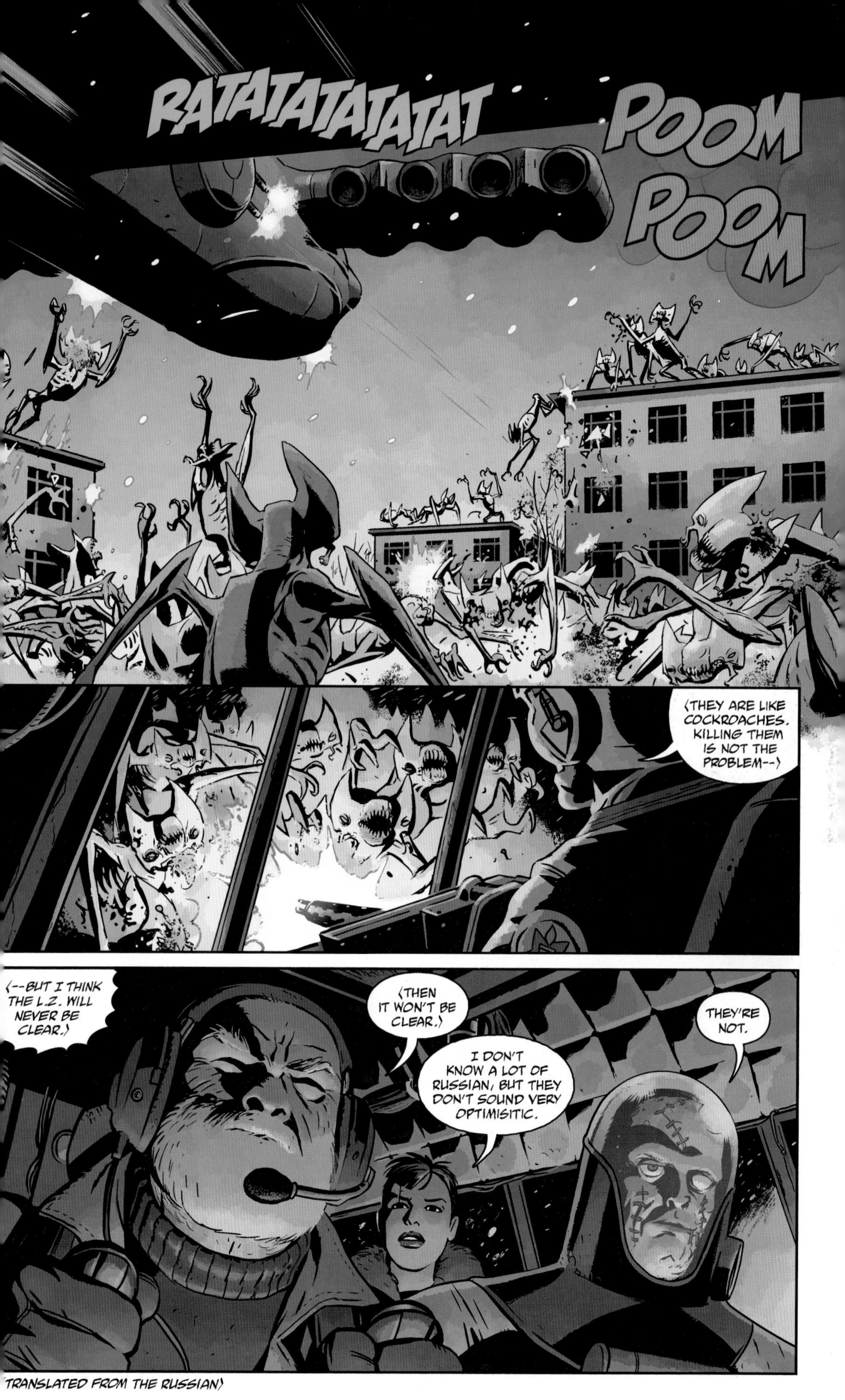
RATATATATATAT
POOM
POOM
‹THEY ARE LIKE COCKROACHES. KILLING THEM IS NOT THE PROBLEM--›
‹--BUT I THINK THE L.Z. WILL NEVER BE CLEAR.›
‹THEN IT WON'T BE CLEAR.›
I DON'T KNOW A LOT OF RUSSIAN, BUT THEY DON'T SOUND VERY OPTIMISITIC.
THEY'RE NOT.

‹TRANSLATED FROM THE RUSSIAN›

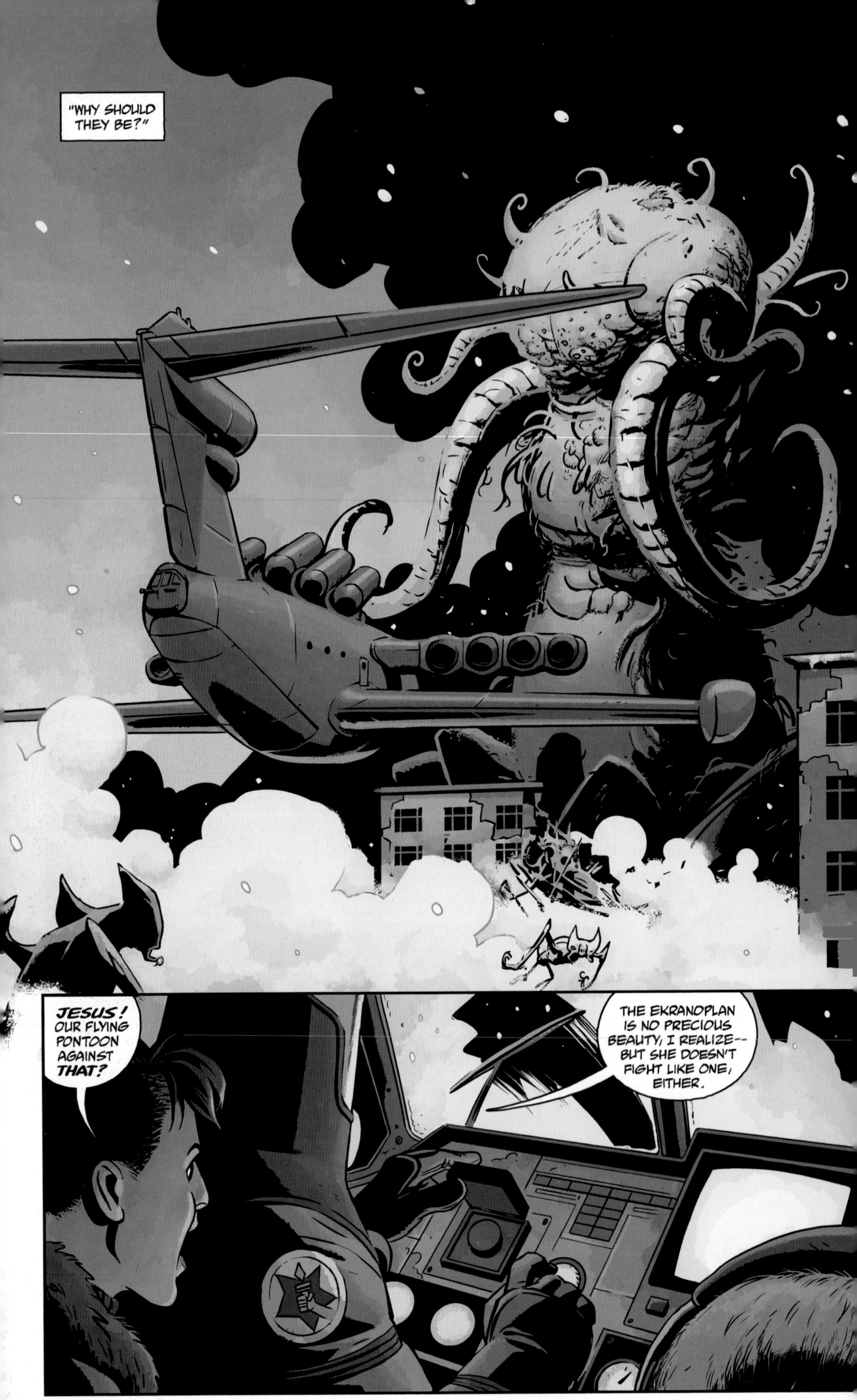
"WHY SHOULD THEY BE?"
JESUS! OUR FLYING PONTOON AGAINST THAT?
THE EKRANOPLAN IS NO PRECIOUS BEAUTY, I REALIZE-- BUT SHE DOESN'T FIGHT LIKE ONE, EITHER.

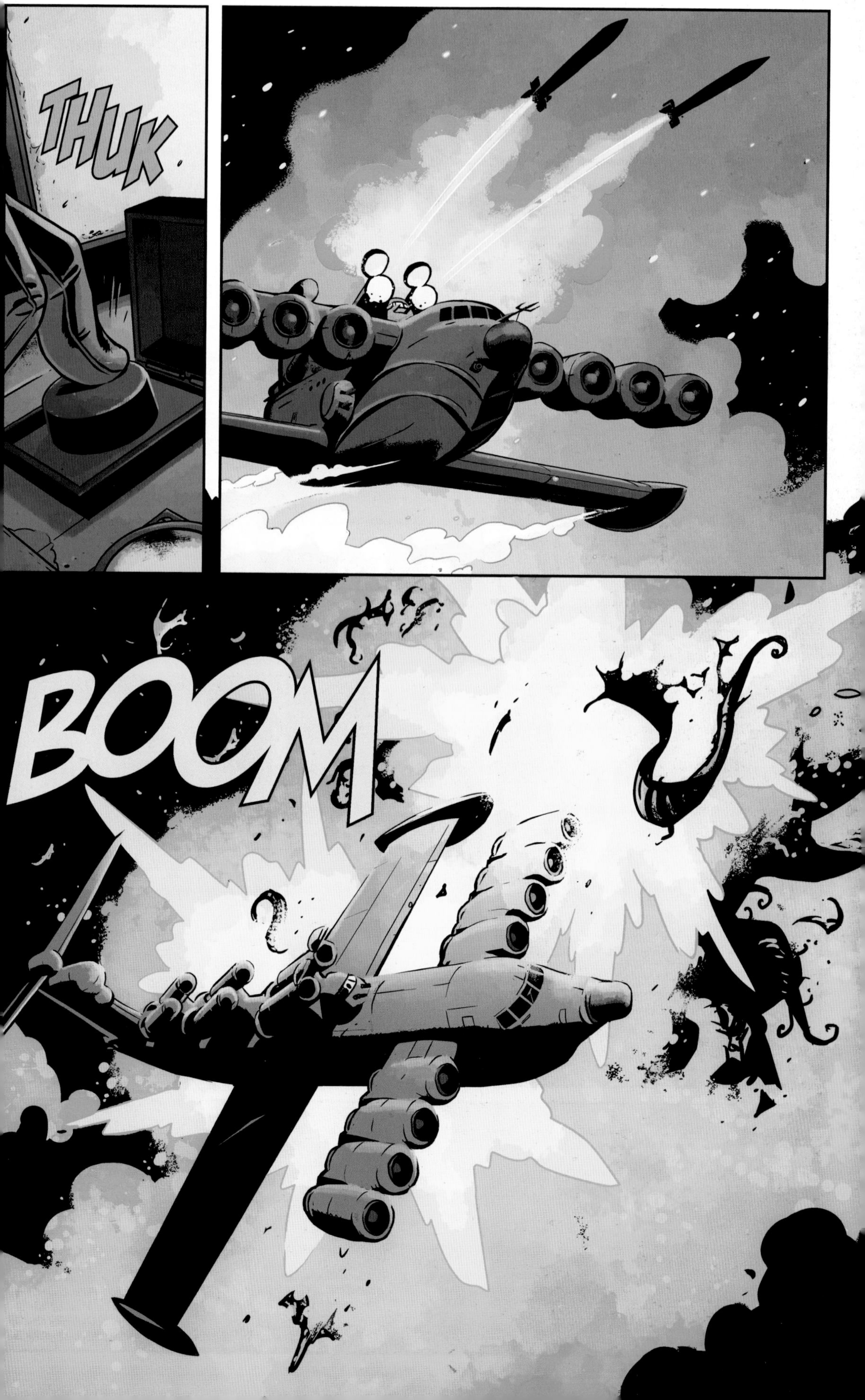
THUK
BOOM

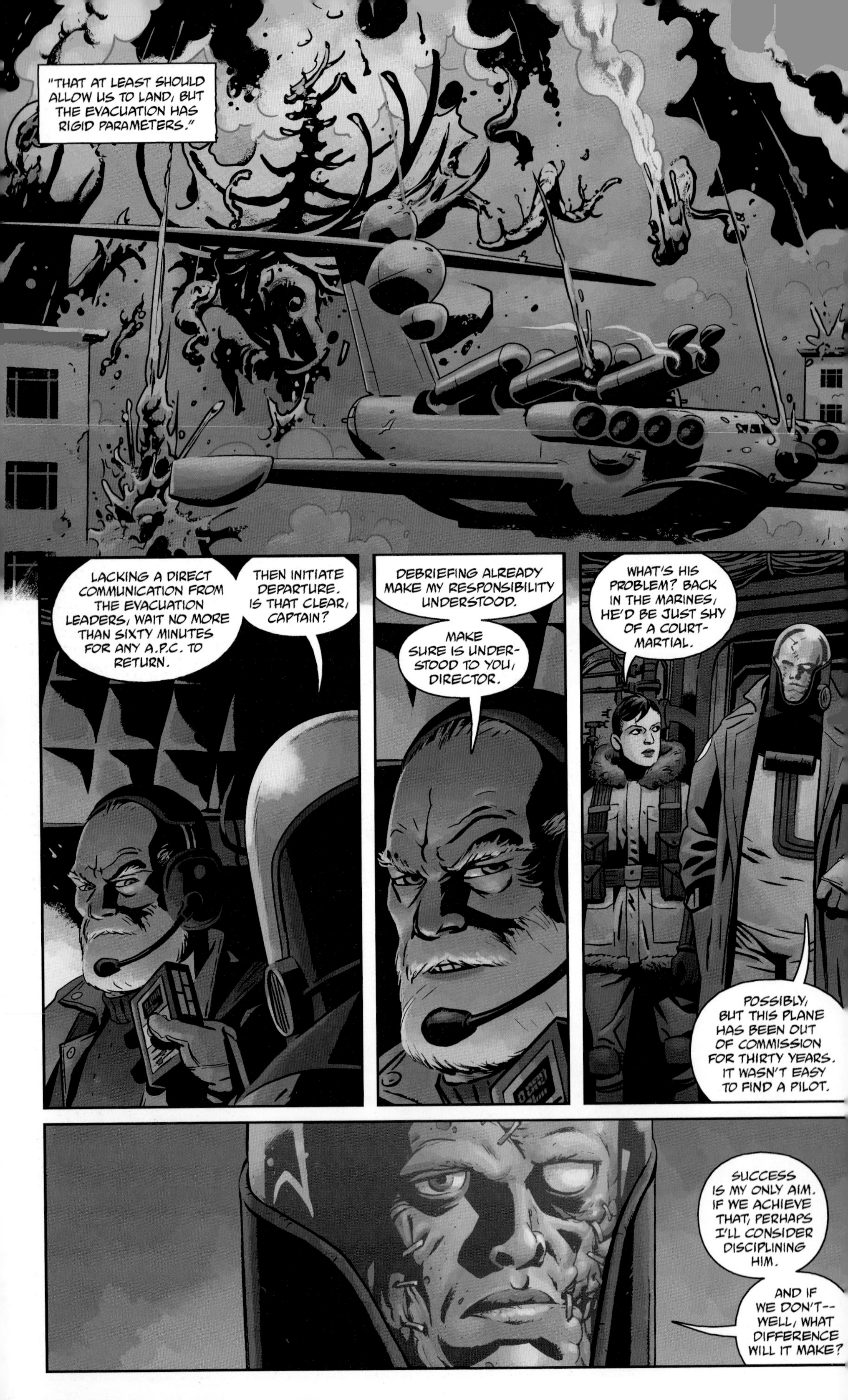
"THAT AT LEAST SHOULD ALLOW US TO LAND, BUT THE EVACUATION HAS RIGID PARAMETERS."
LACKING A DIRECT COMMUNICATION FROM THE EVACUATION LEADERS, WAIT NO MORE THAN SIXTY MINUTES FOR ANY A.P.C. TO RETURN.
THEN INITIATE DEPARTURE. IS THAT CLEAR, CAPTAIN?
DEBRIEFING ALREADY MAKE MY RESPONSIBILITY UNDERSTOOD.
MAKE SURE IS UNDERSTOOD TO YOU, DIRECTOR.
WHAT'S HIS PROBLEM? BACK IN THE MARINES, HE'D BE JUST SHY OF A COURT-MARTIAL.
POSSIBLY, BUT THIS PLANE HAS BEEN OUT OF COMMISSION FOR THIRTY YEARS. IT WASN'T EASY TO FIND A PILOT.
SUCCESS IS MY ONLY AIM. IF WE ACHIEVE THAT, PERHAPS I'LL CONSIDER DISCIPLINING HIM.
AND IF WE DON'T--WELL, WHAT DIFFERENCE WILL IT MAKE?

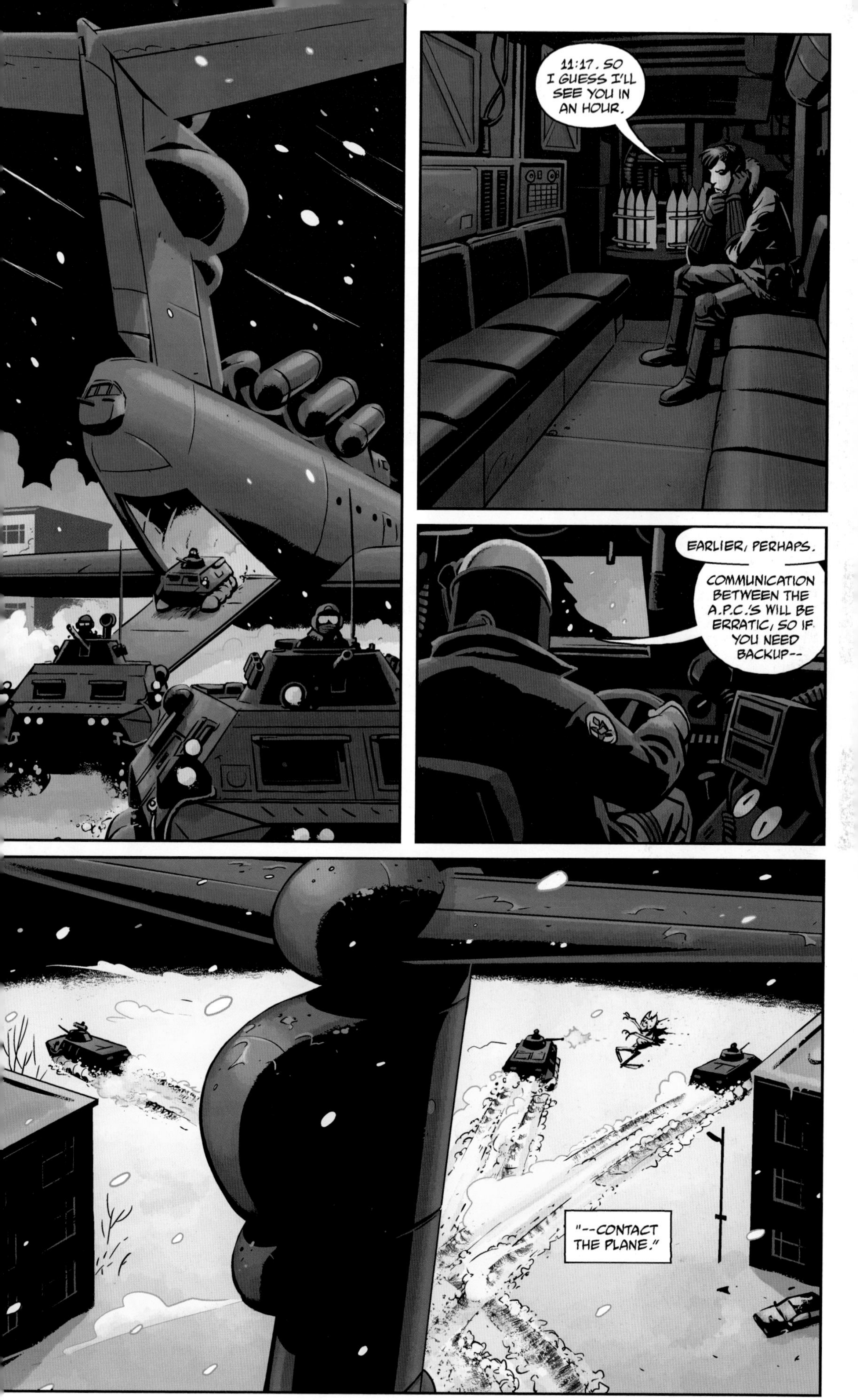
11:17. SO I GUESS I'LL SEE YOU IN AN HOUR.
EARLIER, PERHAPS.
COMMUNICATION BETWEEN THE A.P.C.'S WILL BE ERRATIC, SO IF YOU NEED BACKUP--
"--CONTACT THE PLANE."

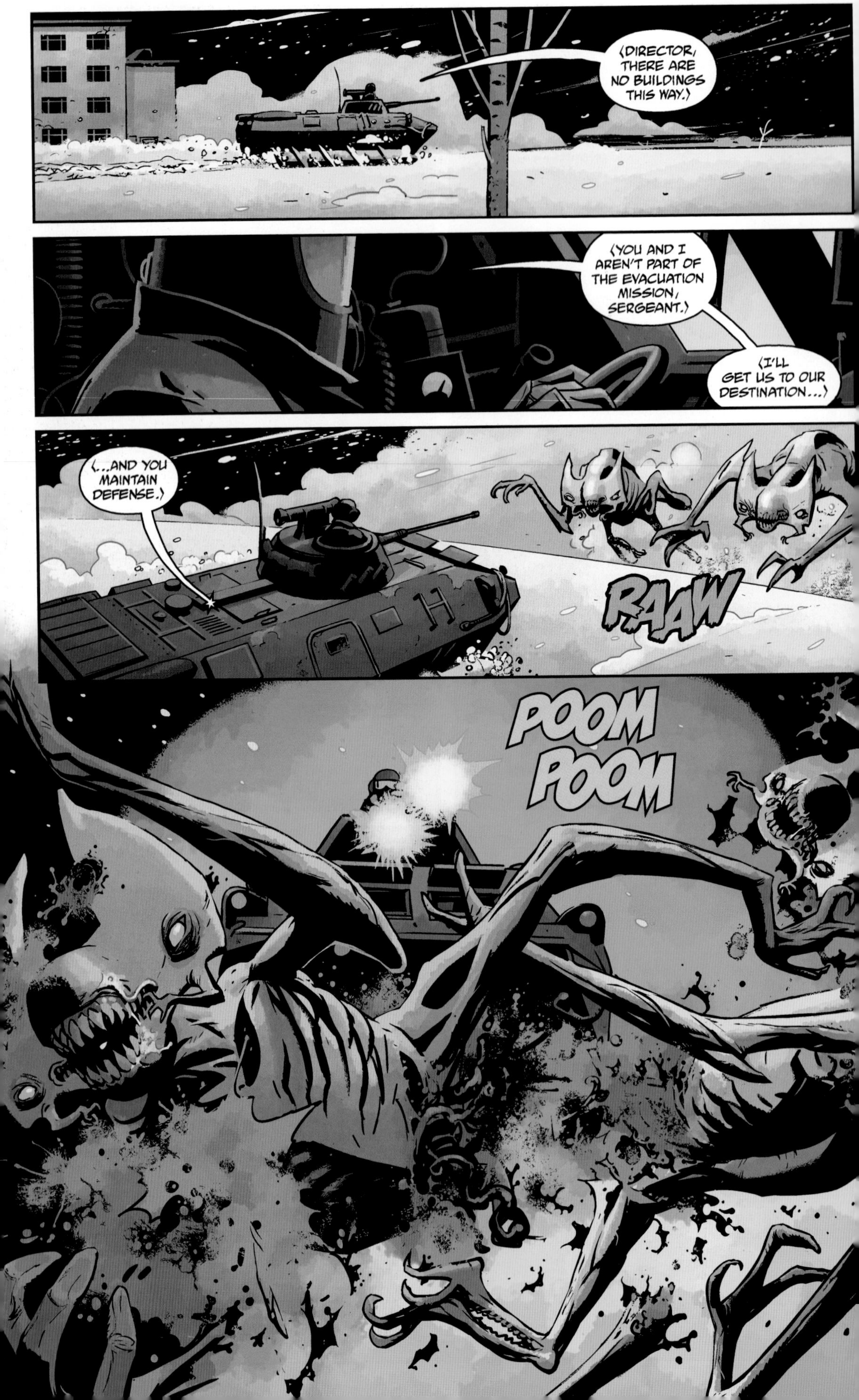

⟨DIRECTOR, THERE ARE NO BUILDINGS THIS WAY.⟩
⟨YOU AND I AREN'T PART OF THE EVACUATION MISSION, SERGEANT.⟩
⟨I'LL GET US TO OUR DESTINATION...⟩
⟨...AND YOU MAINTAIN DEFENSE.⟩
RAAW
POOM
POOM

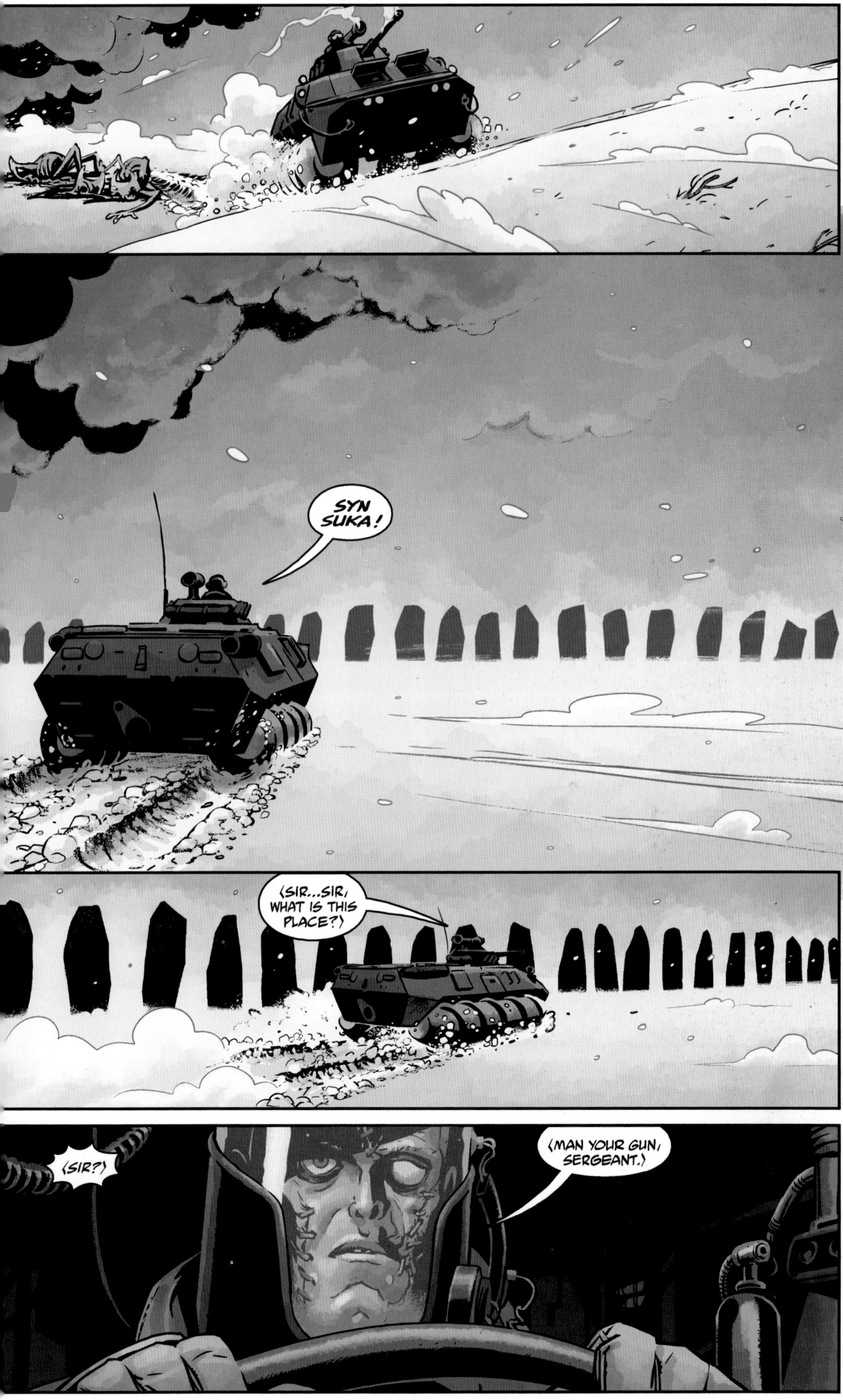
SYN SUKA!
⟨SIR...SIR, WHAT IS THIS PLACE?⟩
⟨SIR?⟩
⟨MAN YOUR GUN, SERGEANT.⟩

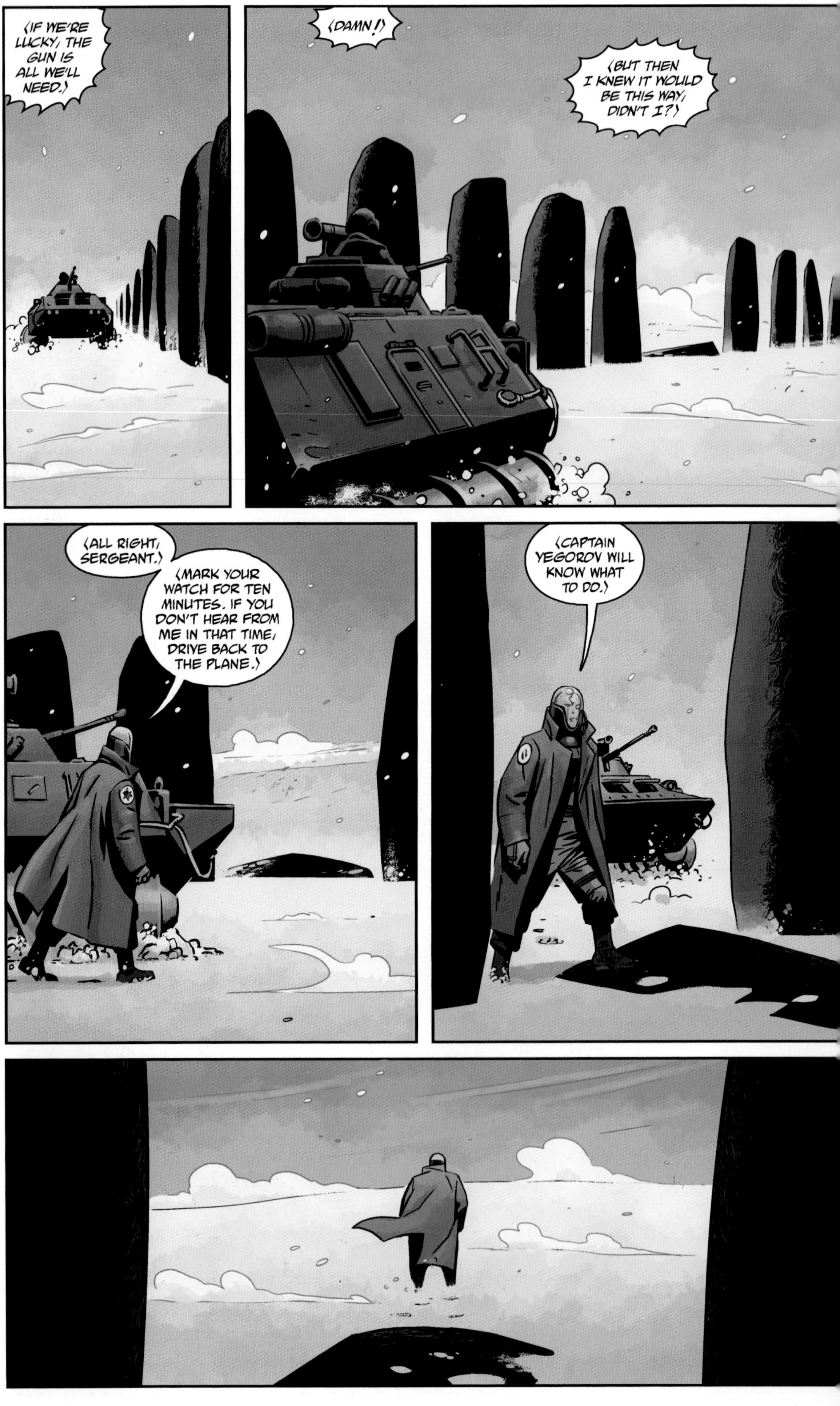
⟨IF WE'RE LUCKY, THE GUN IS ALL WE'LL NEED.⟩
⟨DAMN!⟩
⟨BUT THEN I KNEW IT WOULD BE THIS WAY, DIDN'T I?⟩
⟨ALL RIGHT, SERGEANT.⟩
⟨MARK YOUR WATCH FOR TEN MINUTES. IF YOU DON'T HEAR FROM ME IN THAT TIME, DRIVE BACK TO THE PLANE.⟩
⟨CAPTAIN YEGOROV WILL KNOW WHAT TO DO.⟩

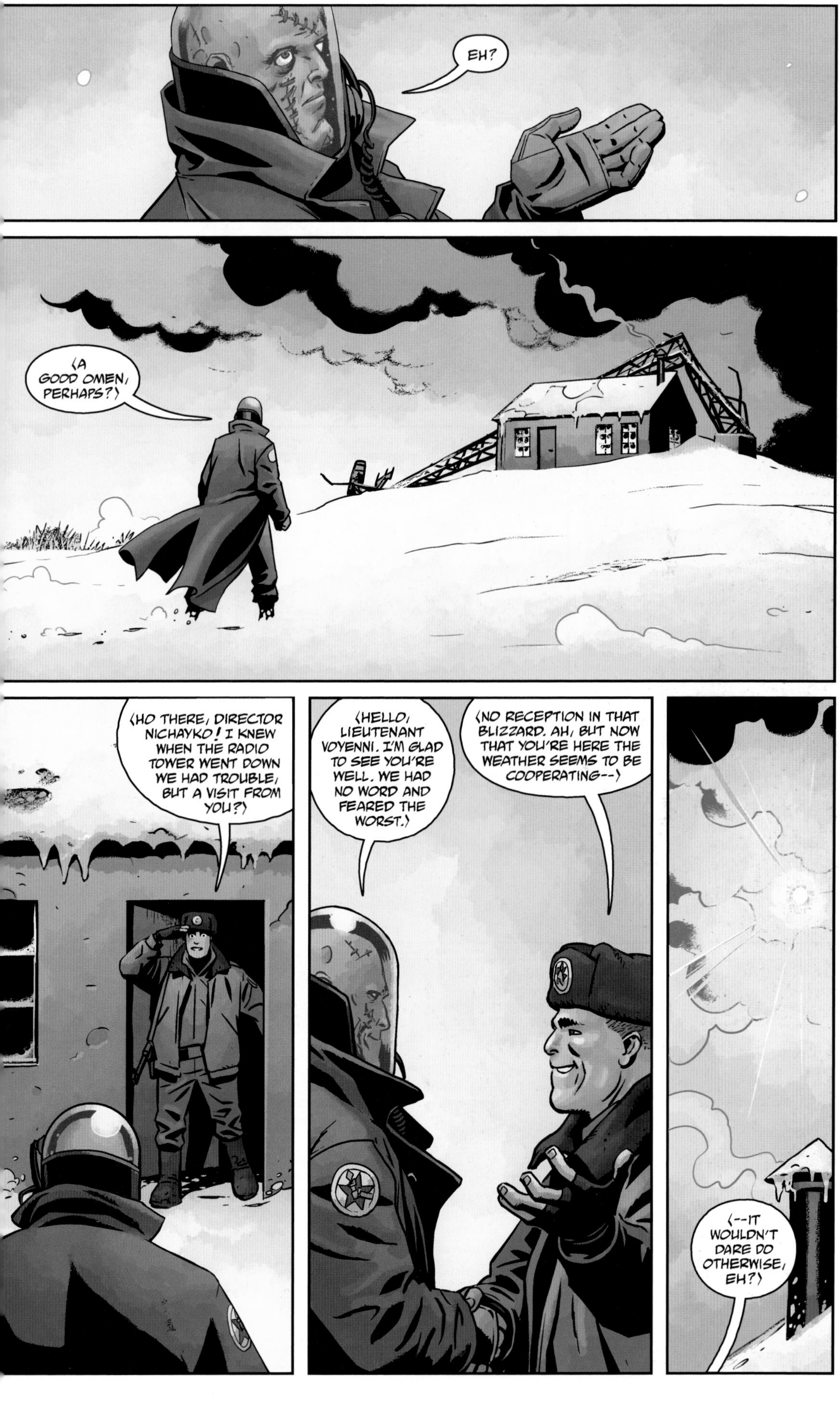
EH?
‹A GOOD OMEN, PERHAPS?›
‹HO THERE, DIRECTOR NICHAYKO! I KNEW WHEN THE RADIO TOWER WENT DOWN WE HAD TROUBLE, BUT A VISIT FROM YOU?›
‹HELLO, LIEUTENANT VOYENNI. I'M GLAD TO SEE YOU'RE WELL. WE HAD NO WORD AND FEARED THE WORST.›
‹NO RECEPTION IN THAT BLIZZARD. AH, BUT NOW THAT YOU'RE HERE THE WEATHER SEEMS TO BE COOPERATING--›
‹--IT WOULDN'T DARE DO OTHERWISE, EH?›

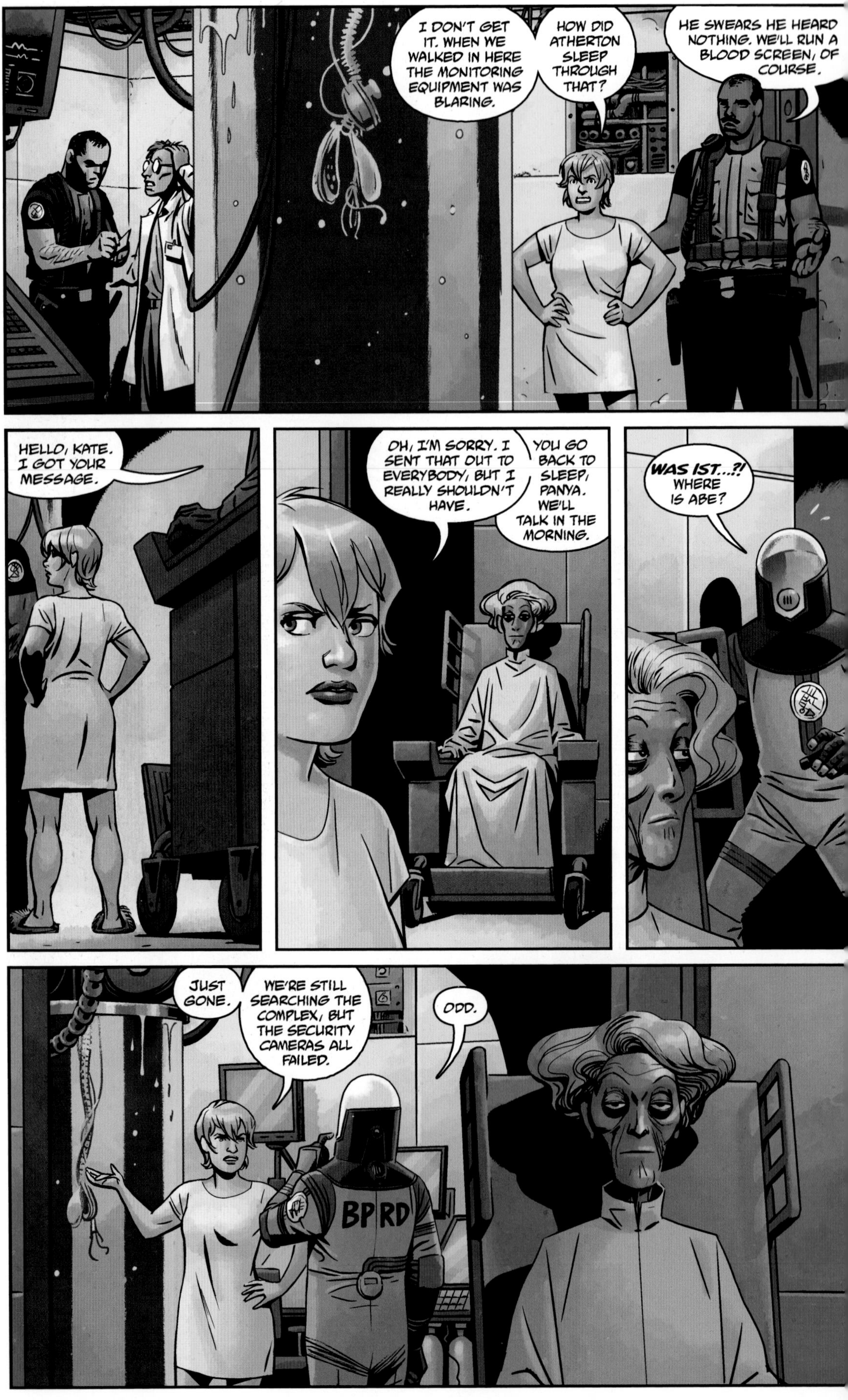
I DON'T GET IT. WHEN WE WALKED IN HERE THE MONITORING EQUIPMENT WAS BLARING.
HOW DID ATHERTON SLEEP THROUGH THAT?
HE SWEARS HE HEARD NOTHING. WE'LL RUN A BLOOD SCREEN, OF COURSE.
HELLO, KATE. I GOT YOUR MESSAGE.
OH, I'M SORRY. I SENT THAT OUT TO EVERYBODY, BUT I REALLY SHOULDN'T HAVE.
YOU GO BACK TO SLEEP, PANYA. WE'LL TALK IN THE MORNING.
WAS IST...?! WHERE IS ABE?
JUST GONE.
WE'RE STILL SEARCHING THE COMPLEX, BUT THE SECURITY CAMERAS ALL FAILED.
ODD.
BPRD

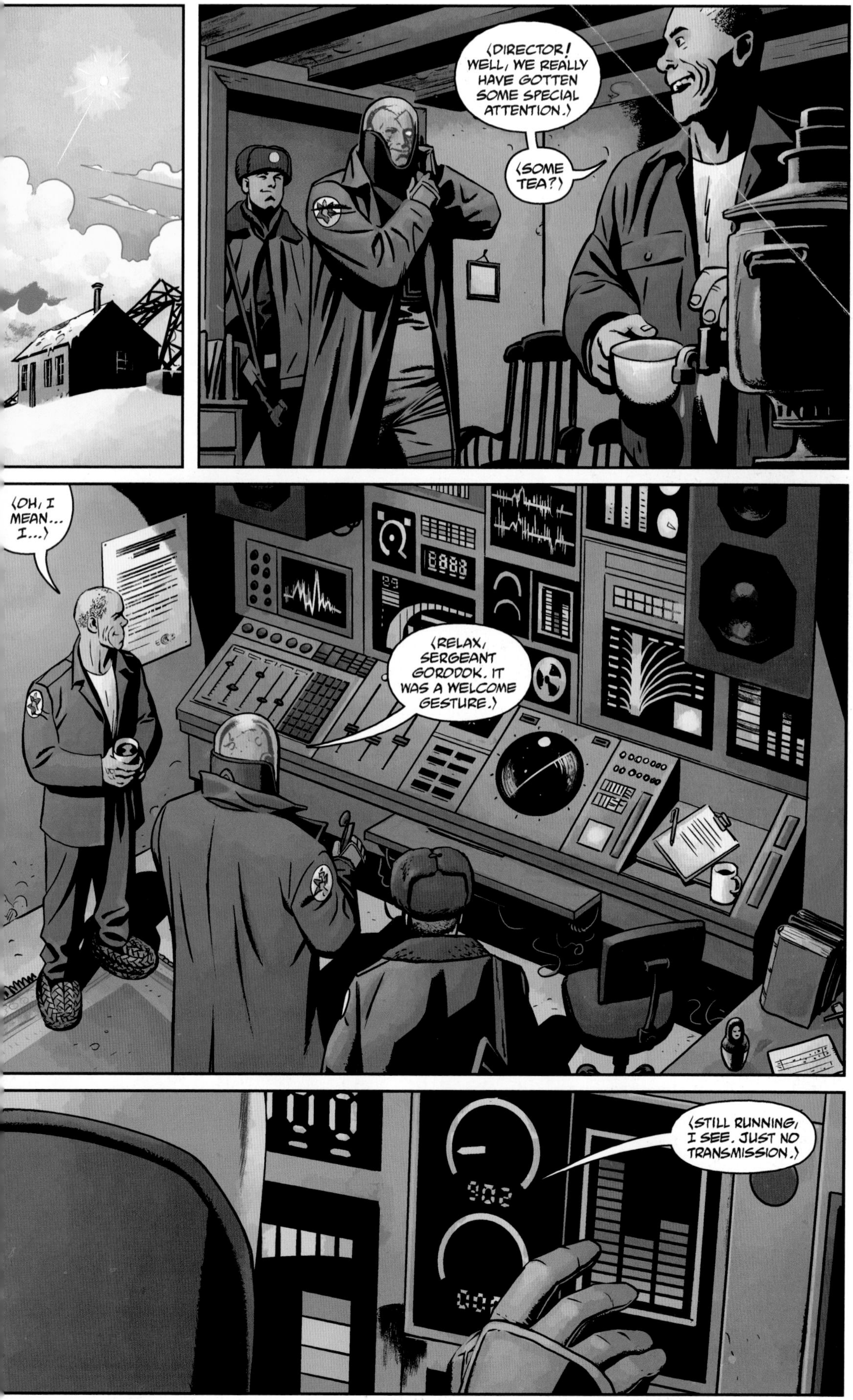

⟨DIRECTOR! WELL, WE REALLY HAVE GOTTEN SOME SPECIAL ATTENTION.⟩
⟨SOME TEA?⟩
⟨OH, I MEAN... I...⟩
⟨RELAX, SERGEANT GORODOK. IT WAS A WELCOME GESTURE.⟩
⟨STILL RUNNING, I SEE. JUST NO TRANSMISSION.⟩

⟨NOT VERY FAR, BUT EVEN WITHOUT THE TOWER WE GET A BROADCAST RADIUS OF ABOUT ONE HUNDRED METERS.⟩

⟨OUT TO THE FENCE. GOOD. BETTER THAN I EXPECTED.⟩

⟨BUT THEN, WE CAN'T AFFORD TO MOVE THE AUDIO FILE FOR NOW.⟩

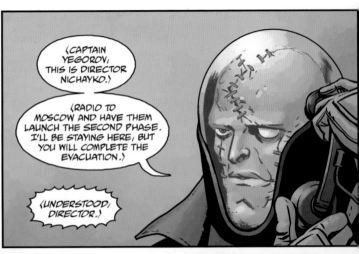

⟨CAPTAIN YEGOROV, THIS IS DIRECTOR NICHAYKO.⟩

⟨RADIO TO MOSCOW AND HAVE THEM LAUNCH THE SECOND PHASE. I'LL BE STAYING HERE, BUT YOU WILL COMPLETE THE EVACUATION.⟩

⟨UNDERSTOOD, DIRECTOR.⟩

⟨WELL THEN, NO TEA FOR ME, BUT YOU HAVE A CHESS SET, YES?⟩

⟨YOU KNOW, DIRECTOR, I'VE BEEN HERE TWO YEARS, VOYENNI ALMOST THREE.⟩

⟨WE BROADCAST THAT AUDIO FILE, DAY AND NIGHT, FORBIDDEN TO LISTEN TO IT, BUT WE DEFEND IT WITH OUR LIVES.⟩

⟨AND NOW, WITH YOU HERE... IT WOULD BE NICE TO KNOW WHAT IS SO IMPORTANT ABOUT OUR BROADCAST, SIR.⟩

⟨ARE YOU ASKING FOR HONESTY FROM RUSSIAN BUREAUCRACY?⟩

⟨NO. FROM YOU.⟩

⟨AH, I SEE HOW IT IS.⟩

⟨ACTUALLY, IT'S A GOOD DAY FOR YOU TO KNOW THE TRUTH.⟩

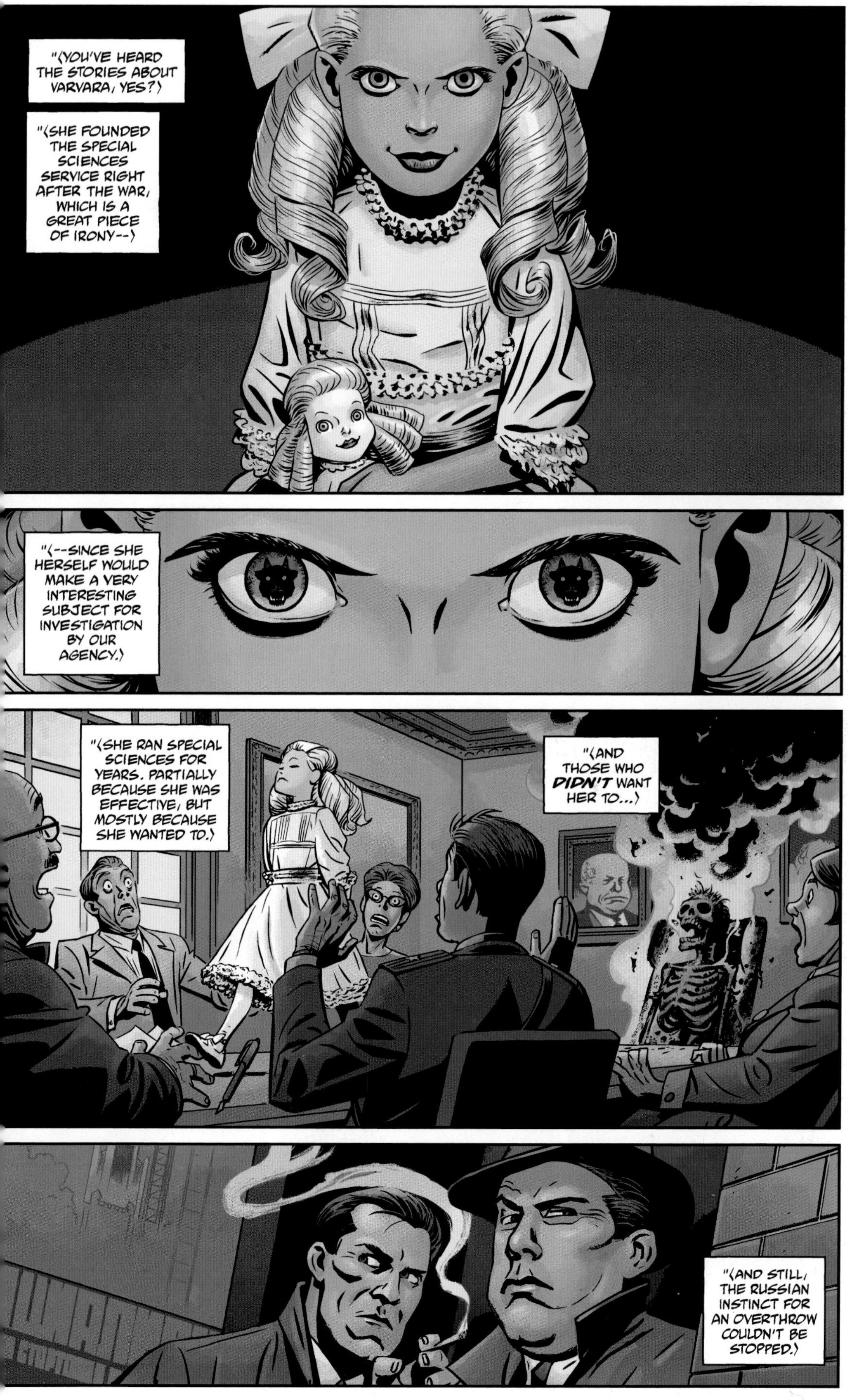
"⟨YOU'VE HEARD THE STORIES ABOUT VARVARA, YES?⟩
"⟨SHE FOUNDED THE SPECIAL SCIENCES SERVICE RIGHT AFTER THE WAR, WHICH IS A GREAT PIECE OF IRONY--⟩
"⟨--SINCE SHE HERSELF WOULD MAKE A VERY INTERESTING SUBJECT FOR INVESTIGATION BY OUR AGENCY.⟩
"⟨SHE RAN SPECIAL SCIENCES FOR YEARS. PARTIALLY BECAUSE SHE WAS EFFECTIVE, BUT MOSTLY BECAUSE SHE WANTED TO.⟩
"⟨AND THOSE WHO ***DIDN'T*** WANT HER TO...⟩
"⟨AND STILL, THE RUSSIAN INSTINCT FOR AN OVERTHROW COULDN'T BE STOPPED.⟩

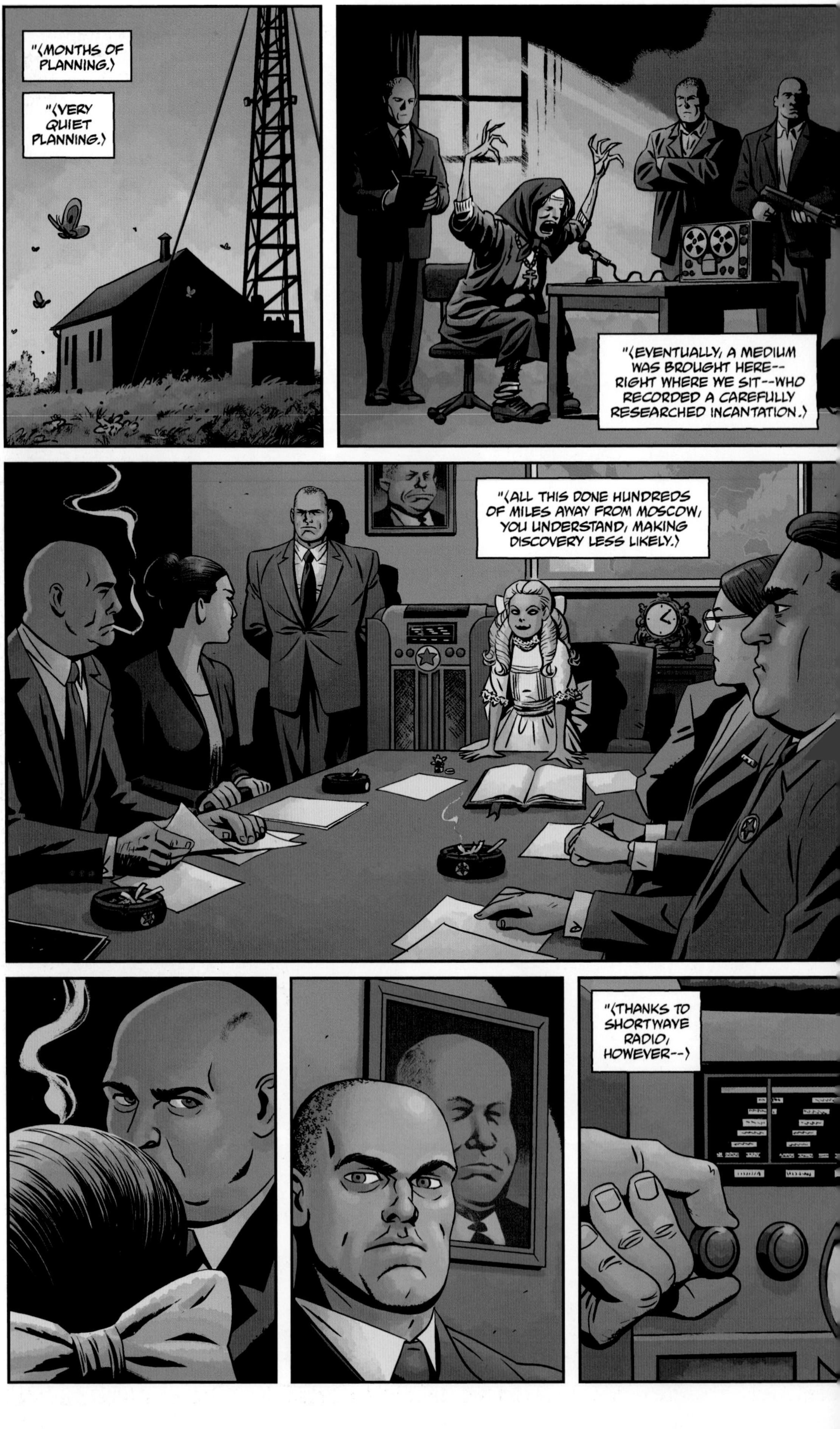
"⟨MONTHS OF PLANNING.⟩
"⟨VERY QUIET PLANNING.⟩
"⟨EVENTUALLY, A MEDIUM WAS BROUGHT HERE-- RIGHT WHERE WE SIT--WHO RECORDED A CAREFULLY RESEARCHED INCANTATION.⟩
"⟨ALL THIS DONE HUNDREDS OF MILES AWAY FROM MOSCOW, YOU UNDERSTAND, MAKING DISCOVERY LESS LIKELY.⟩
"⟨THANKS TO SHORTWAVE RADIO, HOWEVER--⟩

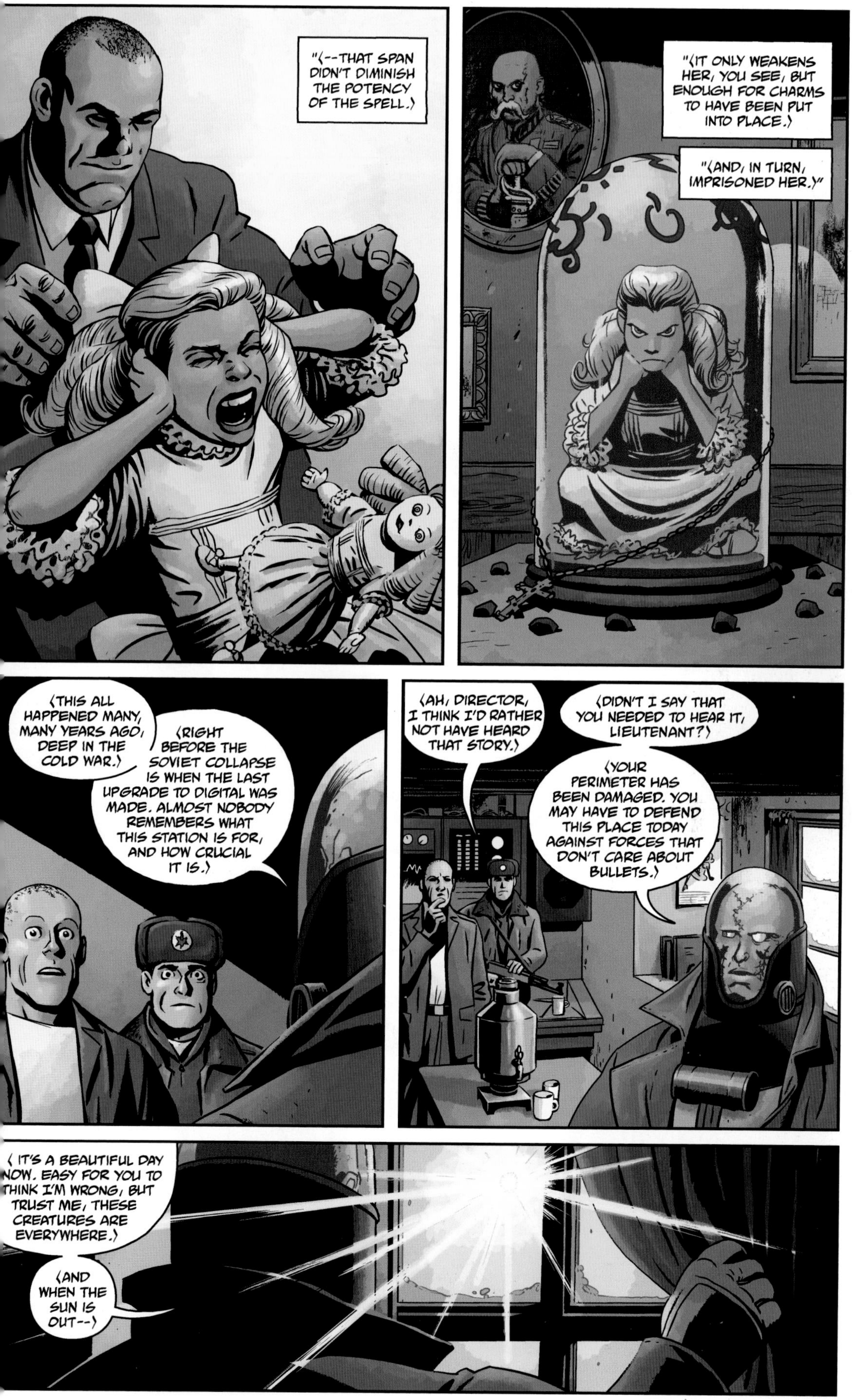
"⟨--THAT SPAN DIDN'T DIMINISH THE POTENCY OF THE SPELL.⟩
"⟨IT ONLY WEAKENS HER, YOU SEE, BUT ENOUGH FOR CHARMS TO HAVE BEEN PUT INTO PLACE.⟩
"⟨AND, IN TURN, IMPRISONED HER.⟩"
⟨THIS ALL HAPPENED MANY, MANY YEARS AGO, DEEP IN THE COLD WAR.⟩
⟨RIGHT BEFORE THE SOVIET COLLAPSE IS WHEN THE LAST UPGRADE TO DIGITAL WAS MADE. ALMOST NOBODY REMEMBERS WHAT THIS STATION IS FOR, AND HOW CRUCIAL IT IS.⟩
⟨AH, DIRECTOR, I THINK I'D RATHER NOT HAVE HEARD THAT STORY.⟩
⟨DIDN'T I SAY THAT YOU NEEDED TO HEAR IT, LIEUTENANT?⟩
⟨YOUR PERIMETER HAS BEEN DAMAGED. YOU MAY HAVE TO DEFEND THIS PLACE TODAY AGAINST FORCES THAT DON'T CARE ABOUT BULLETS.⟩
⟨ IT'S A BEAUTIFUL DAY NOW. EASY FOR YOU TO THINK I'M WRONG, BUT TRUST ME, THESE CREATURES ARE EVERYWHERE.⟩
⟨AND WHEN THE SUN IS OUT--⟩

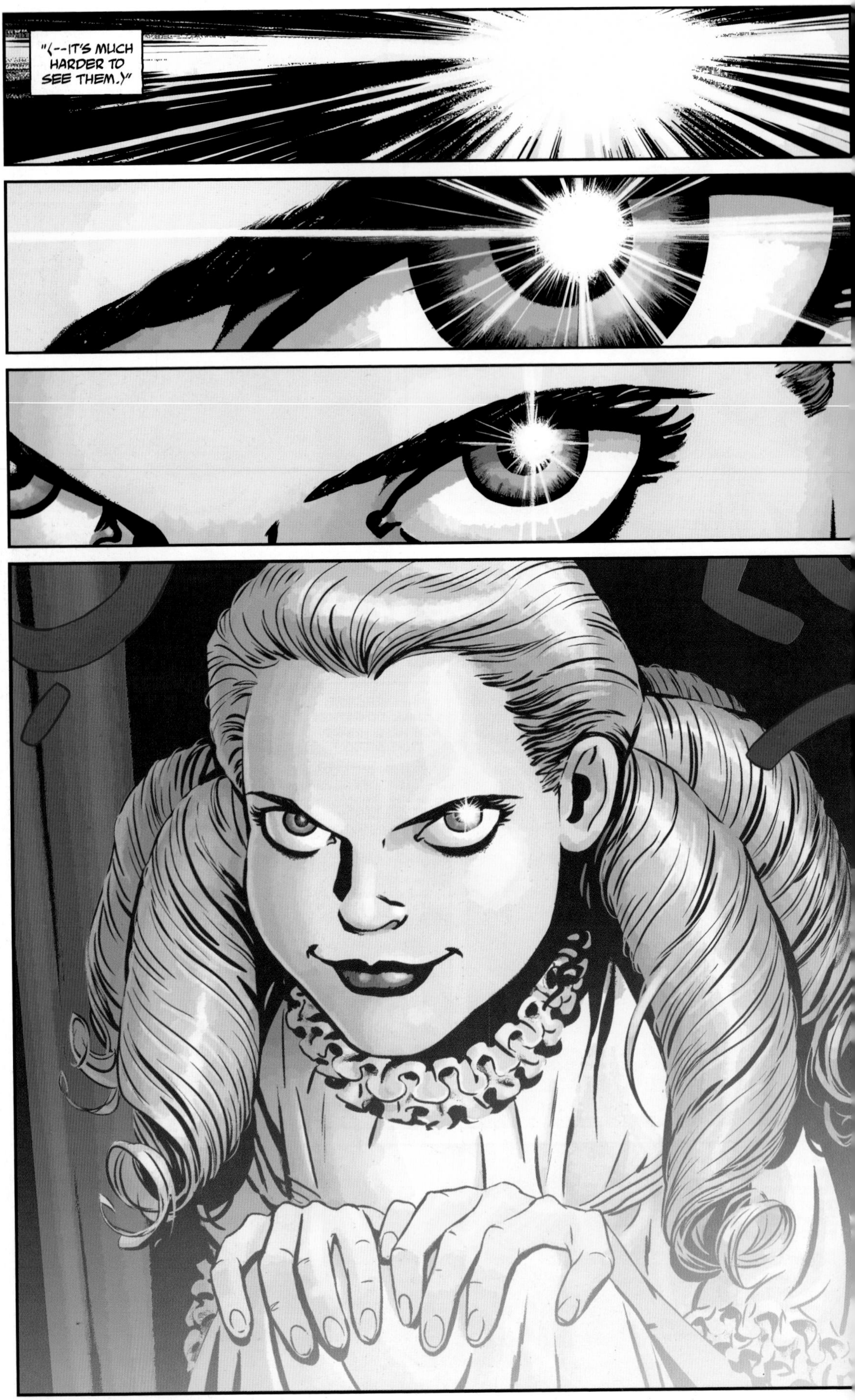
"‹--IT'S MUCH HARDER TO SEE THEM.›"

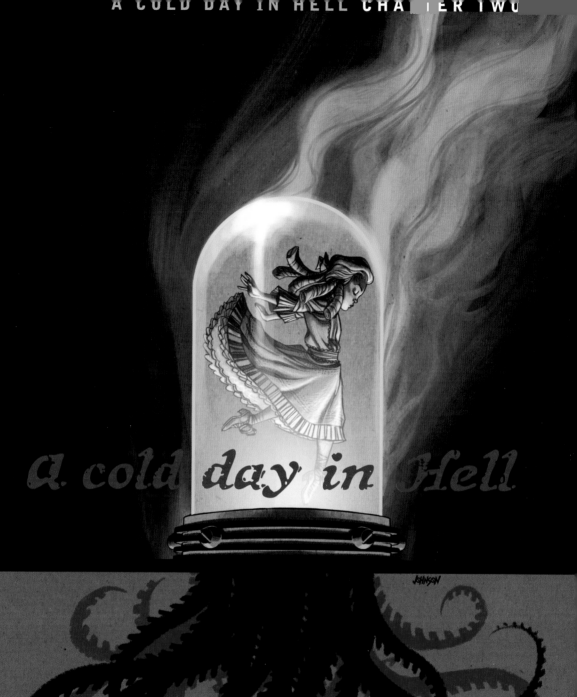

a cold **day in** Hell

JOHNSON

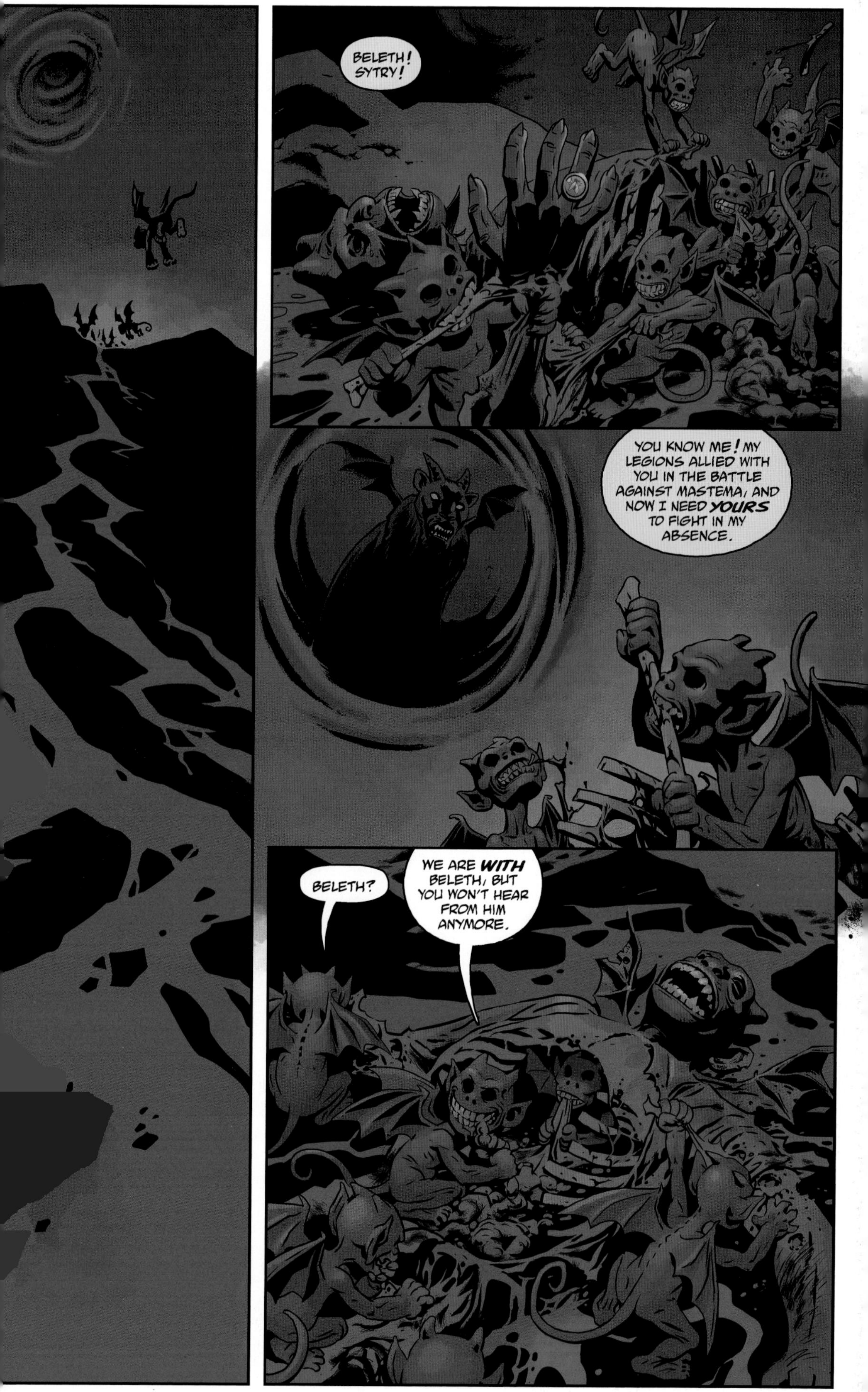

BELETH! SYTRY!
YOU KNOW ME! MY LEGIONS ALLIED WITH YOU IN THE BATTLE AGAINST MASTEMA, AND NOW I NEED YOURS TO FIGHT IN MY ABSENCE.
BELETH?
WE ARE WITH BELETH, BUT YOU WON'T HEAR FROM HIM ANYMORE.

THERE IS NO TIME FOR RIDDLES, SMALL ONE. GO FIND SYTRY! OR RAUM, OR *YOUR* LORD, AND BRING HIM TO ME!

YOU DON'T UNDER-STAND, *OLD* ONE!

NO MASTERS HERE ANYMORE! NO LORDS, NO DUKES, NO ALLIES FOR YOU.

I *AM* AN OLD ONE!

YOU *KNOW* ME. I AM SEVENTH UNDER SATAN, COMMANDER OF SIX THOUSAND LEGIONS IN THE HOUSE OF PRINCES.

BEARER OF THE GRAND CROSS OF THE ORDER OF THE FLY, AND YOU *WILL* HEAR ME!

YES.

YES.

YES, WE HEAR.

COME.

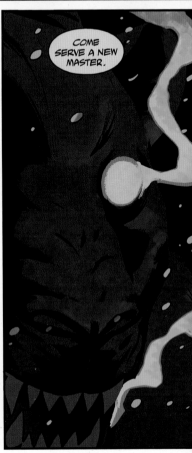

COME SERVE A NEW MASTER.

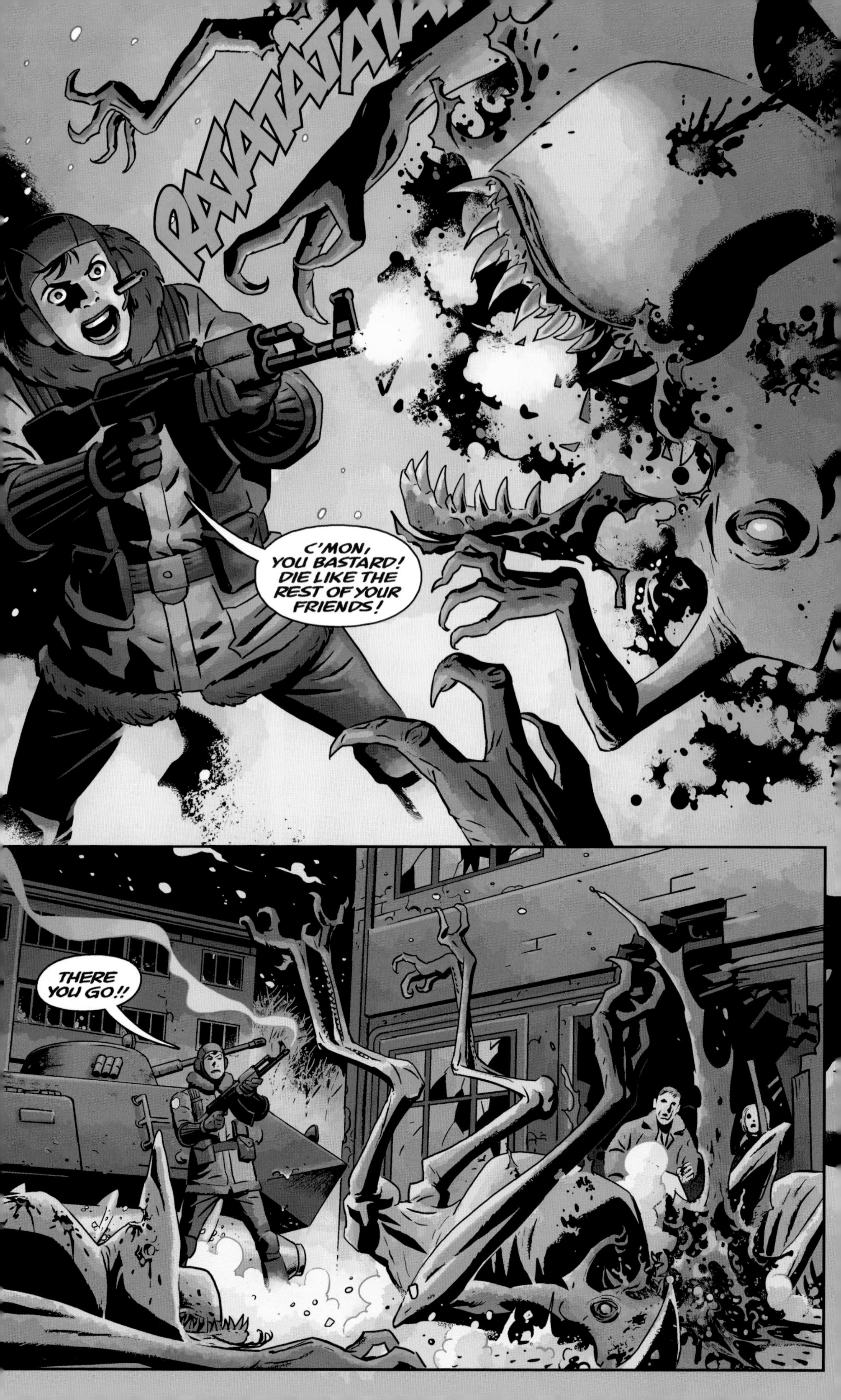
RATATATATA...
C'MON, YOU BASTARD! DIE LIKE THE REST OF YOUR FRIENDS!
THERE YOU GO!!

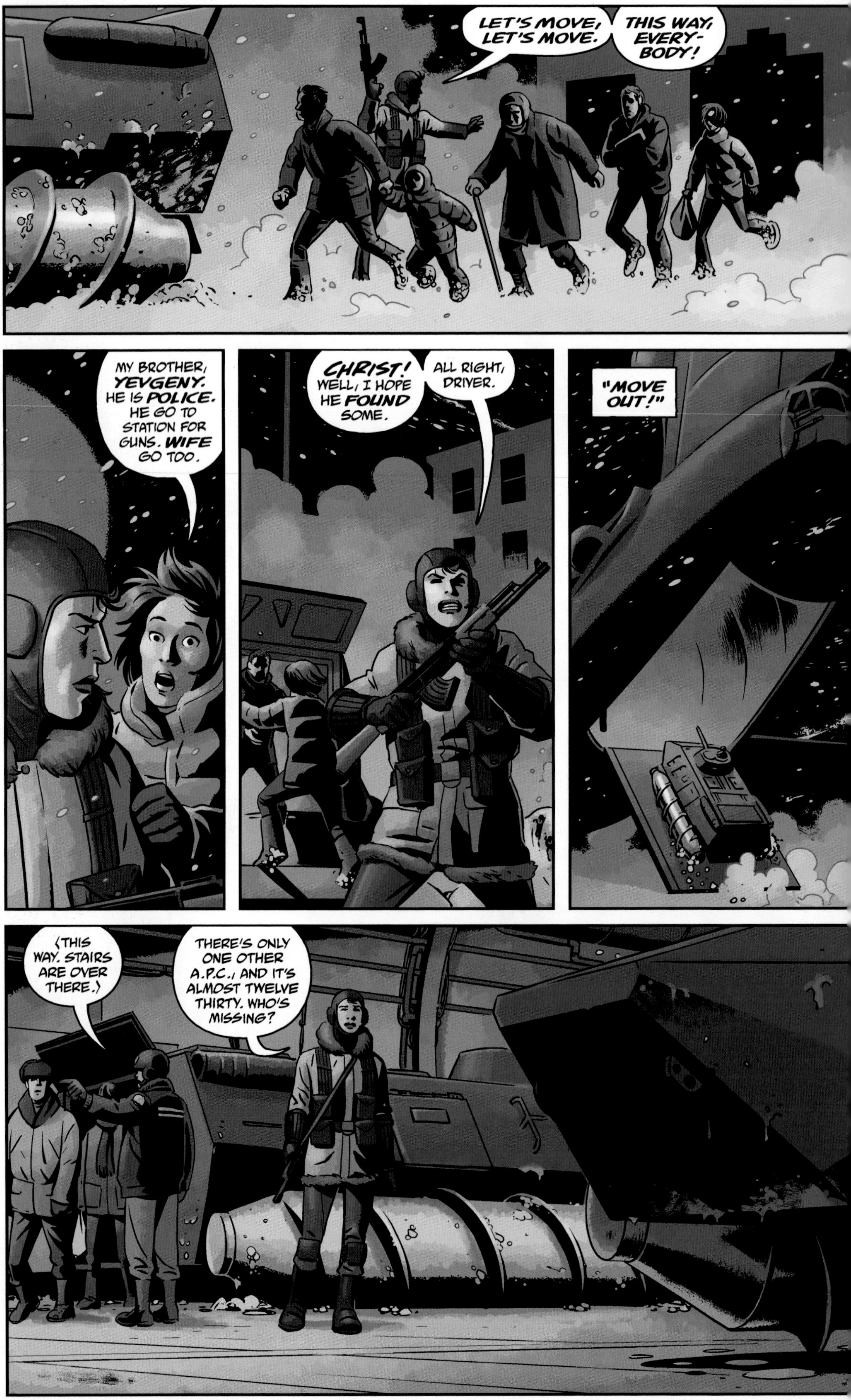
LET'S MOVE, LET'S MOVE.
THIS WAY, EVERY-BODY!
MY BROTHER, YEVGENY. HE IS POLICE. HE GO TO STATION FOR GUNS. WIFE GO TOO.
CHRIST! WELL, I HOPE HE FOUND SOME.
ALL RIGHT, DRIVER.
"MOVE OUT!"
‹THIS WAY. STAIRS ARE OVER THERE.›
THERE'S ONLY ONE OTHER A.P.C., AND IT'S ALMOST TWELVE THIRTY. WHO'S MISSING?

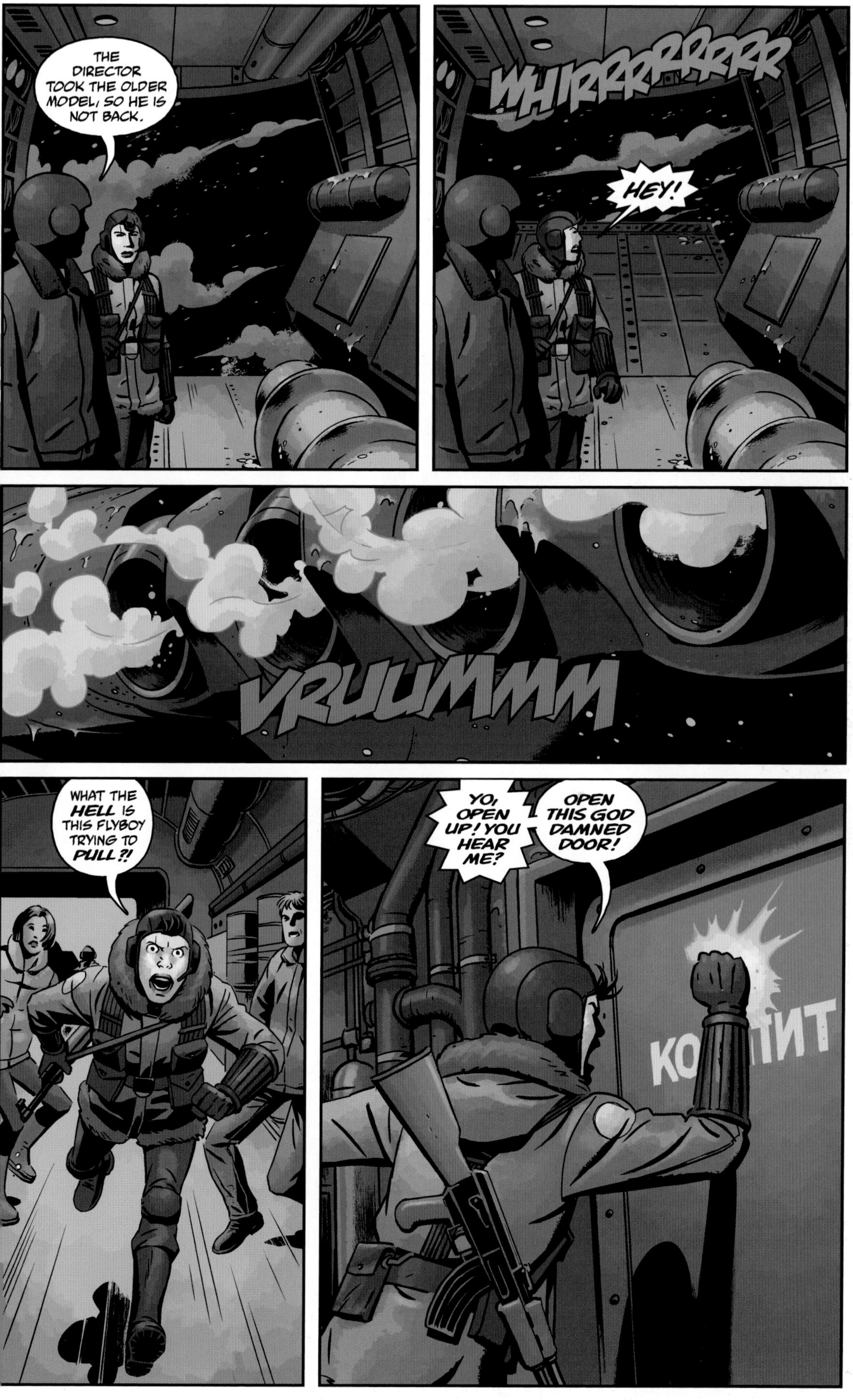
THE DIRECTOR TOOK THE OLDER MODEL, SO HE IS NOT BACK.
WHIRRRRRRRR
HEY!
VRUUMMM
WHAT THE HELL IS THIS FLYBOY TRYING TO PULL?!
YO, OPEN UP! YOU HEAR ME?
OPEN THIS GOD DAMNED DOOR!

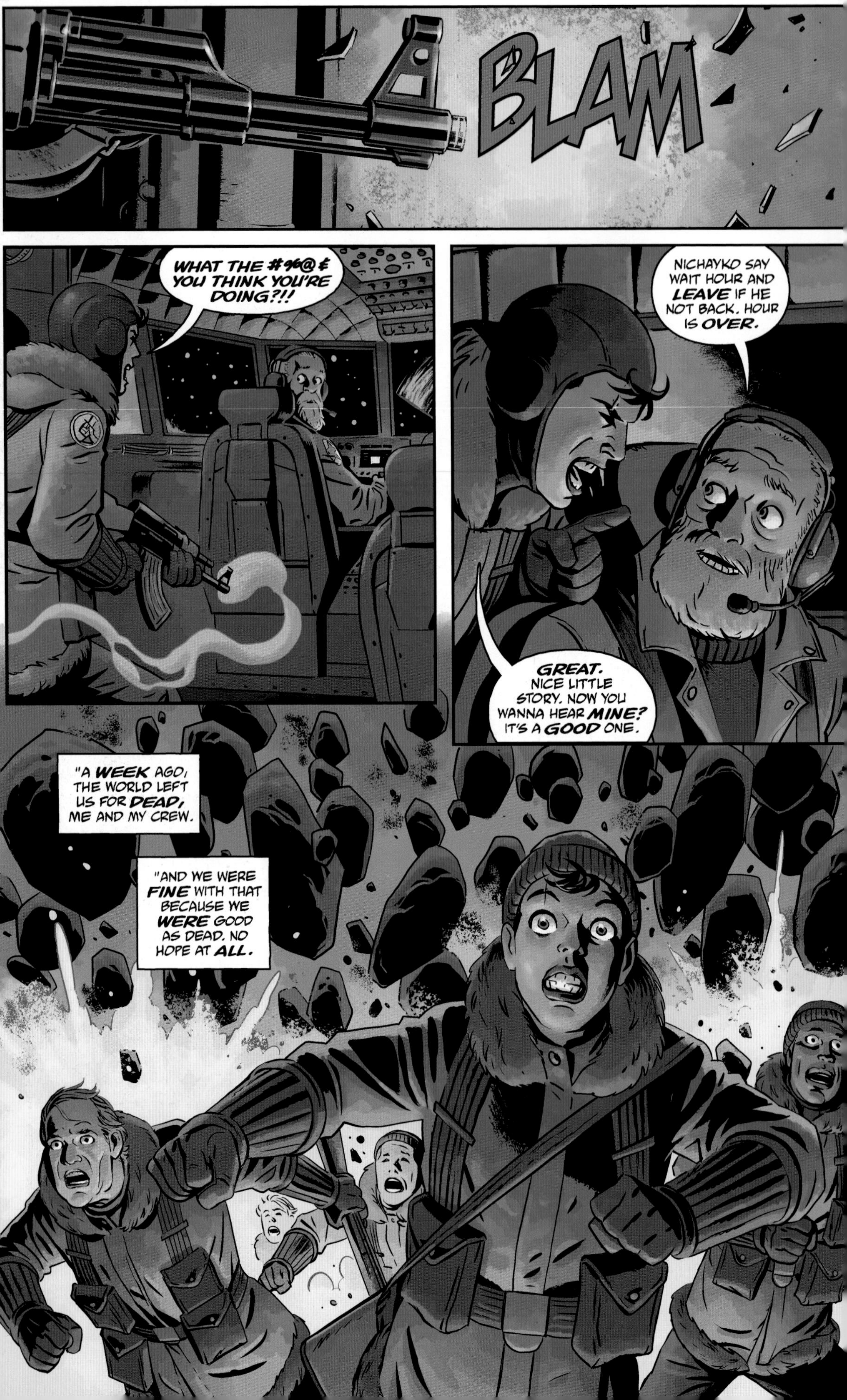

BLAM
WHAT THE #%@ £ YOU THINK YOU'RE DOING?!!
NICHAYKO SAY WAIT HOUR AND LEAVE IF HE NOT BACK. HOUR IS OVER.
GREAT. NICE LITTLE STORY. NOW YOU WANNA HEAR MINE? IT'S A GOOD ONE.
"A WEEK AGO, THE WORLD LEFT US FOR DEAD, ME AND MY CREW.
"AND WE WERE FINE WITH THAT BECAUSE WE WERE GOOD AS DEAD. NO HOPE AT ALL.

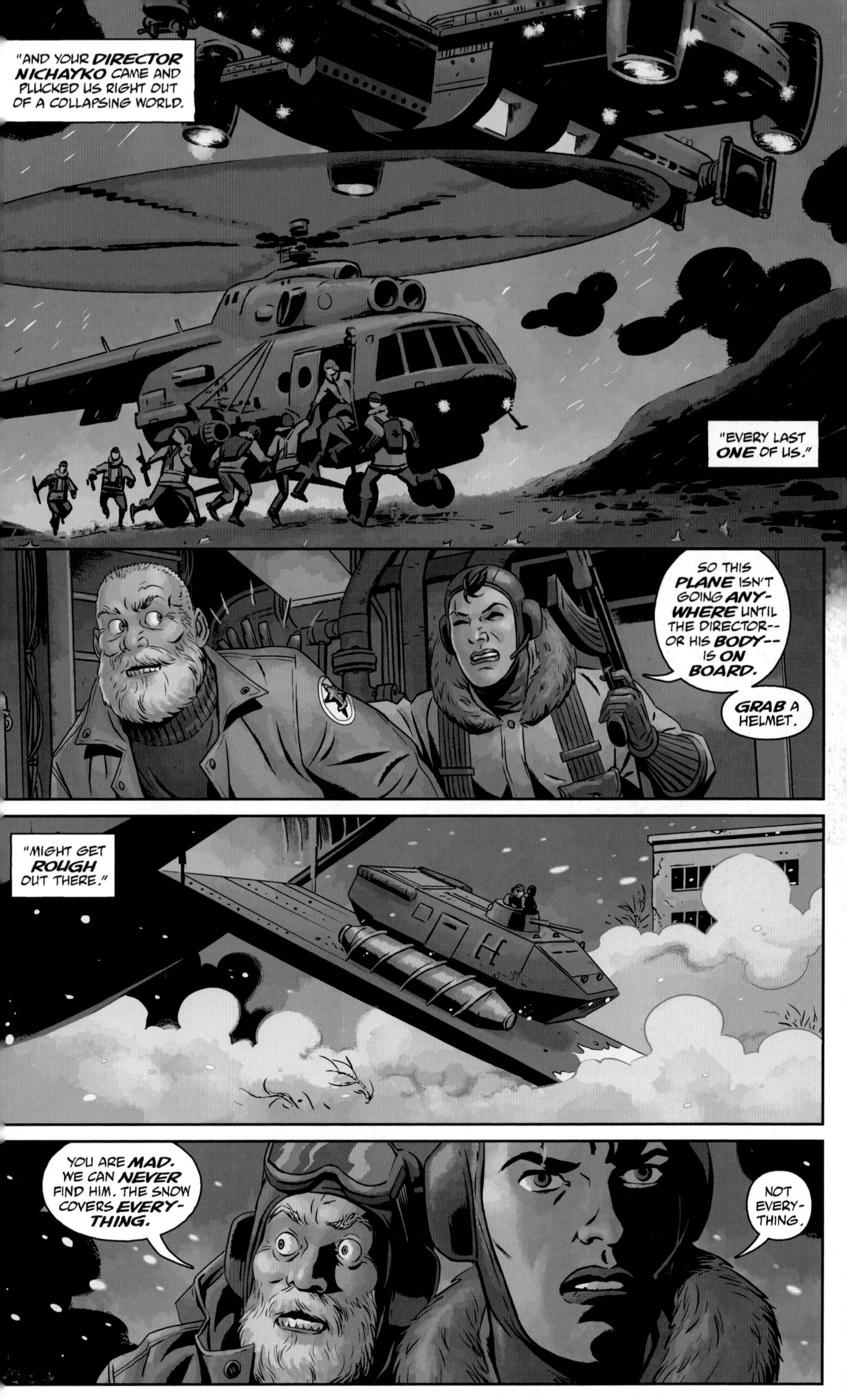
"AND YOUR DIRECTOR NICHAYKO CAME AND PLUCKED US RIGHT OUT OF A COLLAPSING WORLD.
"EVERY LAST ONE OF US."
SO THIS PLANE ISN'T GOING ANYWHERE UNTIL THE DIRECTOR-- OR HIS BODY-- IS ON BOARD.
GRAB A HELMET.
"MIGHT GET ROUGH OUT THERE."
YOU ARE MAD. WE CAN NEVER FIND HIM. THE SNOW COVERS EVERYTHING.
NOT EVERYTHING.

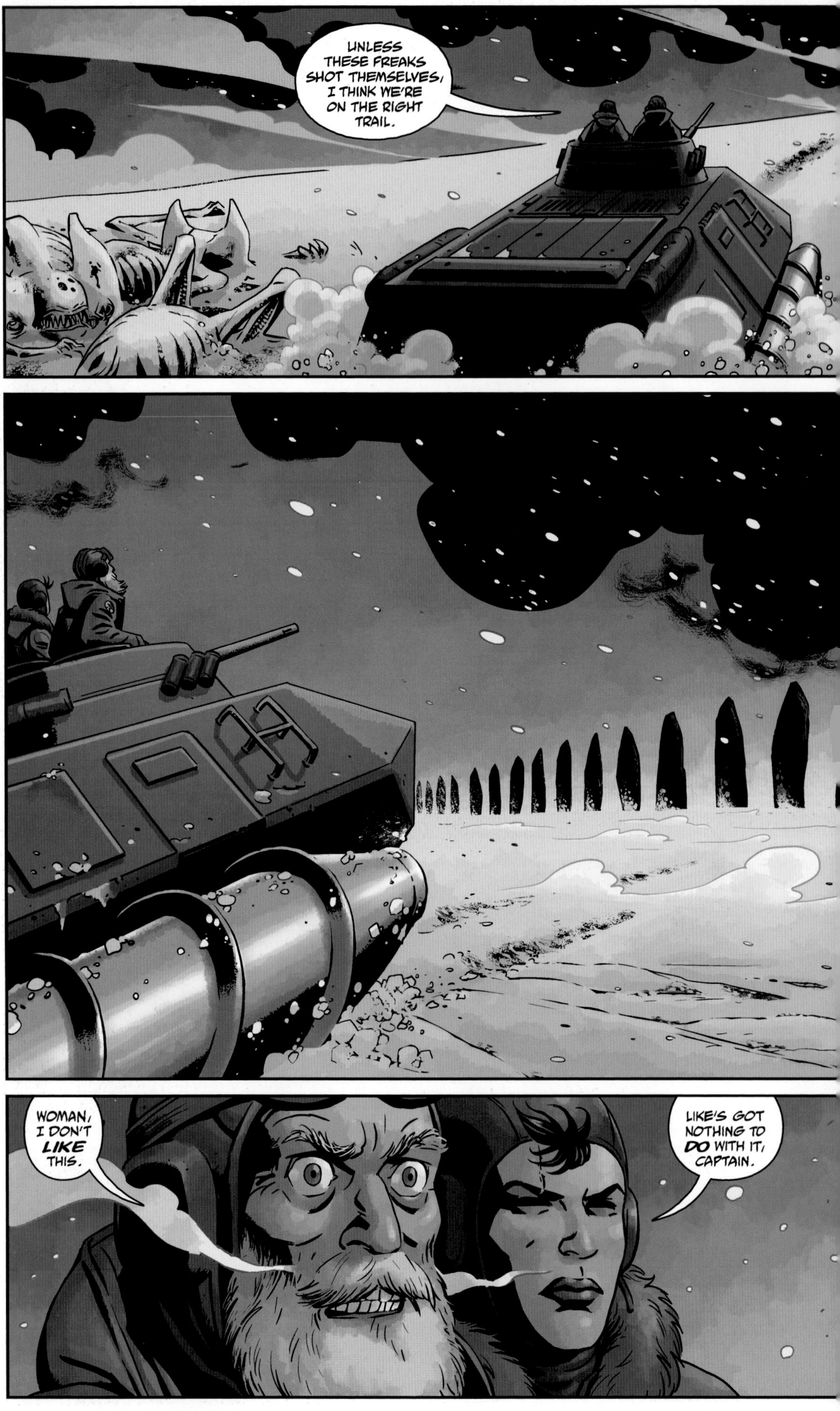
UNLESS THESE FREAKS SHOT THEMSELVES, I THINK WE'RE ON THE RIGHT TRAIL.
WOMAN, I DON'T **LIKE** THIS.
LIKE'S GOT NOTHING TO **DO** WITH IT, CAPTAIN.

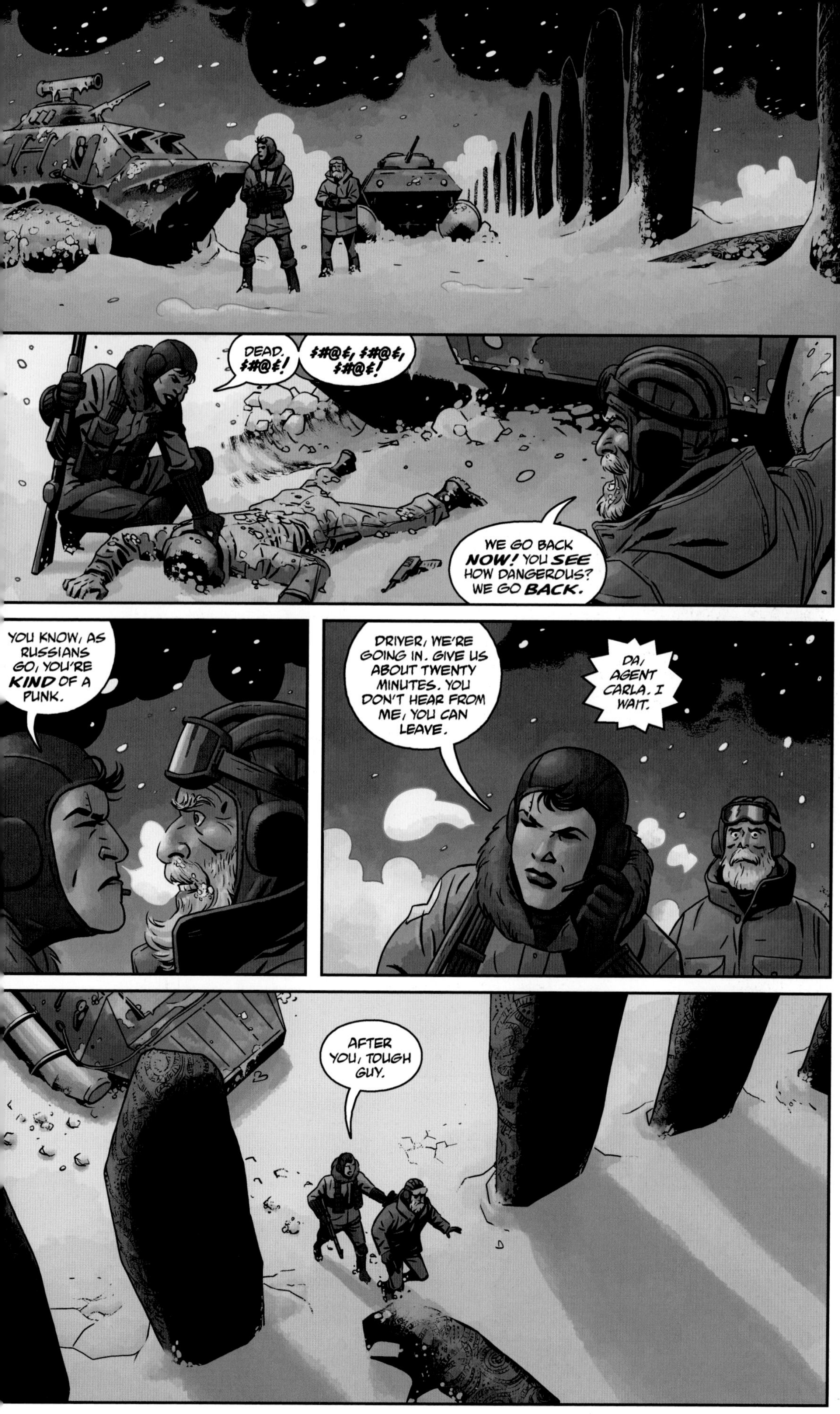
DEAD. $#@&!
$#@&, $#@&, $#@&!
WE GO BACK NOW! YOU SEE HOW DANGEROUS? WE GO BACK.
YOU KNOW, AS RUSSIANS GO, YOU'RE KIND OF A PUNK.
DRIVER, WE'RE GOING IN. GIVE US ABOUT TWENTY MINUTES. YOU DON'T HEAR FROM ME, YOU CAN LEAVE.
DA, AGENT CARLA. I WAIT.
AFTER YOU, TOUGH GUY.

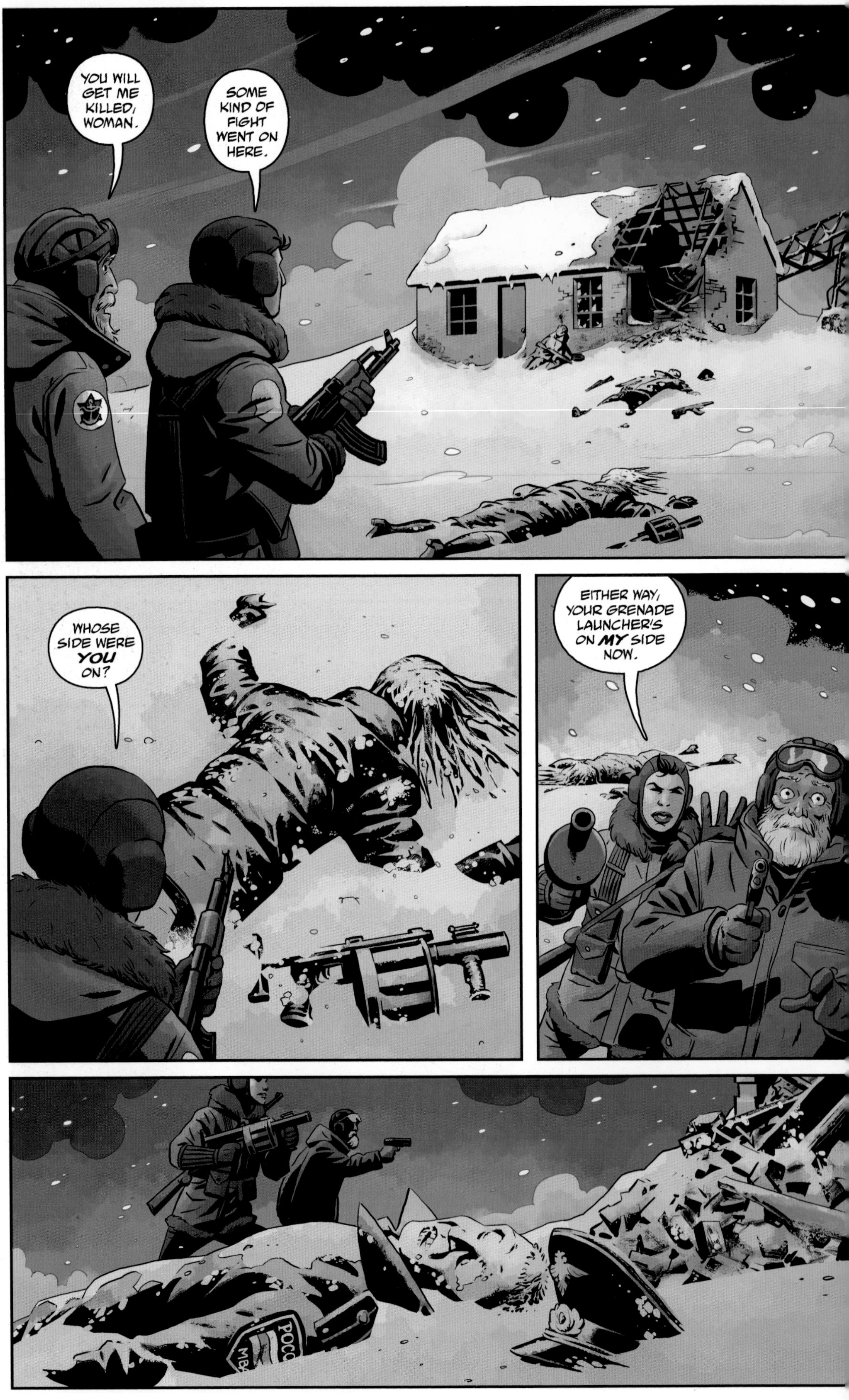
YOU WILL GET ME KILLED, WOMAN.
SOME KIND OF FIGHT WENT ON HERE.
WHOSE SIDE WERE YOU ON?
EITHER WAY, YOUR GRENADE LAUNCHER'S ON MY SIDE NOW.
POCC
MB

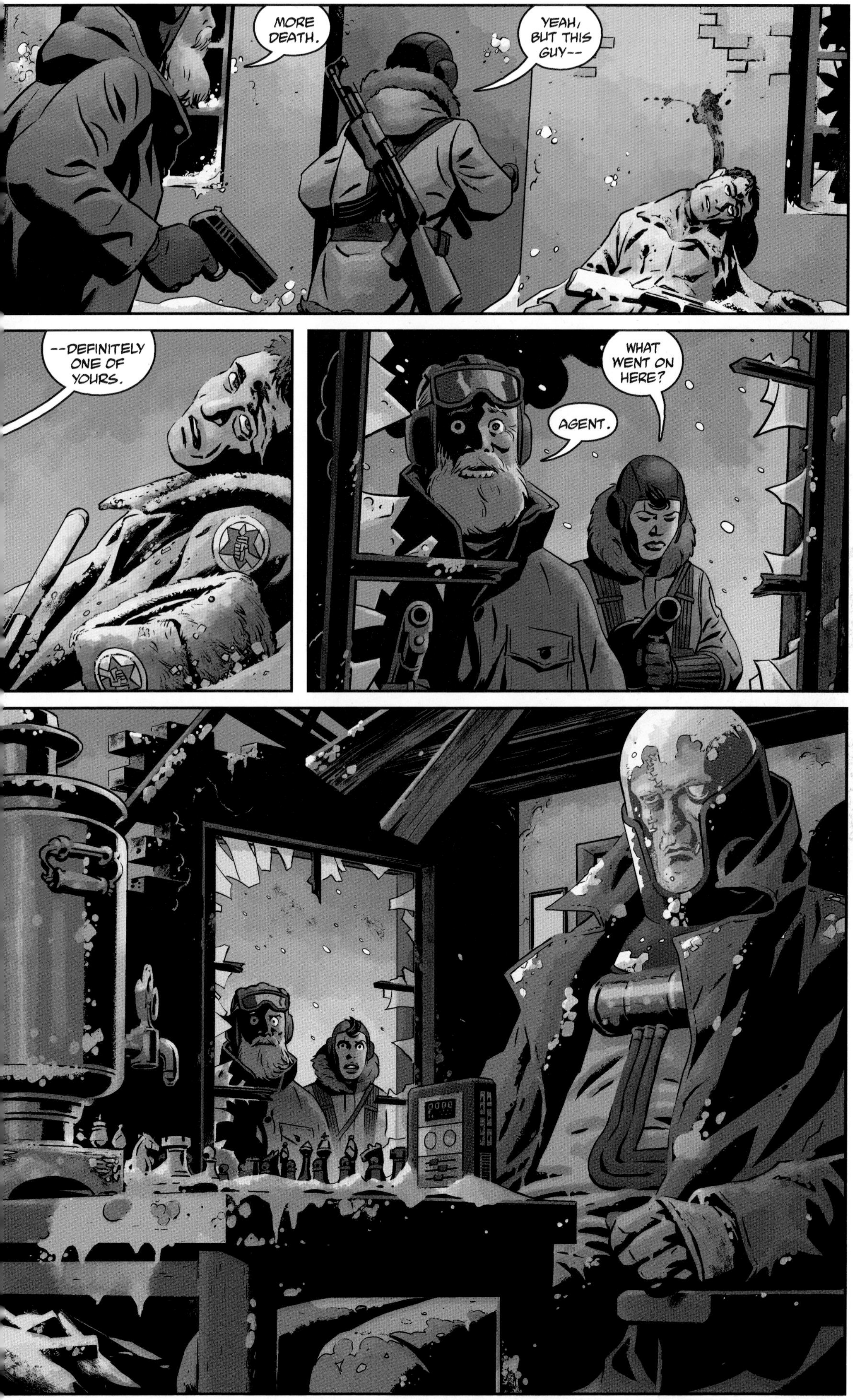
MORE DEATH.
YEAH, BUT THIS GUY--
--DEFINITELY ONE OF YOURS.
WHAT WENT ON HERE?
AGENT.

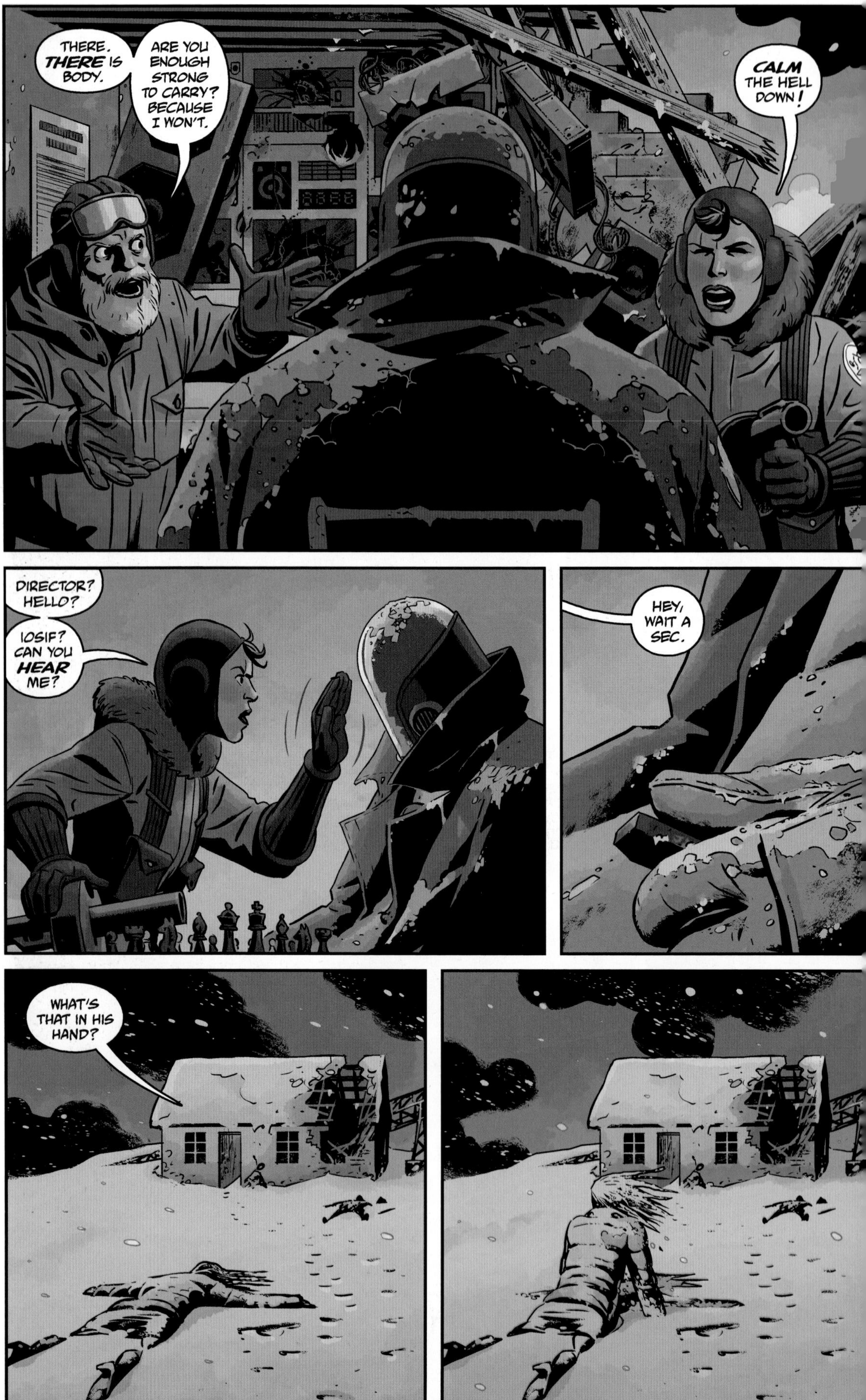

THERE. THERE IS BODY.
ARE YOU ENOUGH STRONG TO CARRY? BECAUSE I WON'T.
CALM THE HELL DOWN!
DIRECTOR? HELLO?
IOSIF? CAN YOU HEAR ME?
HEY, WAIT A SEC.
WHAT'S THAT IN HIS HAND?

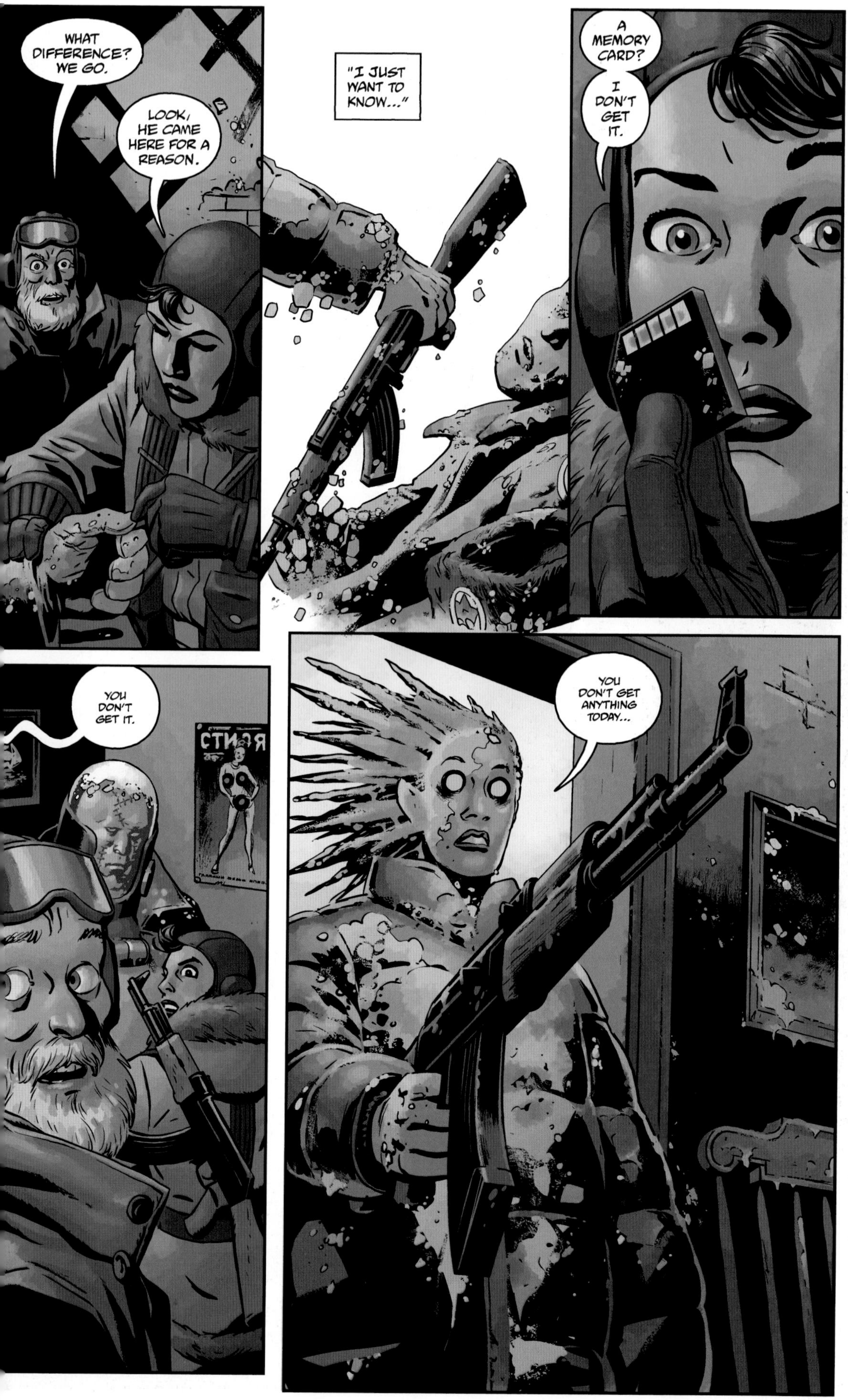
WHAT DIFFERENCE? WE GO.
LOOK, HE CAME HERE FOR A REASON.
"I JUST WANT TO KNOW..."
A MEMORY CARD?
I DON'T GET IT.
YOU DON'T GET IT.
YOU DON'T GET ANYTHING TODAY...

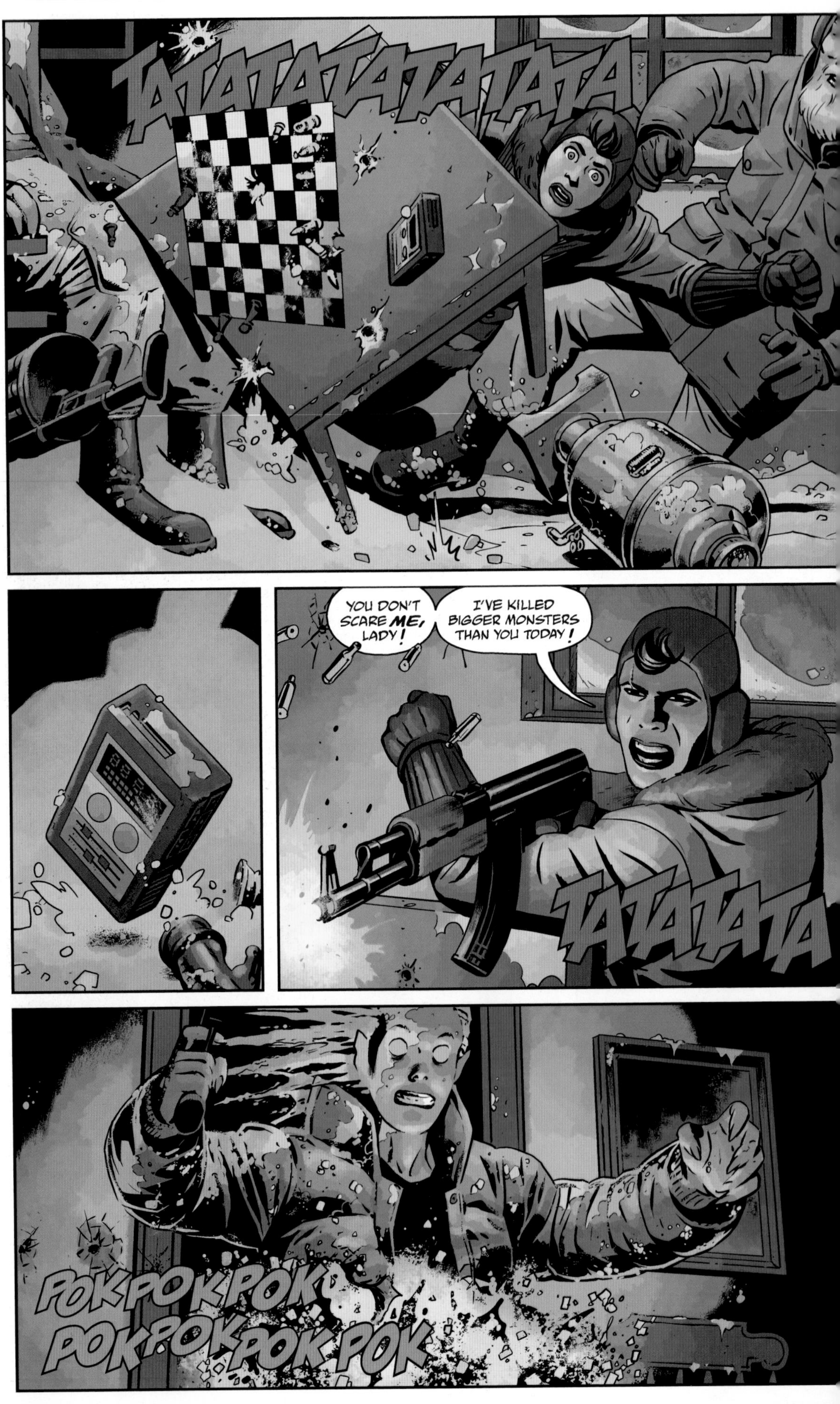
TATATATATATATATA
YOU DON'T SCARE ME, LADY!
I'VE KILLED BIGGER MONSTERS THAN YOU TODAY!
TATATATA
POKPOKPOKPOK POKPOKPOKPOK

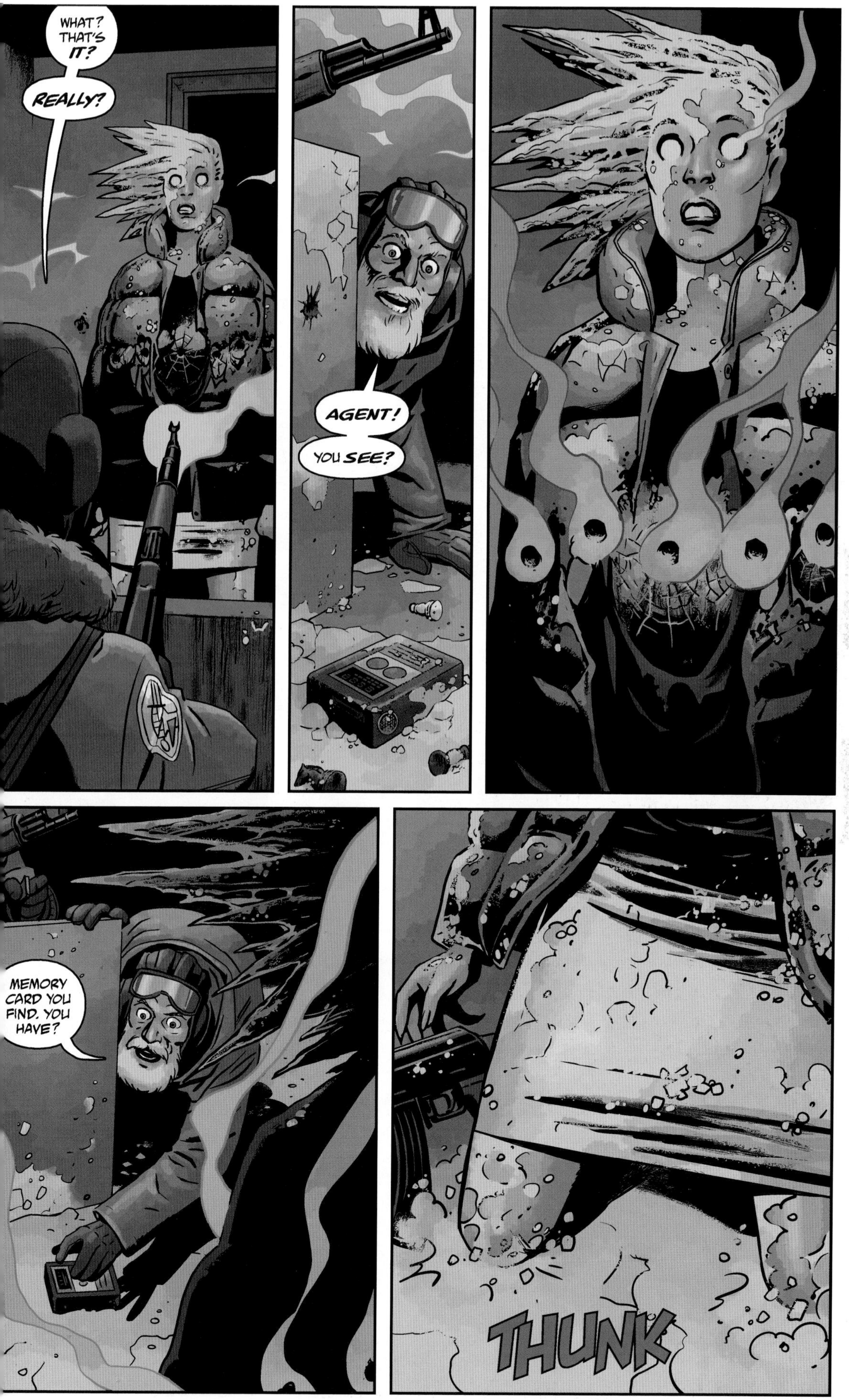
WHAT? THAT'S IT?
REALLY?
AGENT!
YOU SEE?
MEMORY CARD YOU FIND. YOU HAVE?
THUNK

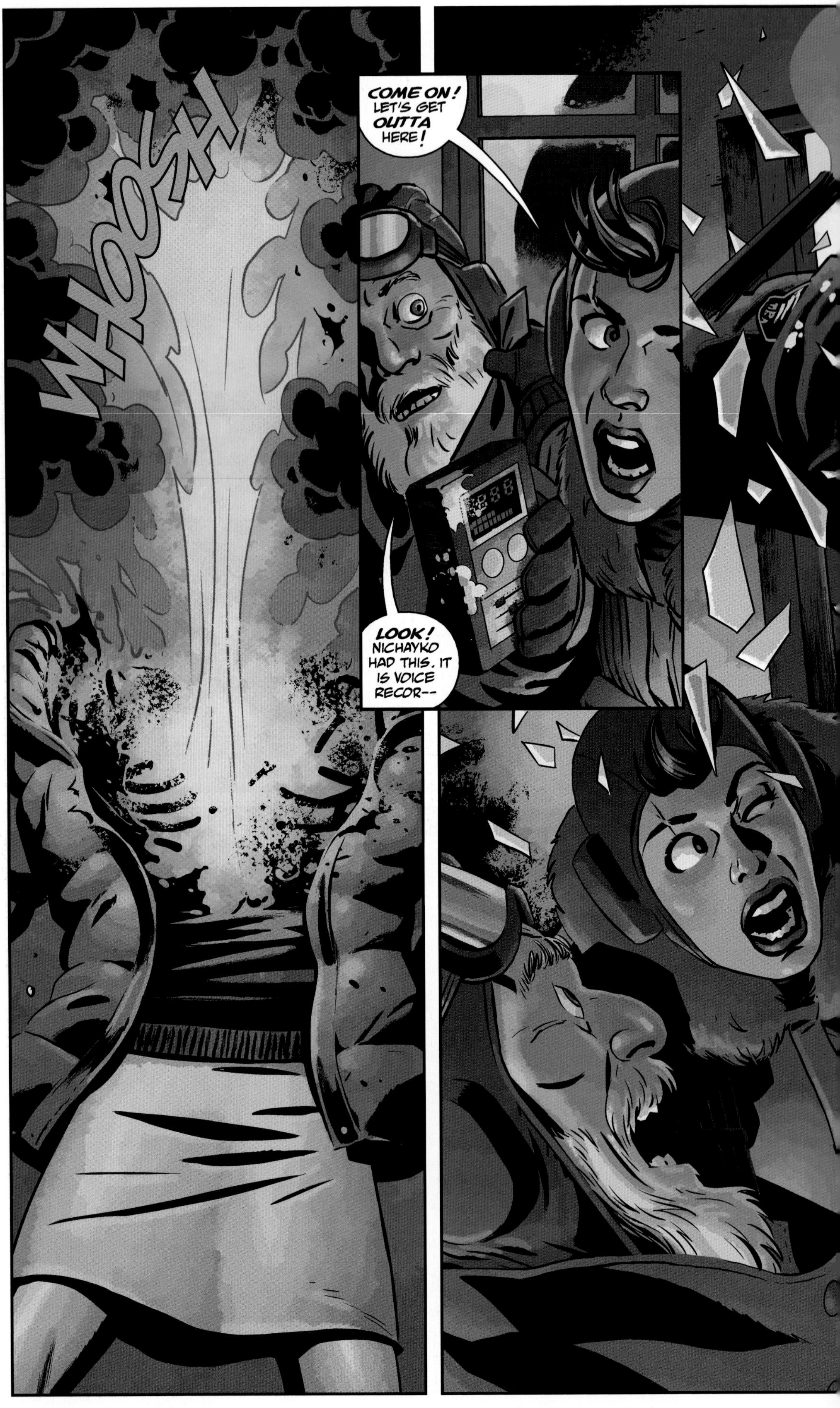
WHOOSH
COME ON! LET'S GET OUTTA HERE!
LOOK! NICHAYKO HAD THIS. IT IS VOICE RECOR--

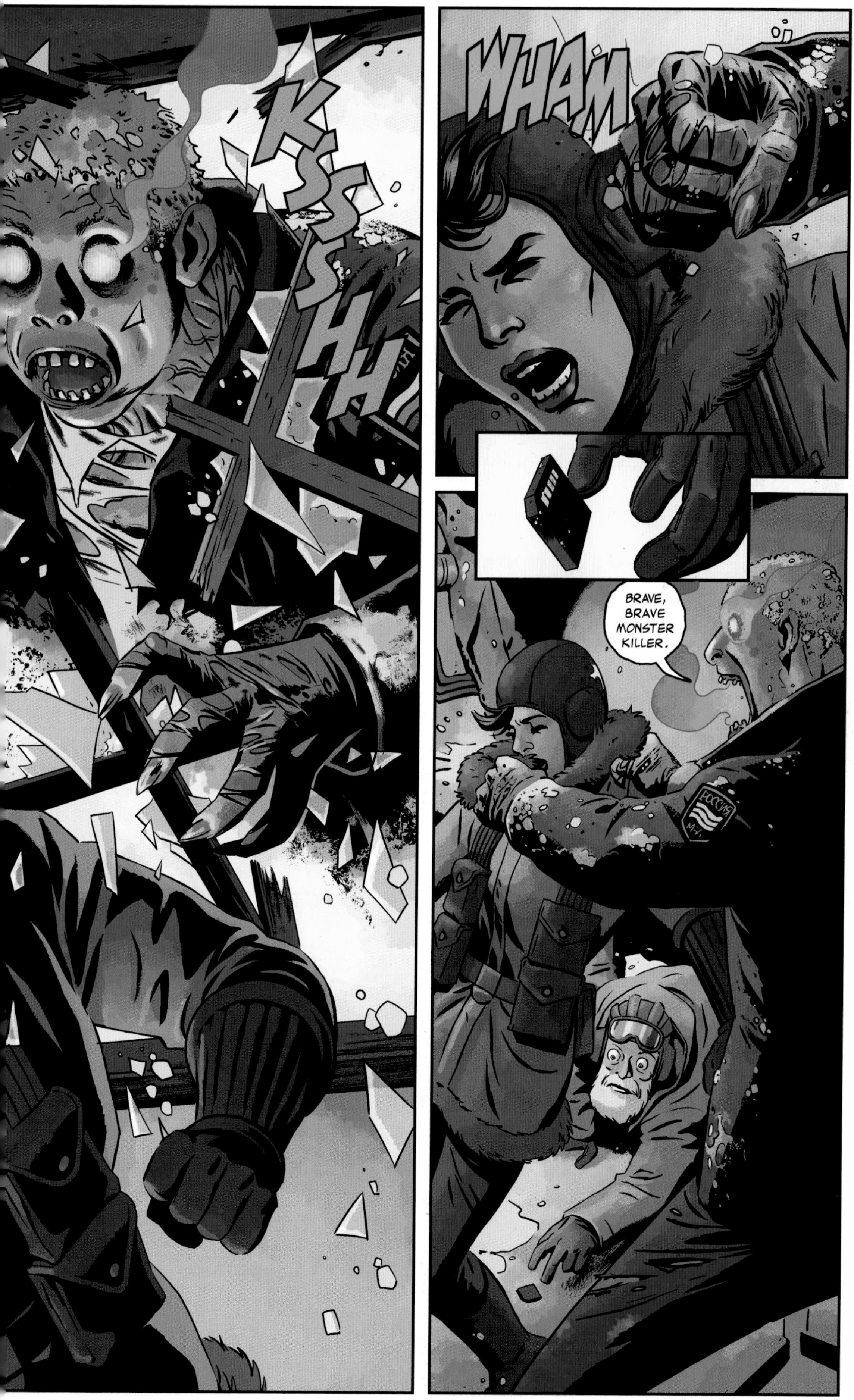
K-SSSHH
WHAM
BRAVE, BRAVE MONSTER KILLER.
РОССИЯ

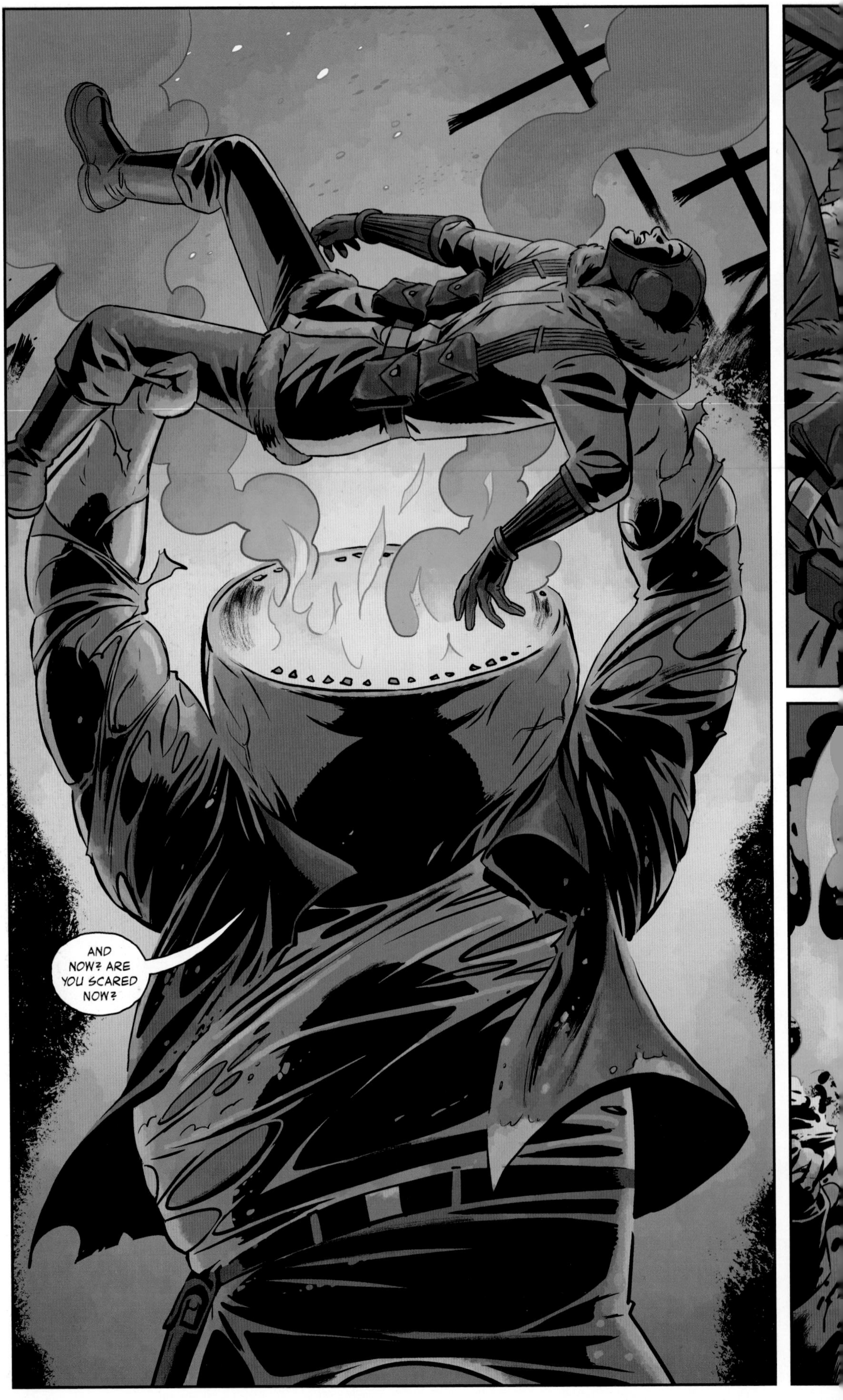
AND NOW? ARE YOU SCARED NOW?

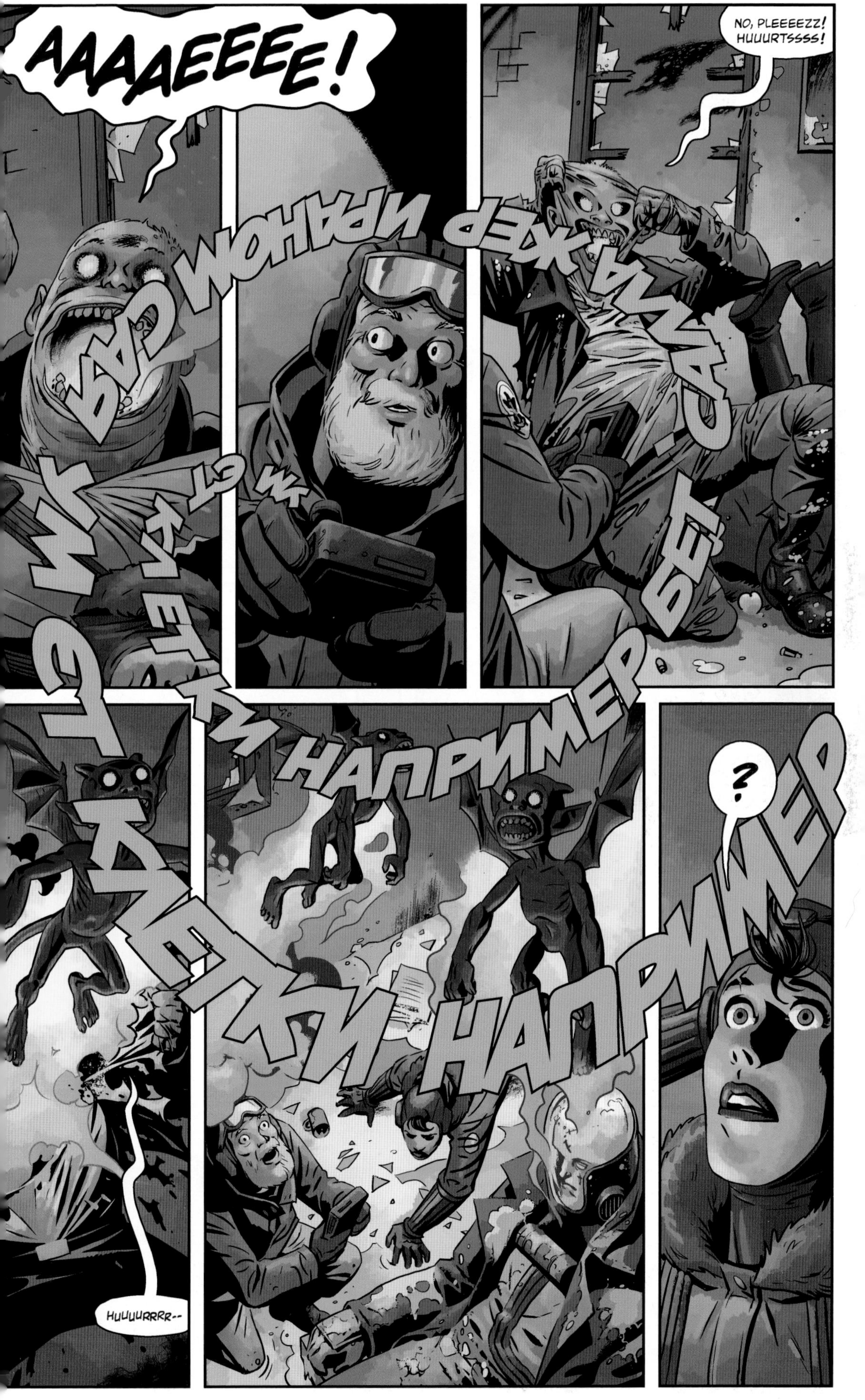
AAAAEEEEE!
NO, PLEEEEZZ! HUUURTSSSS!
НАПРИМЕР
НАПРИМЕР
?
HUUUURRRR--

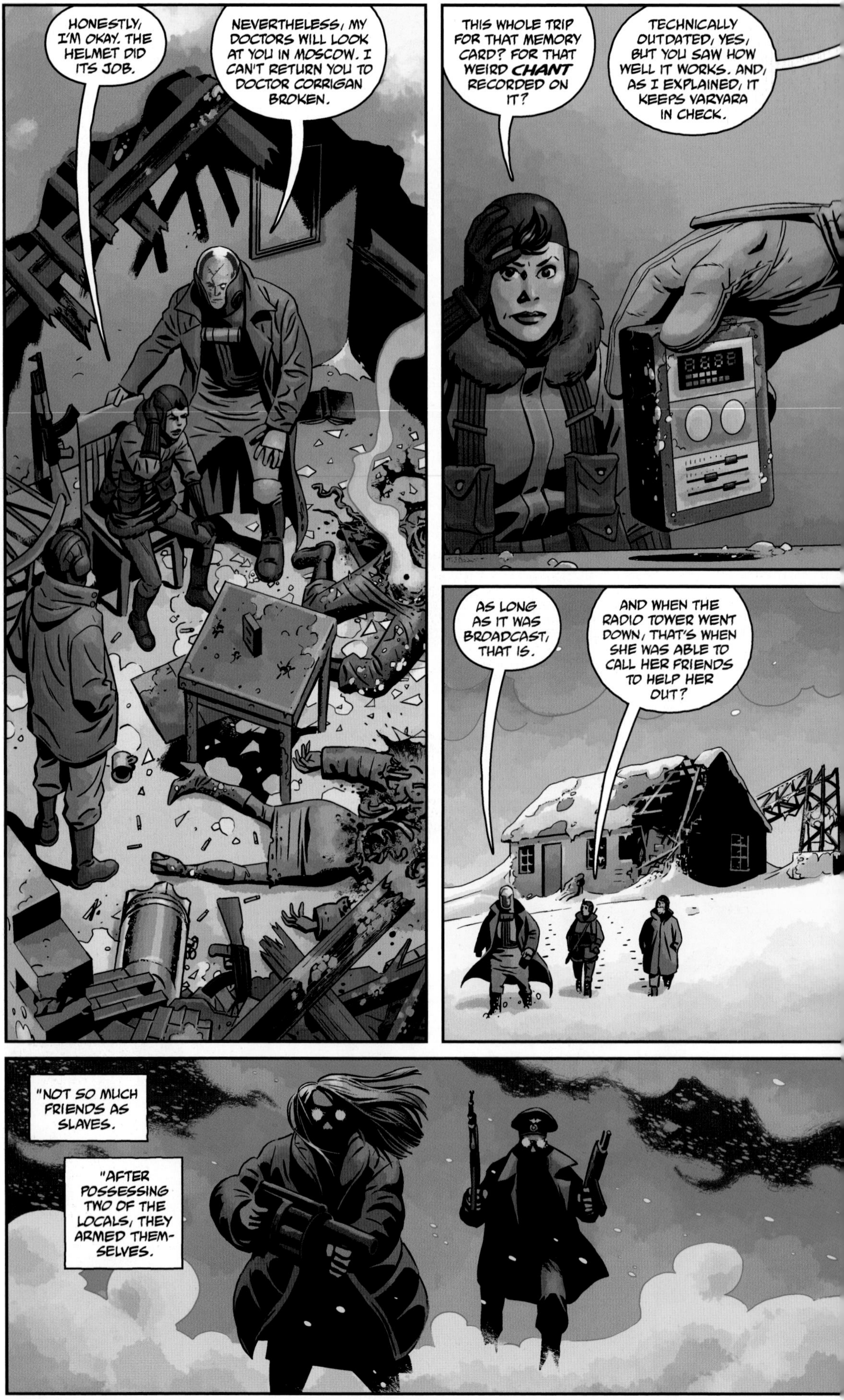
HONESTLY, I'M OKAY. THE HELMET DID ITS JOB.
NEVERTHELESS, MY DOCTORS WILL LOOK AT YOU IN MOSCOW. I CAN'T RETURN YOU TO DOCTOR CORRIGAN BROKEN.
THIS WHOLE TRIP FOR THAT MEMORY CARD? FOR THAT WEIRD CHANT RECORDED ON IT?
TECHNICALLY OUTDATED, YES, BUT YOU SAW HOW WELL IT WORKS. AND, AS I EXPLAINED, IT KEEPS VARYARA IN CHECK.
AS LONG AS IT WAS BROADCAST, THAT IS.
AND WHEN THE RADIO TOWER WENT DOWN, THAT'S WHEN SHE WAS ABLE TO CALL HER FRIENDS TO HELP HER OUT?
"NOT SO MUCH FRIENDS AS SLAVES.
"AFTER POSSESSING TWO OF THE LOCALS, THEY ARMED THEM-SELVES.

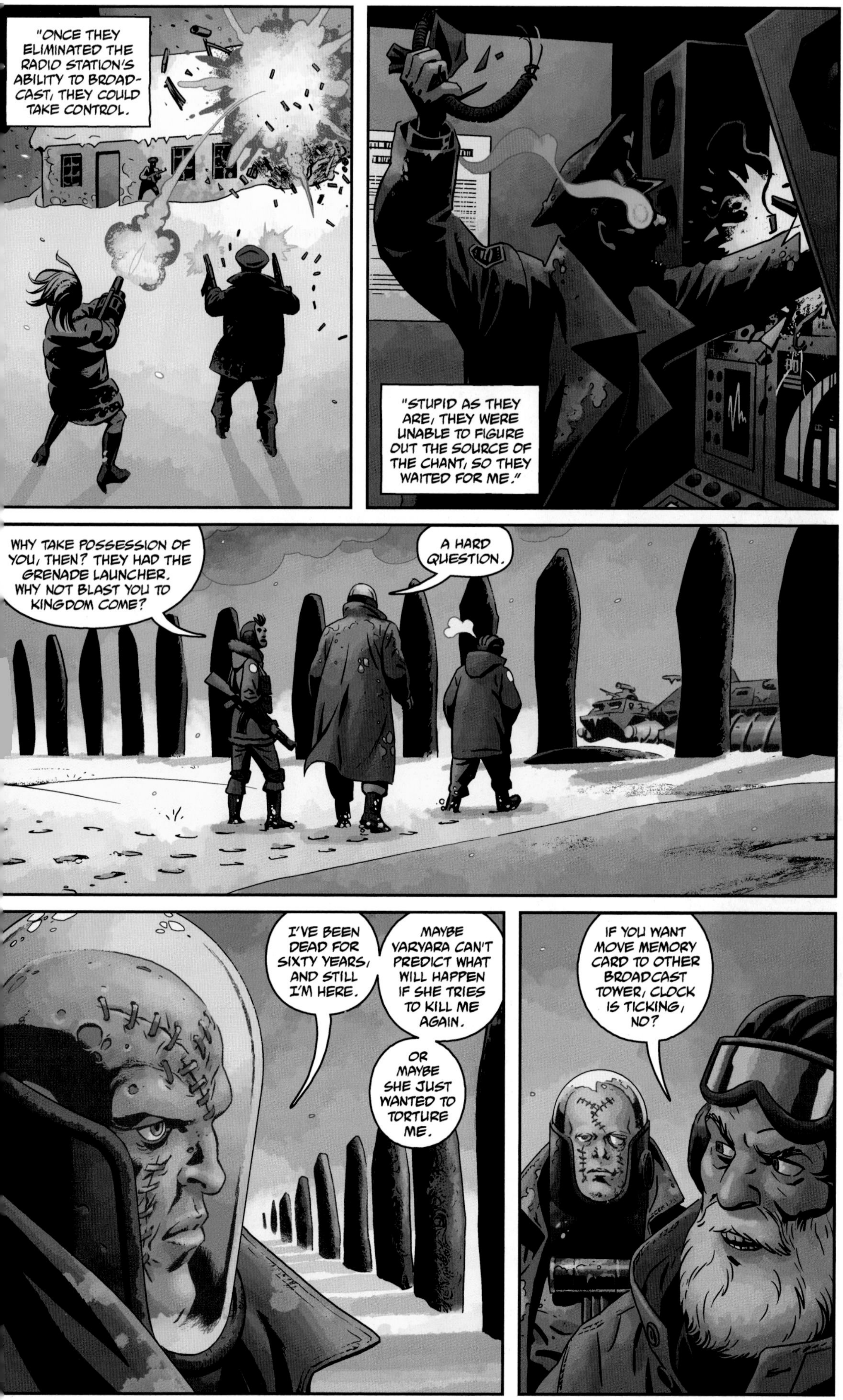
"ONCE THEY ELIMINATED THE RADIO STATION'S ABILITY TO BROAD-CAST, THEY COULD TAKE CONTROL.
"STUPID AS THEY ARE, THEY WERE UNABLE TO FIGURE OUT THE SOURCE OF THE CHANT, SO THEY WAITED FOR ME."
WHY TAKE POSSESSION OF YOU, THEN? THEY HAD THE GRENADE LAUNCHER. WHY NOT BLAST YOU TO KINGDOM COME?
A HARD QUESTION.
I'VE BEEN DEAD FOR SIXTY YEARS, AND STILL I'M HERE.
MAYBE VARYARA CAN'T PREDICT WHAT WILL HAPPEN IF SHE TRIES TO KILL ME AGAIN.
OR MAYBE SHE JUST WANTED TO TORTURE ME.
IF YOU WANT MOVE MEMORY CARD TO OTHER BROADCAST TOWER, CLOCK IS TICKING, NO?

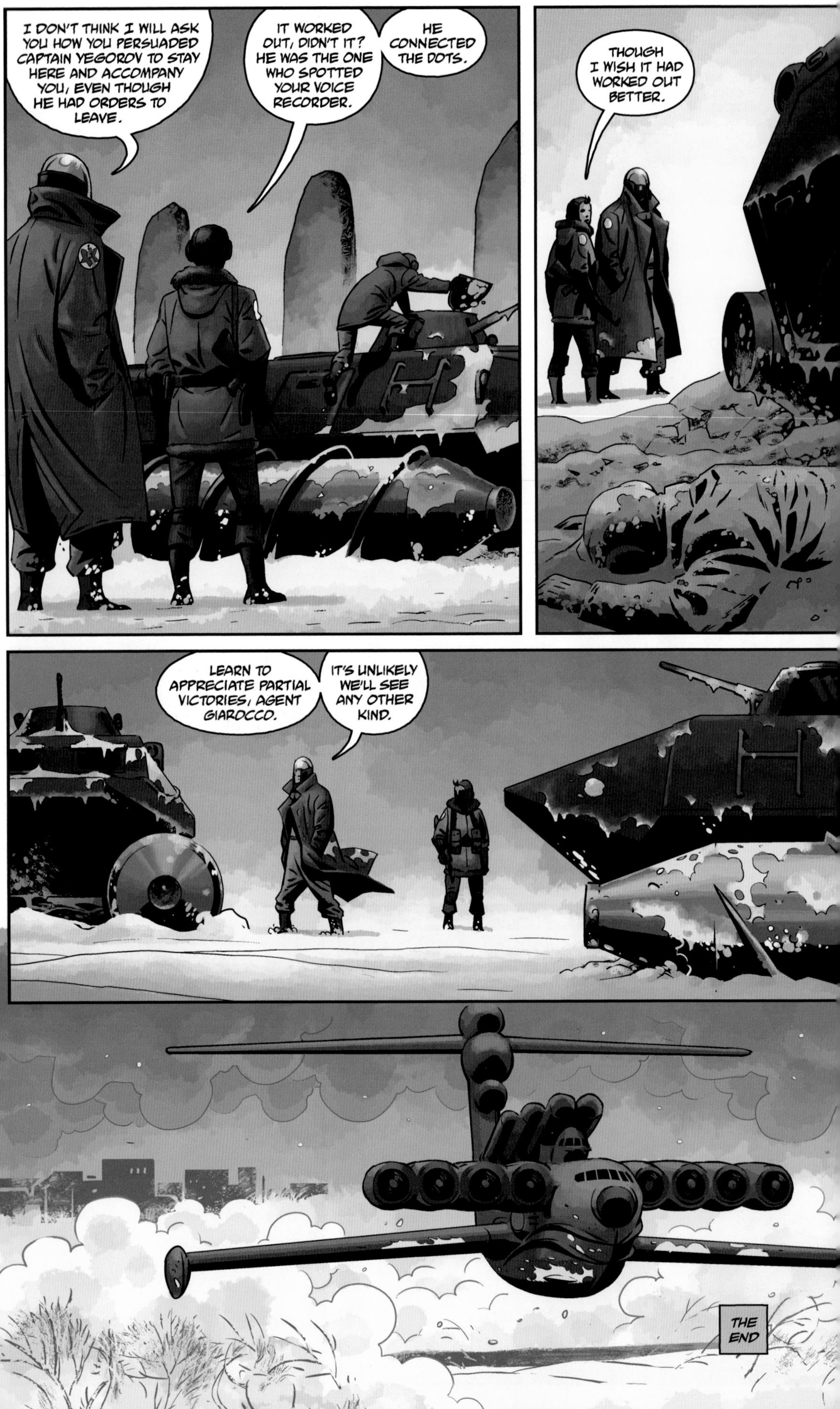
I DON'T THINK I WILL ASK YOU HOW YOU PERSUADED CAPTAIN YEGOROV TO STAY HERE AND ACCOMPANY YOU, EVEN THOUGH HE HAD ORDERS TO LEAVE.
IT WORKED OUT, DIDN'T IT? HE WAS THE ONE WHO SPOTTED YOUR VOICE RECORDER.
HE CONNECTED THE DOTS.
THOUGH I WISH IT HAD WORKED OUT BETTER.
LEARN TO APPRECIATE PARTIAL VICTORIES, AGENT GIAROCCO.
IT'S UNLIKELY WE'LL SEE ANY OTHER KIND.
THE END

# B.P.R.D.

## SKETCHBOOK

*Notes by Scott Allie*

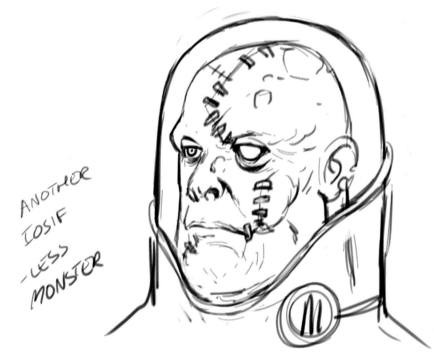

ANOTHER
IOSIF
-LESS
MONSTER

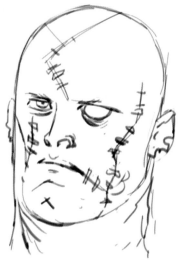

Iosif Nichayko
by Peter Snejbjerg.

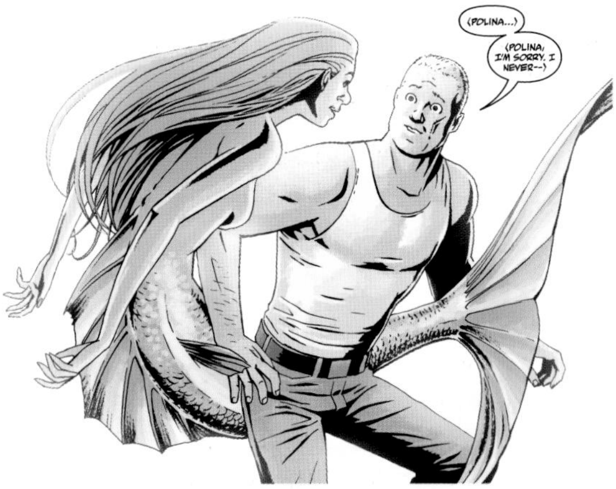
(POLINA...)
(POLINA, I'M SORRY, I NEVER--)

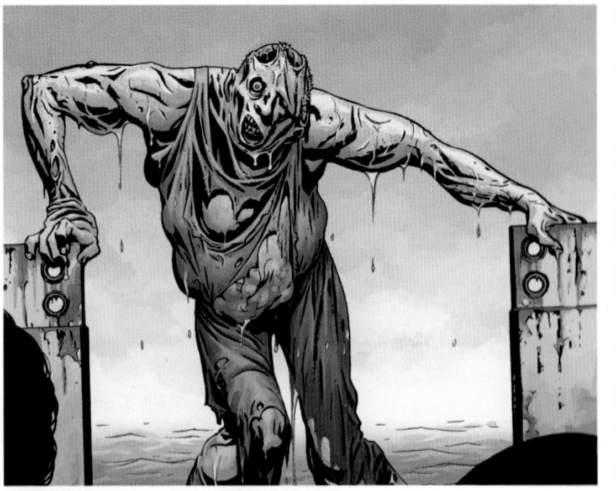

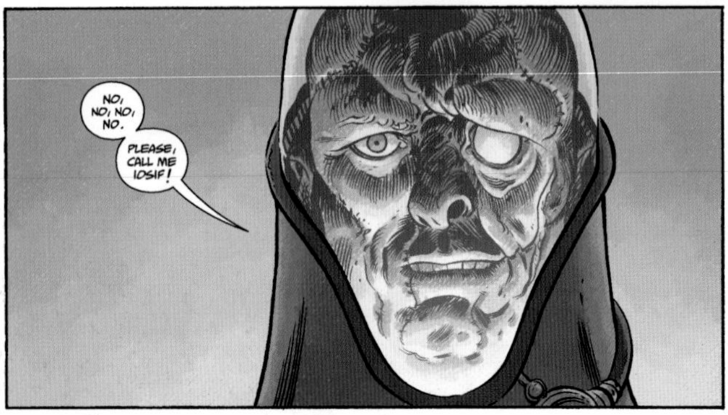
NO, NO, NO, NO.
PLEASE, CALL ME IOSIF!

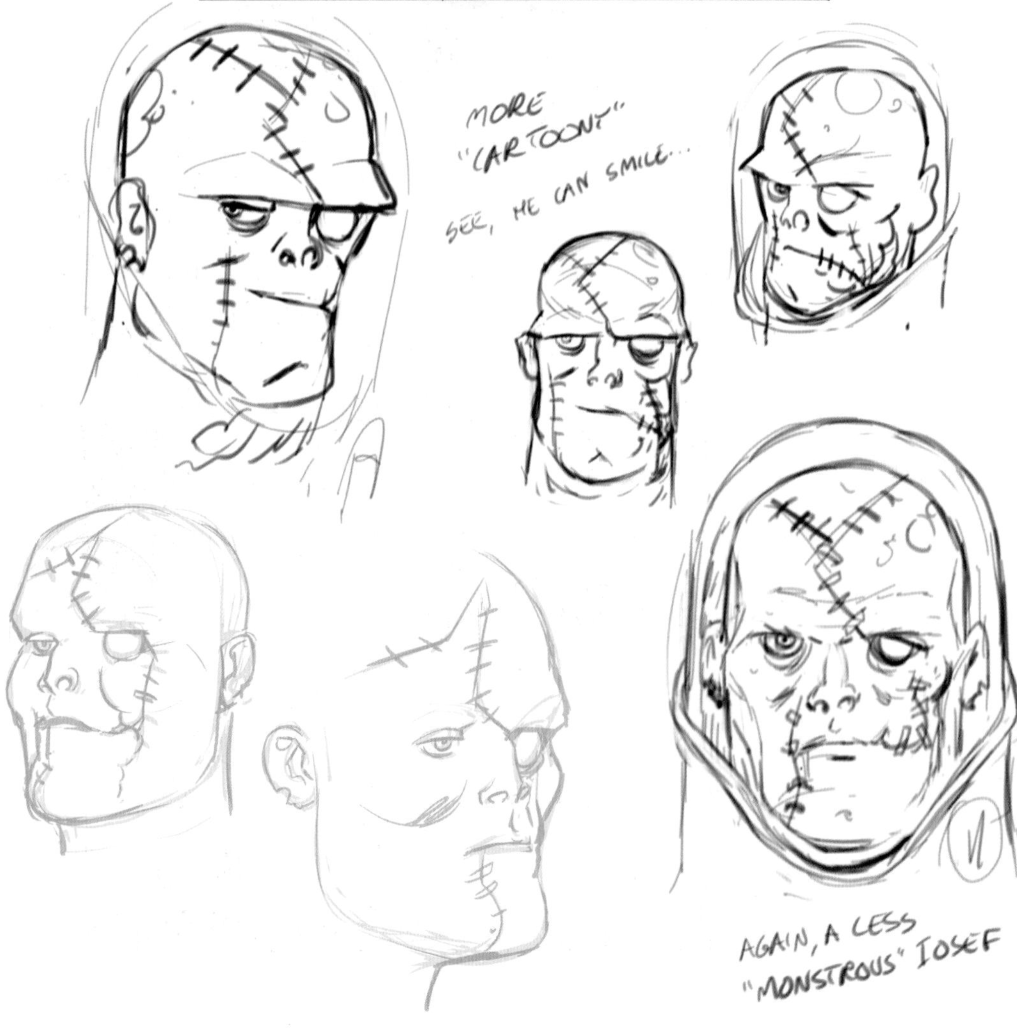
MORE "CARTOONY"
SEE, HE CAN SMILE...
AGAIN, A LESS "MONSTROUS" IOSEF

Peter Snejbjerg was the first artist to draw Iosif, in *The Abyssal Plain* (2010), collected in *Abe Sapien* Volume 2 (facing, top, colors by Bjarne Hansen). When Iosif came back as the undead director of Russia's Special Sciences Service, Tyler Crook was the first one to draw him (*B.P.R.D. Hell on Earth: Russia*, 2011, facing, center panel, colors by Dave Stewart). When Peter returned for *A Cold Day in Hell*, we asked him to revise Iosif's design, taking us through many versions for the right mix of dead but expressive.

This page: Peter's thumbnails, followed by a tighter inked version, equivalent to the pencil stage for other artists, before Peter tightens further and adds detail and texture.

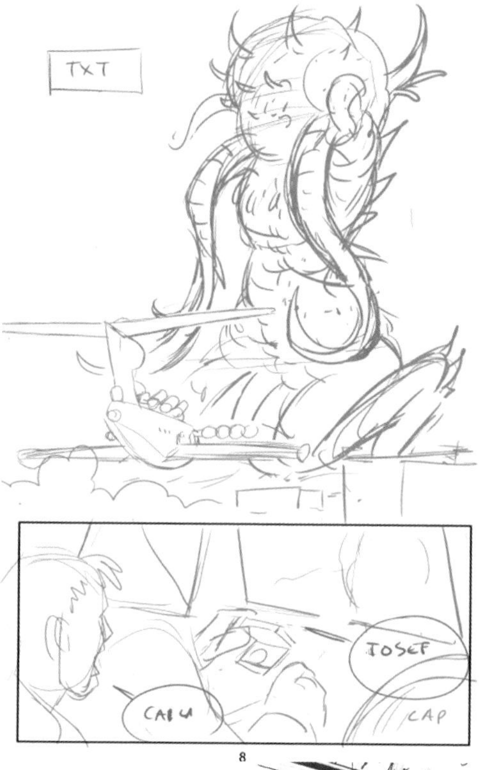
TXT
JOSEF
CAP
8

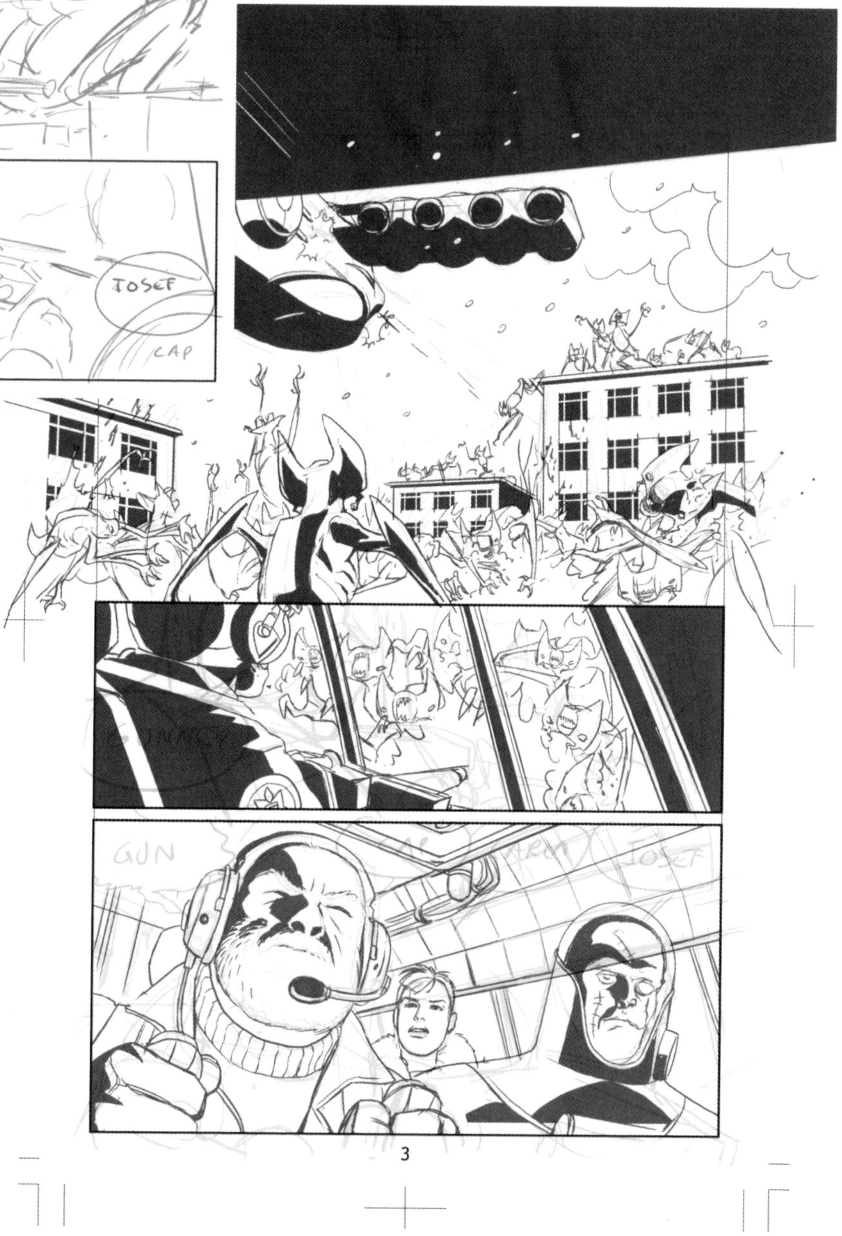
GUN
3

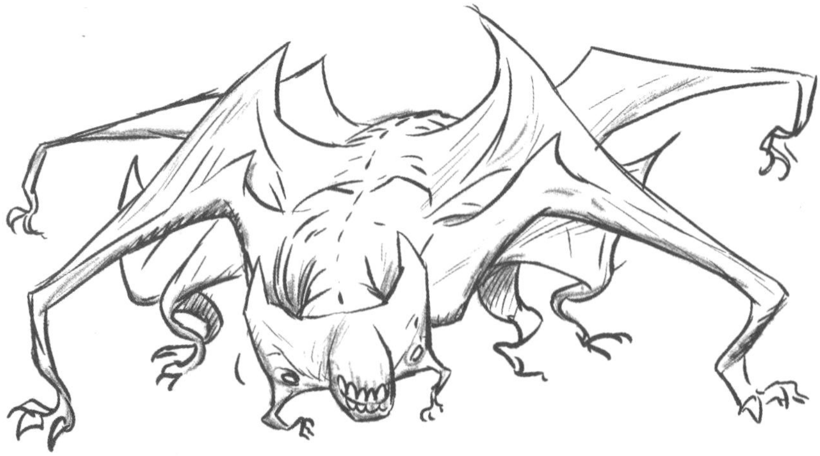

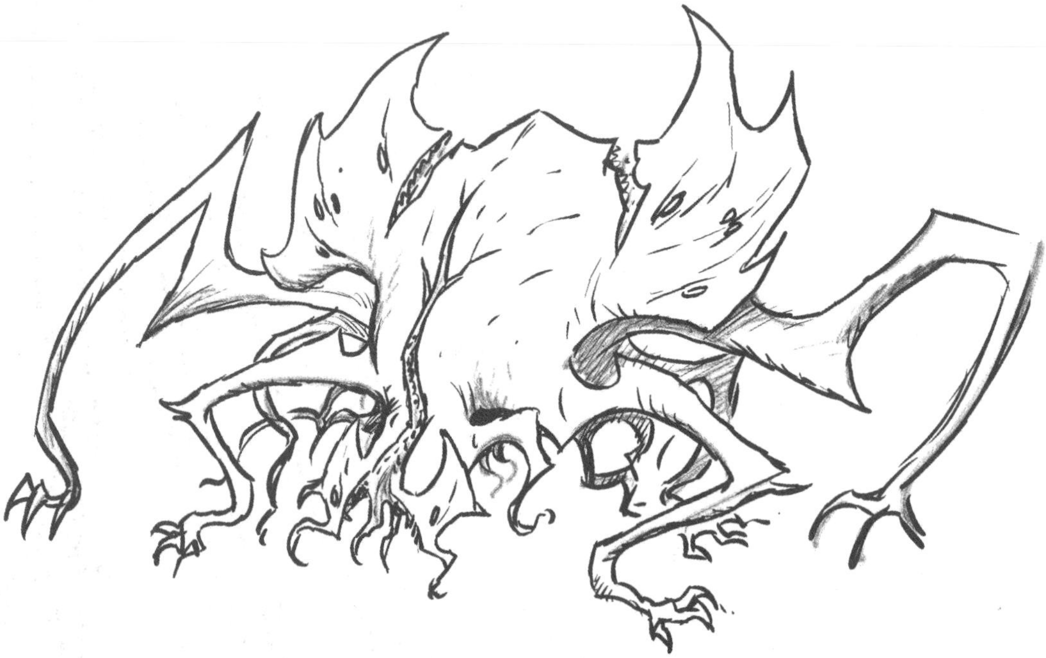

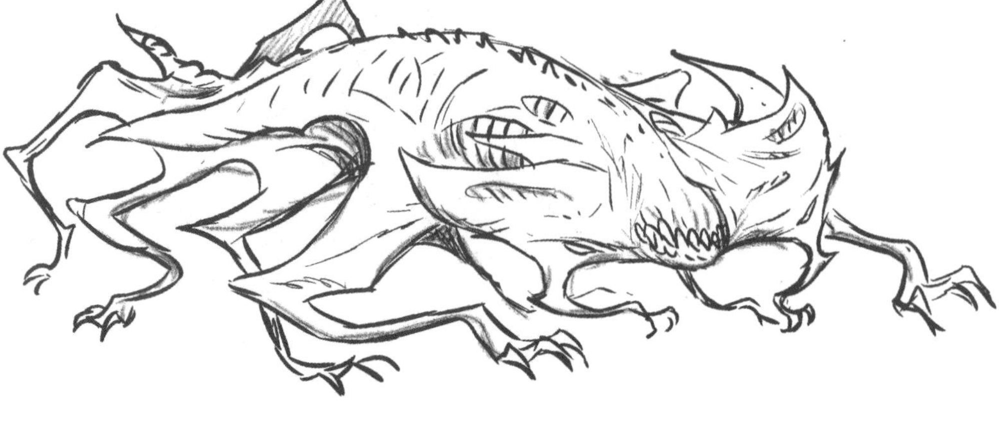

Peter studies hammerheads.

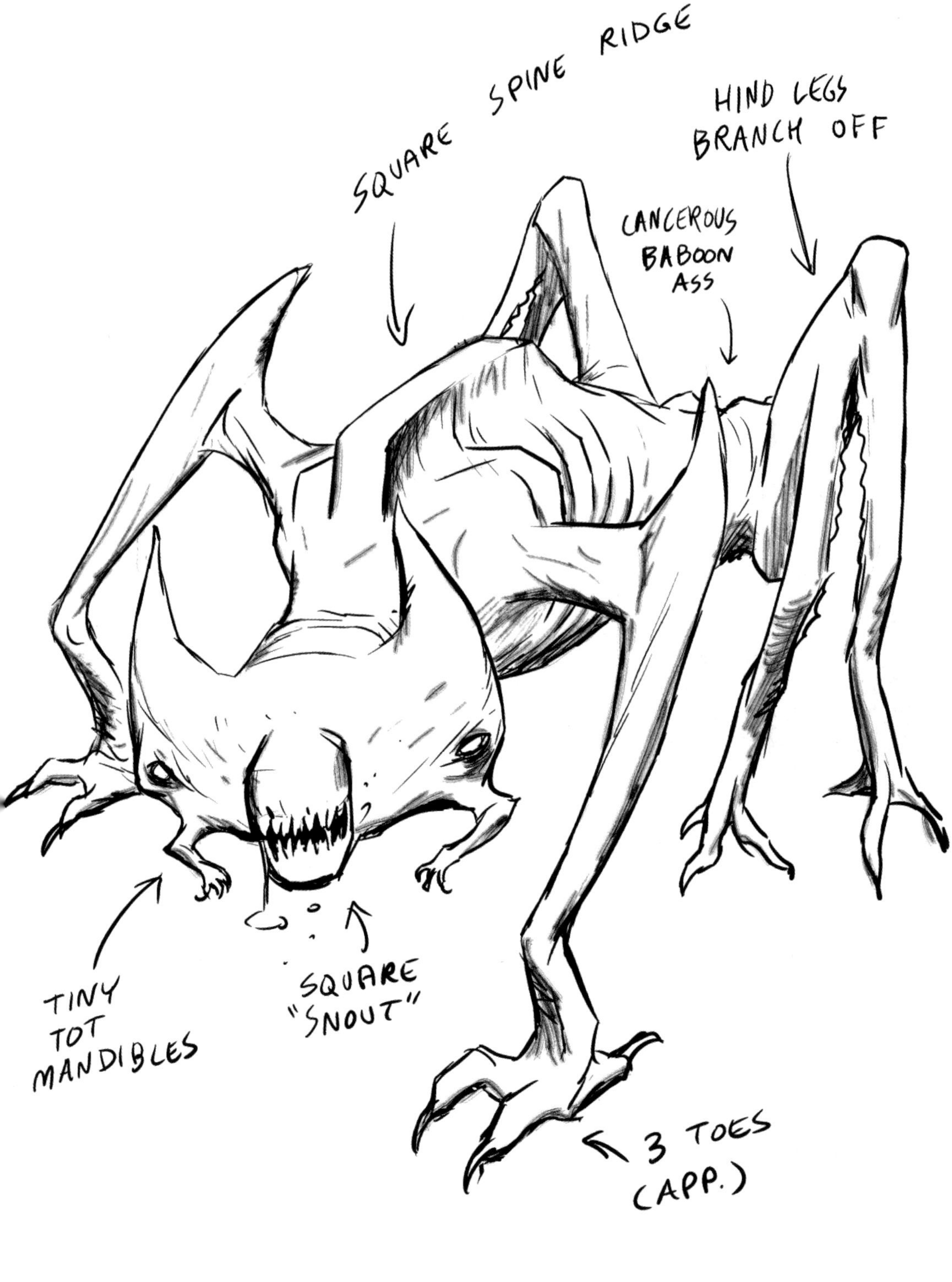

SQUARE SPINE RIDGE
HIND LEGS BRANCH OFF
CANCEROUS BABOON ASS
TINY TOT MANDIBLES
SQUARE "SNOUT"
3 TOES (APP.)

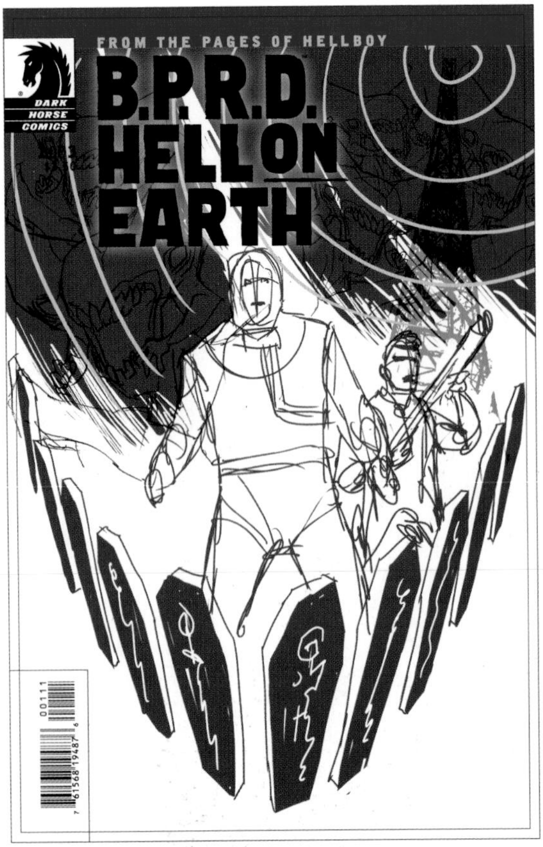
FROM THE PAGES OF HELLBOY
DARK HORSE COMICS
B.P.R.D.
HELL ON
EARTH

Dave Johnson's sketches for the covers of *A Cold Day in Hell* #1–#2. Compare to the final covers reprinted in this volume as chapter breaks. With these two covers, Dave's initial sketches were just what we wanted, whereas the following three covers went through greater changes.

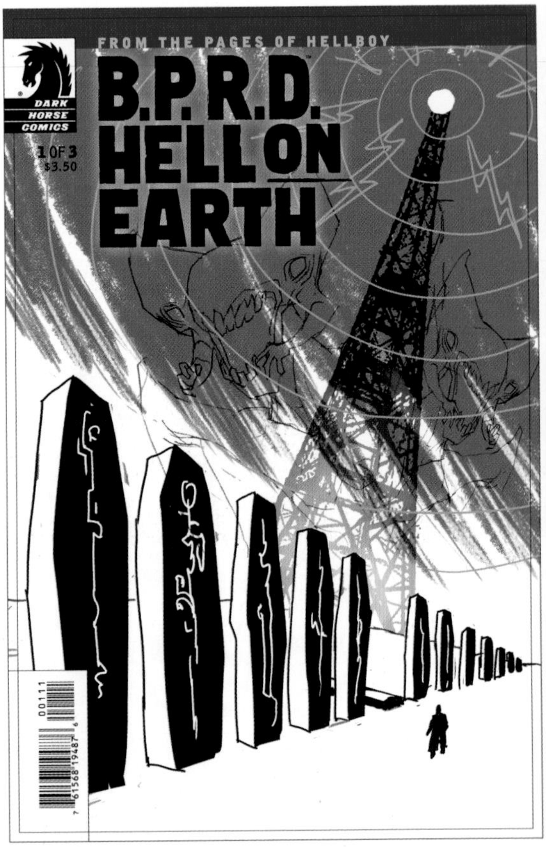
FROM THE PAGES OF HELLBOY
DARK HORSE COMICS
1 OF 3
$3.50
B.P.R.D.
HELL ON
EARTH

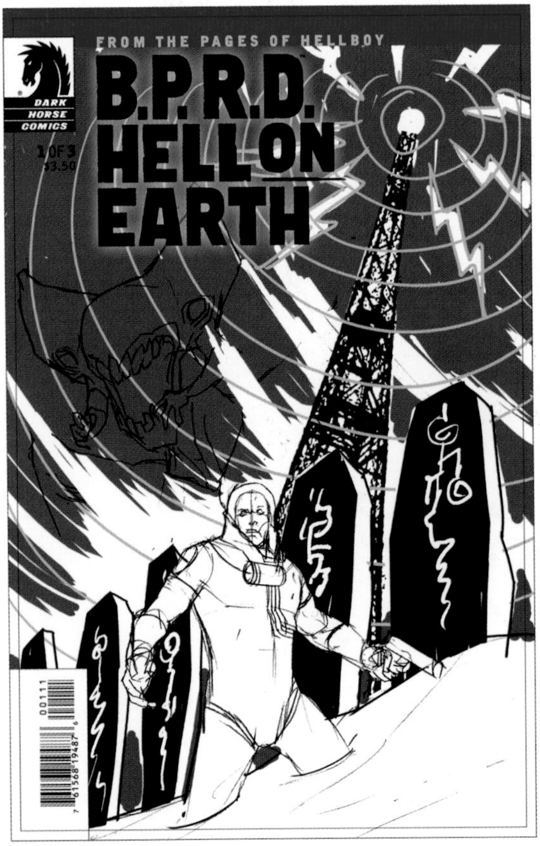
FROM THE PAGES OF HELLBOY
DARK HORSE COMICS
1 OF 3
$3.50
B.P.R.D.
HELL ON
EARTH

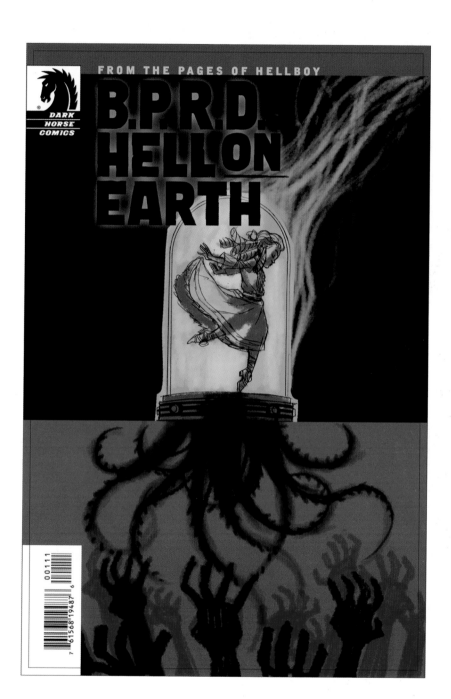

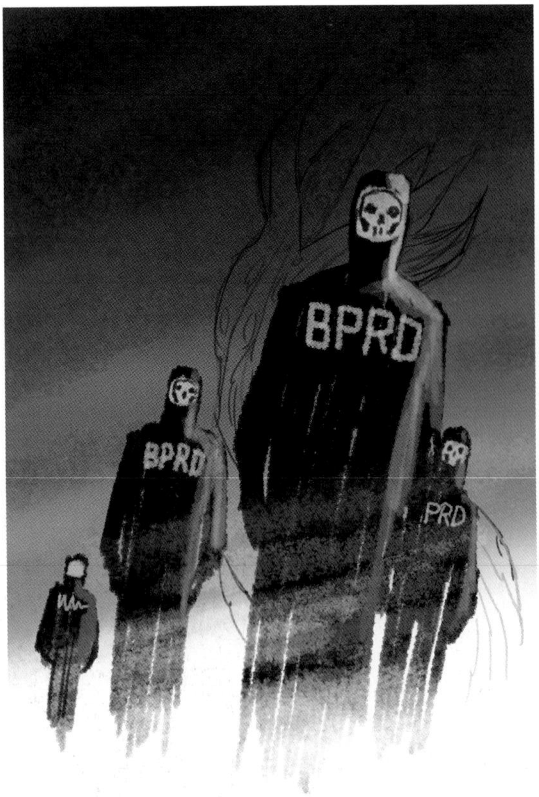

BPRD
BPRD
PRD

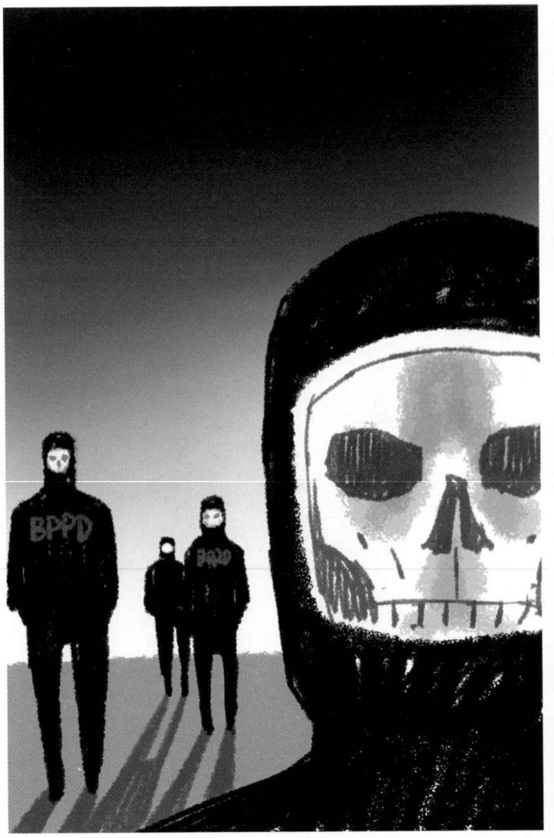

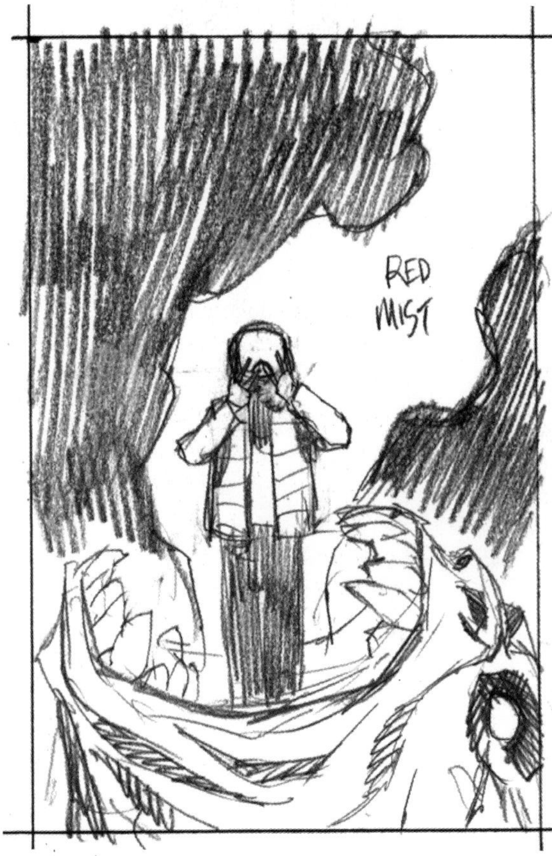

RED MIST

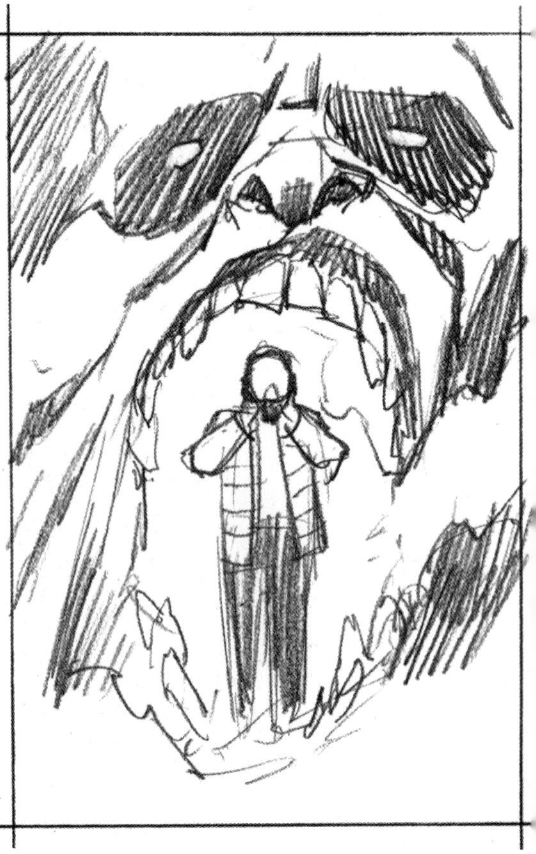

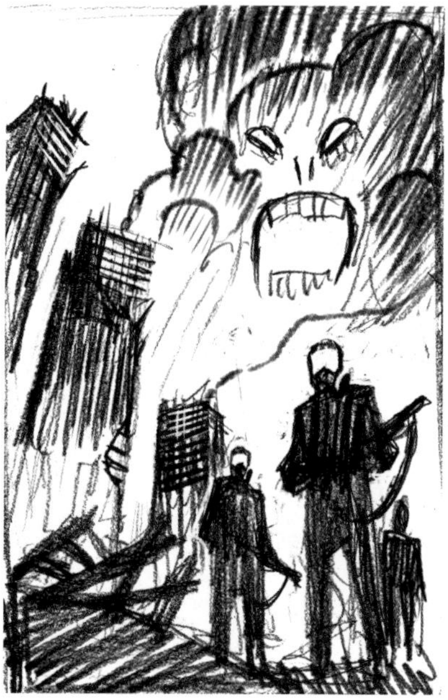

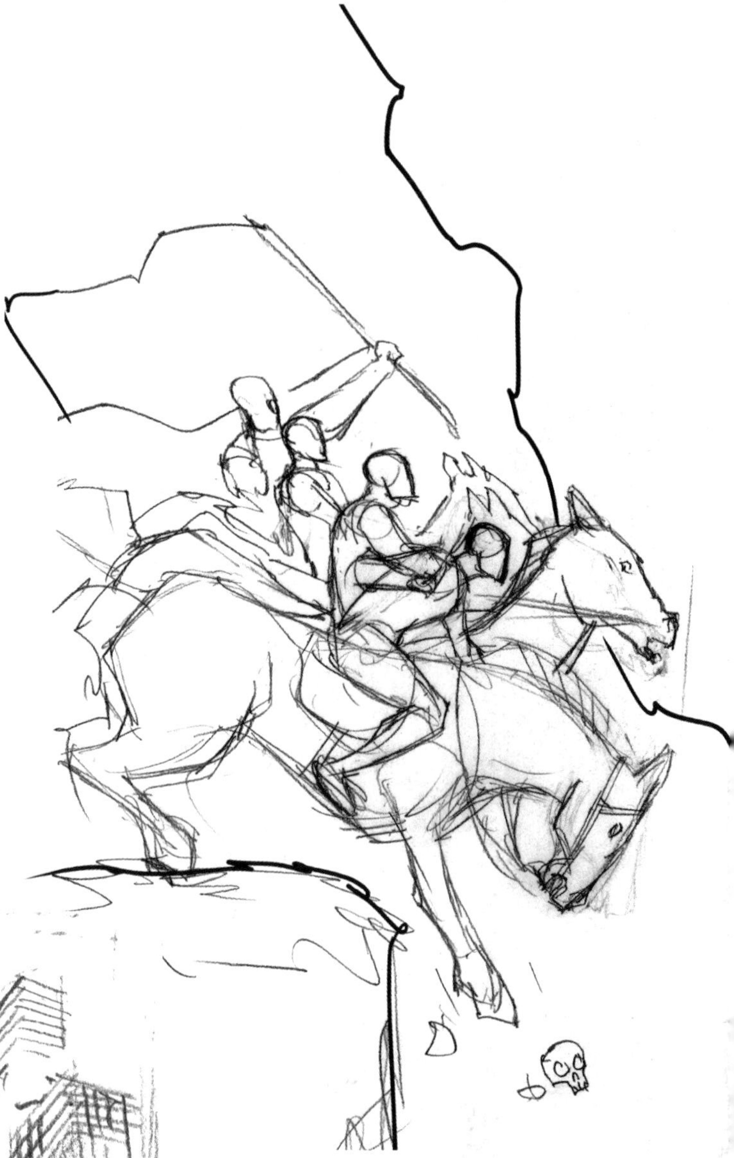

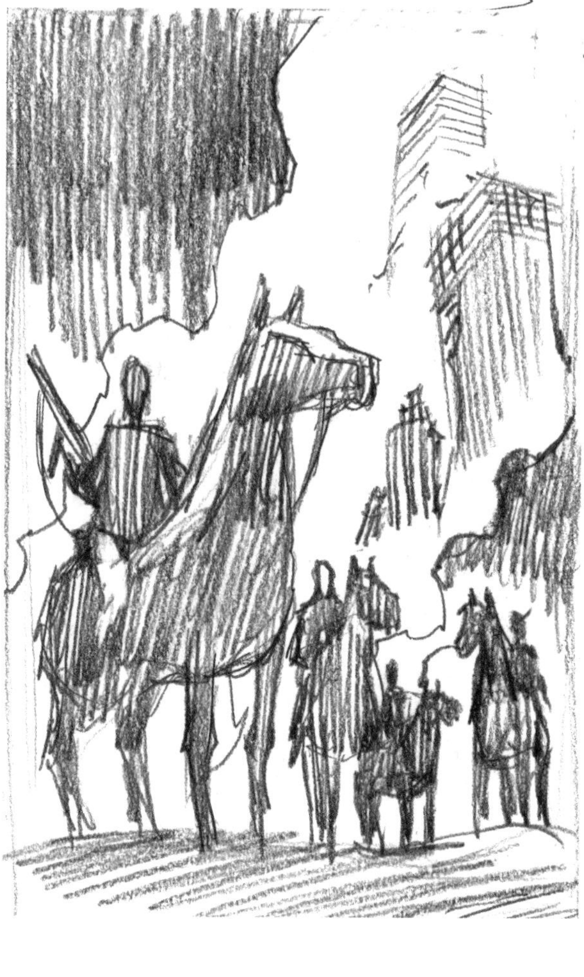

Facing: Dave Johnson's cover sketches for *Wasteland* #1–#2. John Arcudi suggested a Four Horsemen of the Apocalypse theme for part 3 of *Wasteland* (this page), and we went through very literal ideas about War and Pestilence, etc., before settling on a simpler approach to four horsemen.

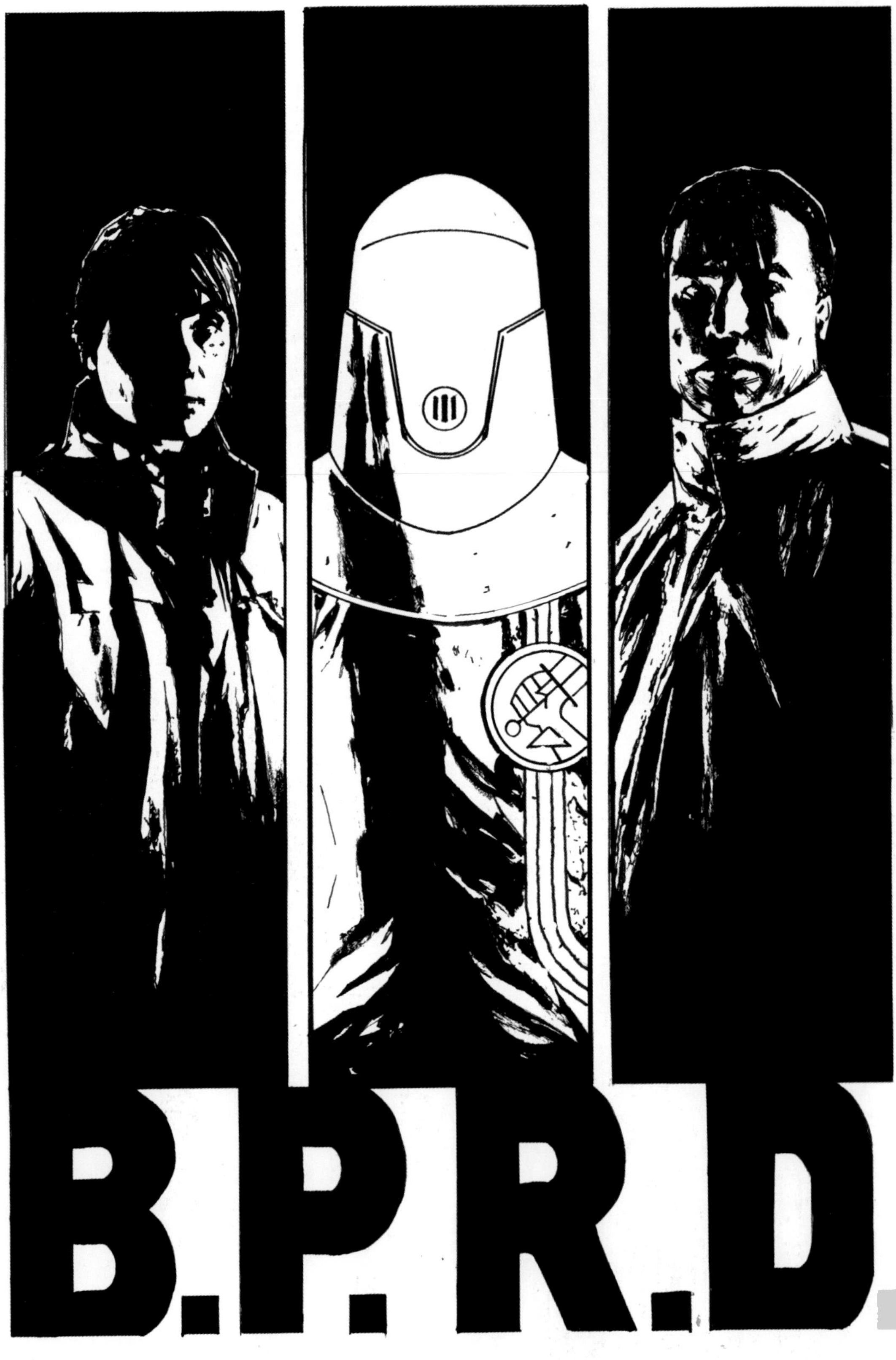
B.P.R.D

Laurence Campbell's realistic style was a departure for us on *B.P.R.D.*, and we wondered how he would handle the most fantastical elements, but these Ogdru Hem designs (facing) reassured us.

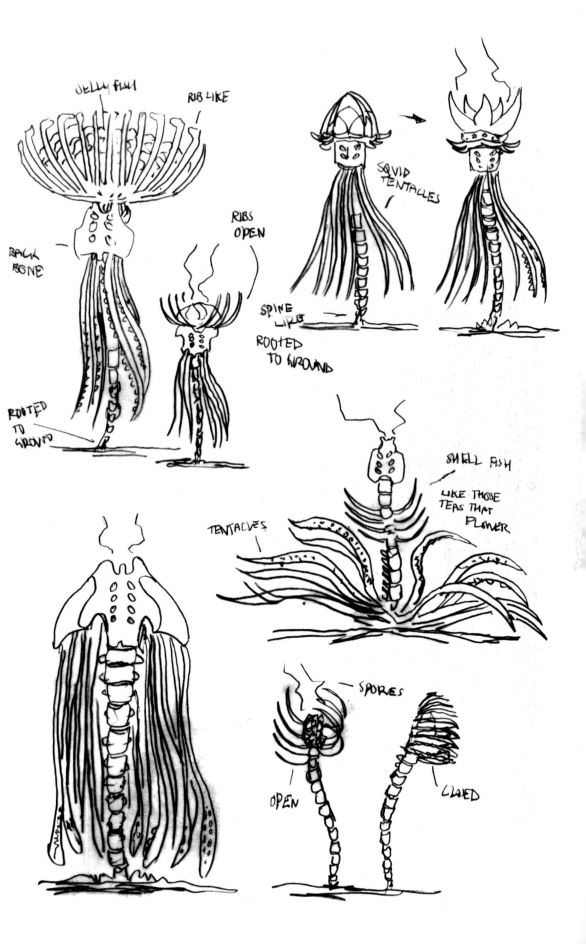

JELLY FISH

RIB LIKE

RIBS OPEN

SQUID TENTACLES

BACK BONE

SPINE LIKE

ROOTED TO GROUND

ROOTED TO GROUND

SHELL FISH

LIKE THOSE TEAS THAT FLOWER

TENTACLES

SPORES

OPEN

CLOSED

Before doing the monster design on the preceding page, Laurence offered two options for the helicopter accident in chapter 1 of *Wasteland*, pages 4–5. The two versions at the top are his rough layouts. Below, Laurence's "pencils" for the two-page-spread version of the scene. However, we asked him to do the version with two separate pages, so the monster wouldn't be in the fold. The raw finished art for page 5 is on the facing page.

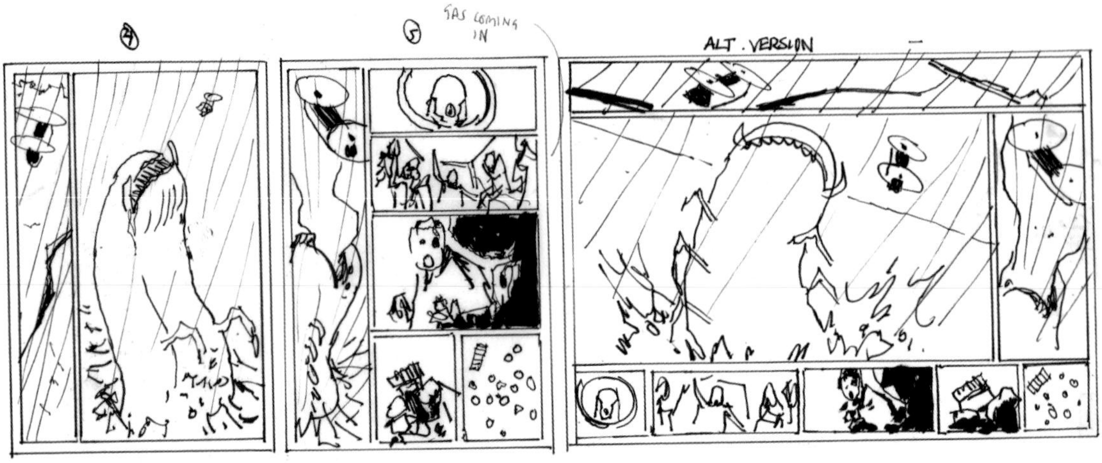

SAS COMING IN
ALT. VERSION


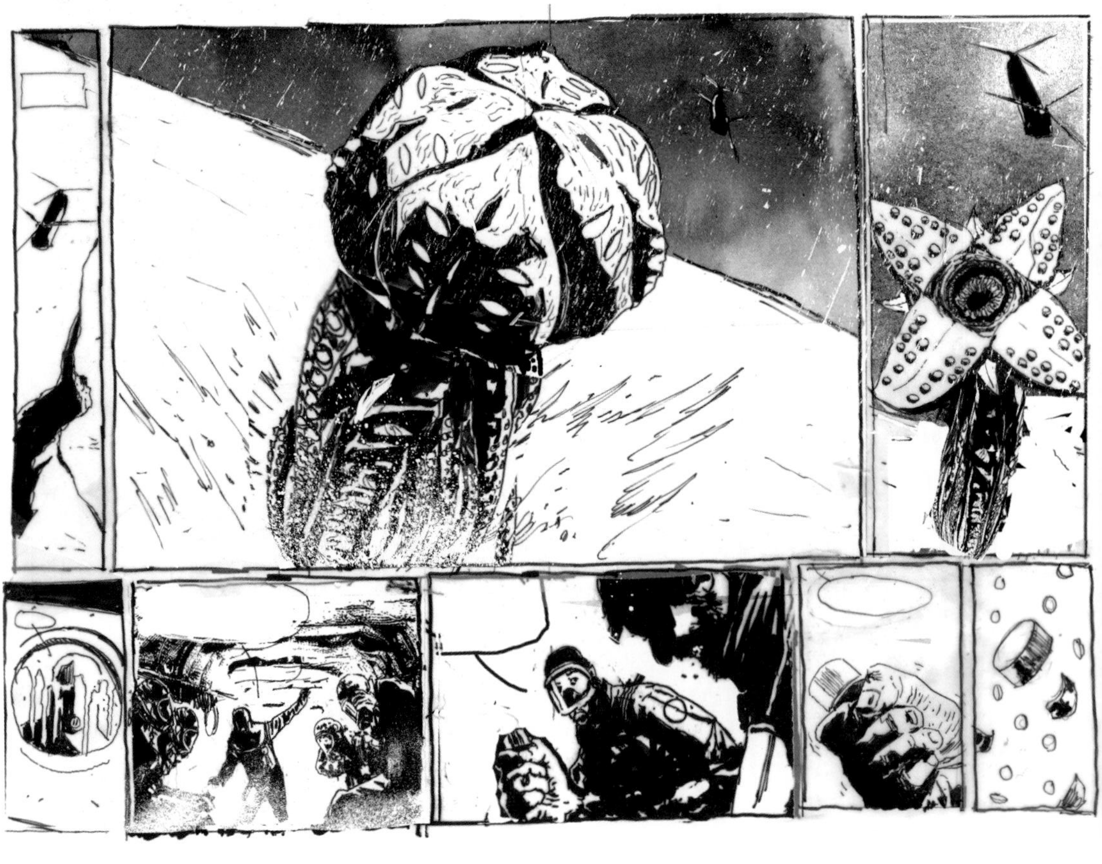

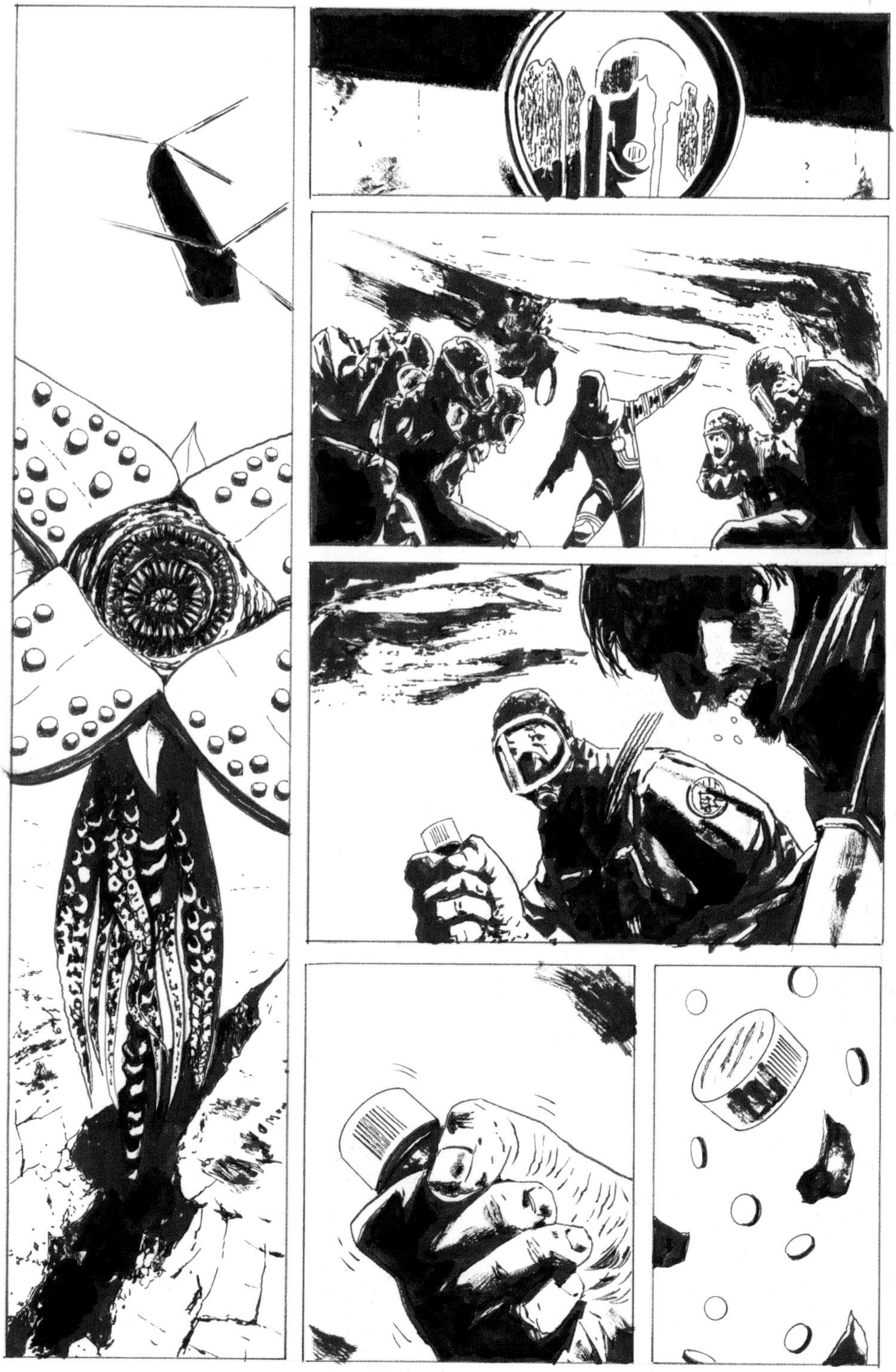

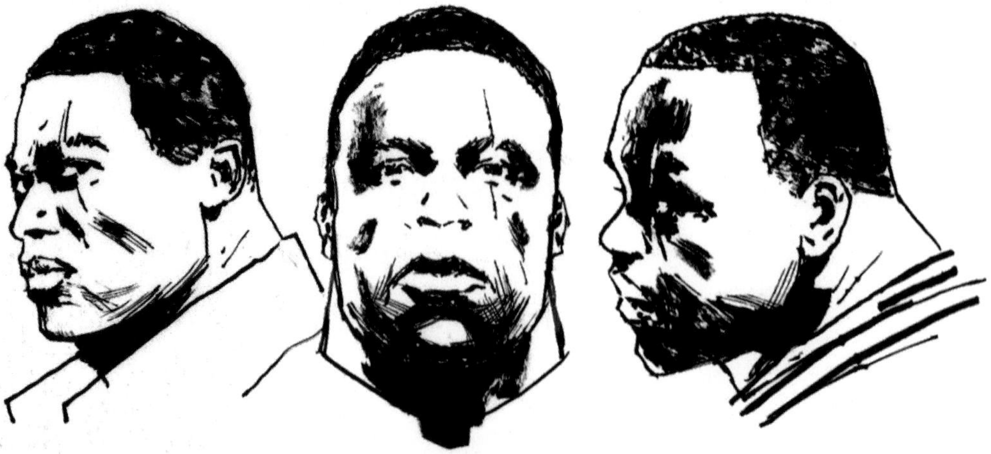
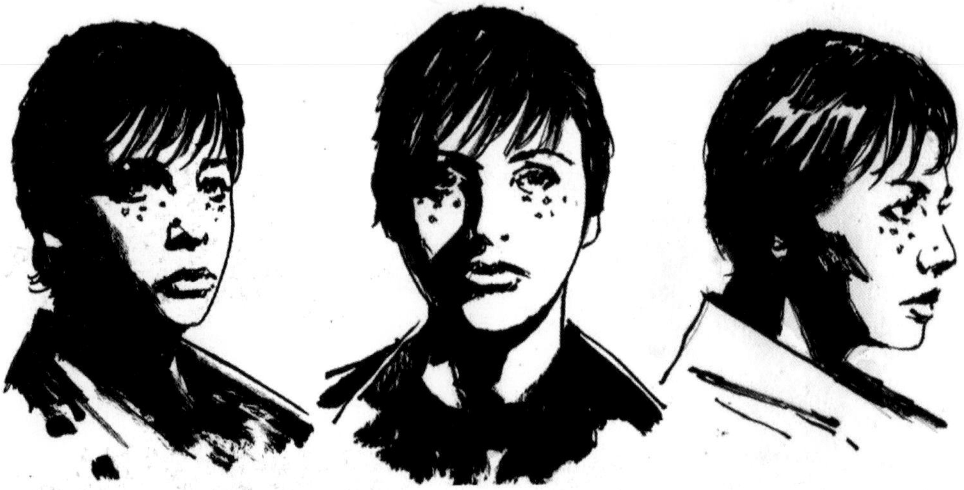
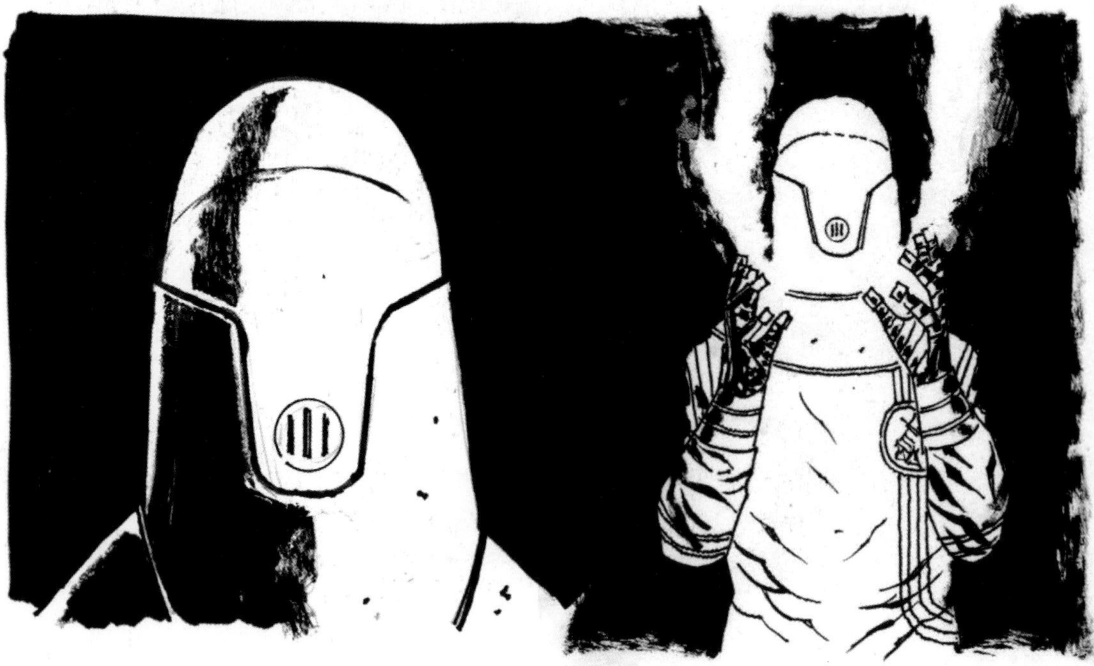

Heroes and villains by Laurence Campbell. Following pages: Laurence's pinups of various Mignola characters, including his piece for Multiversity.com's promotion for *Abe Sapien: Dark and Terrible.*

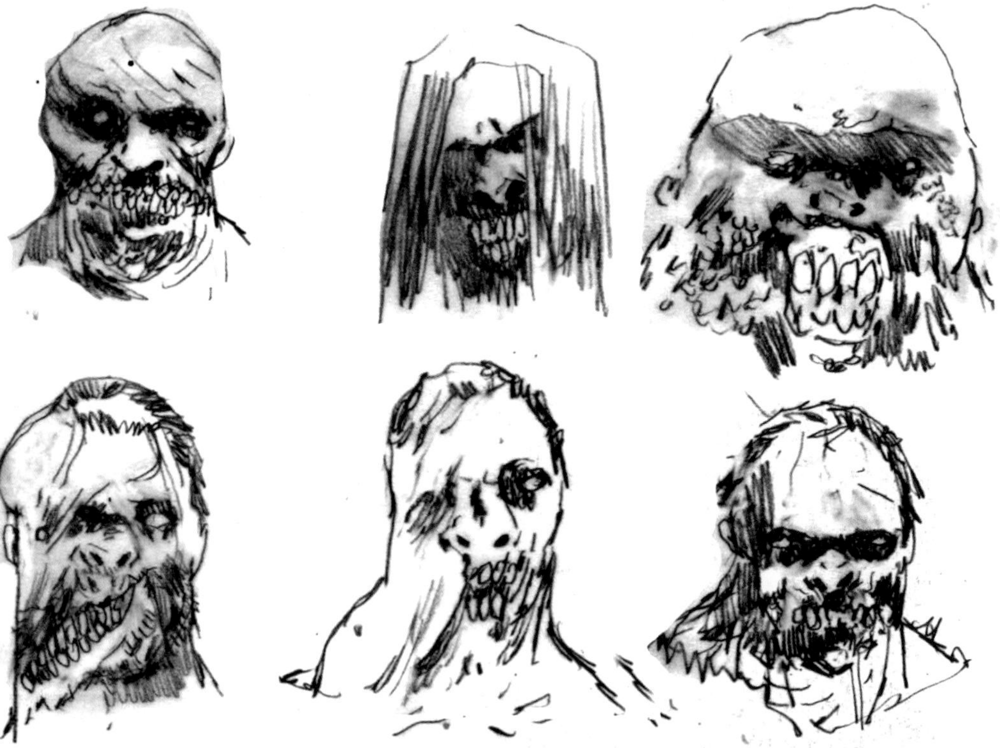

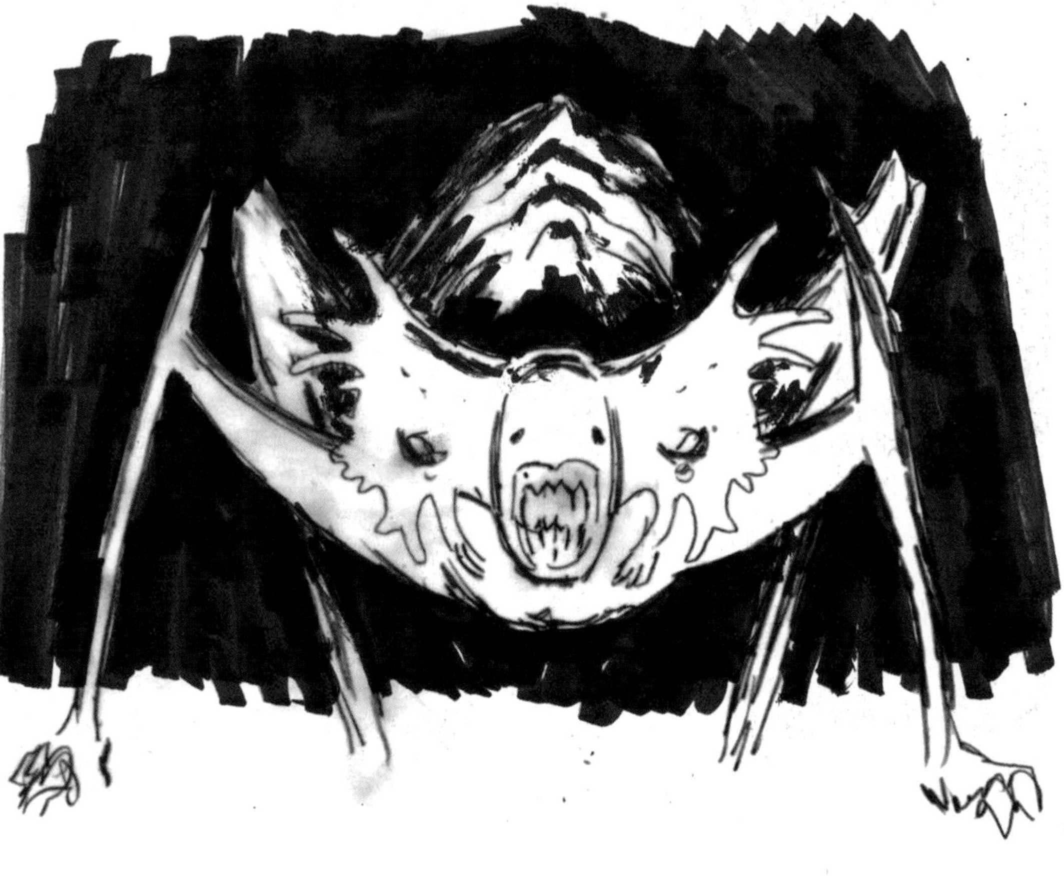

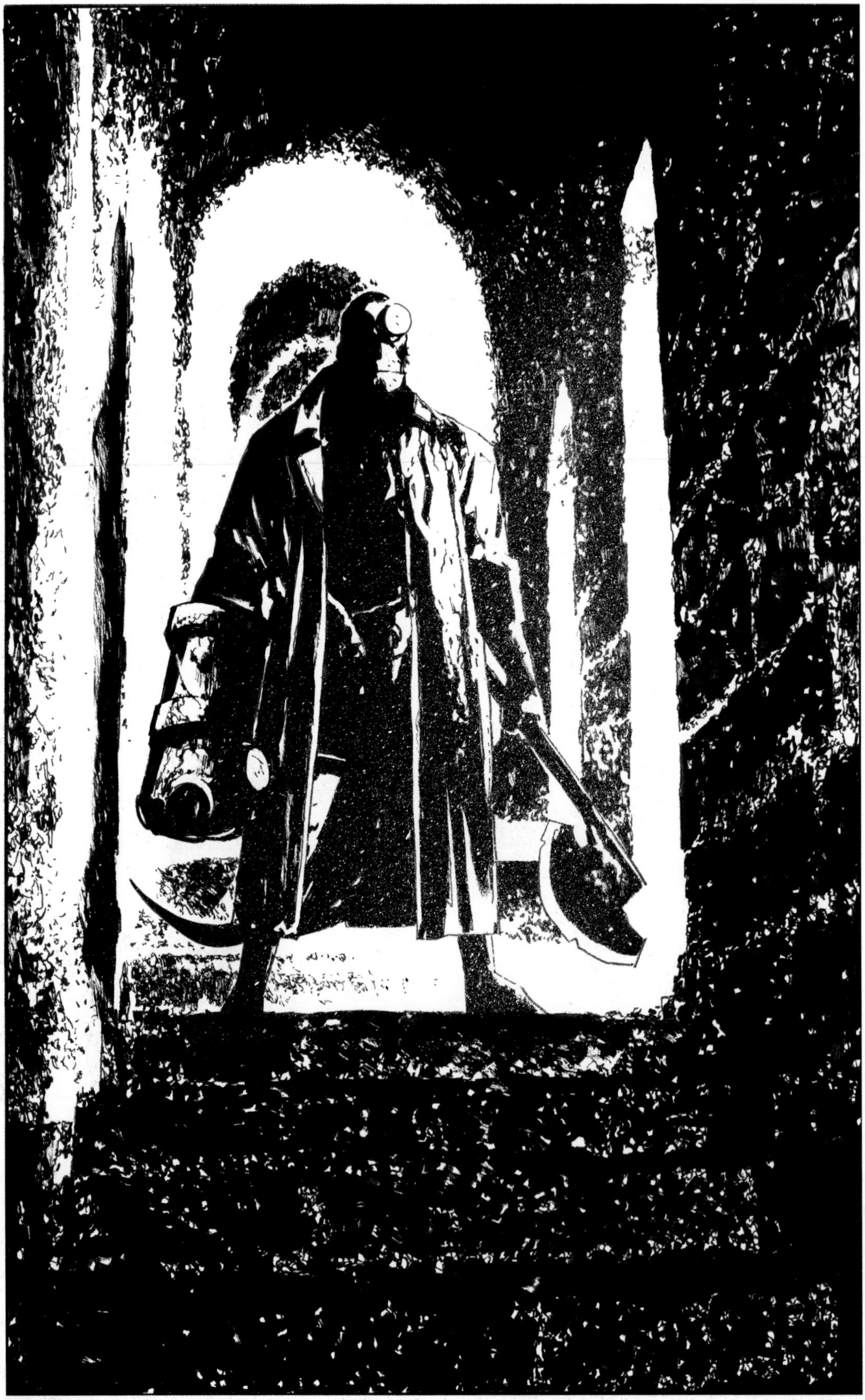

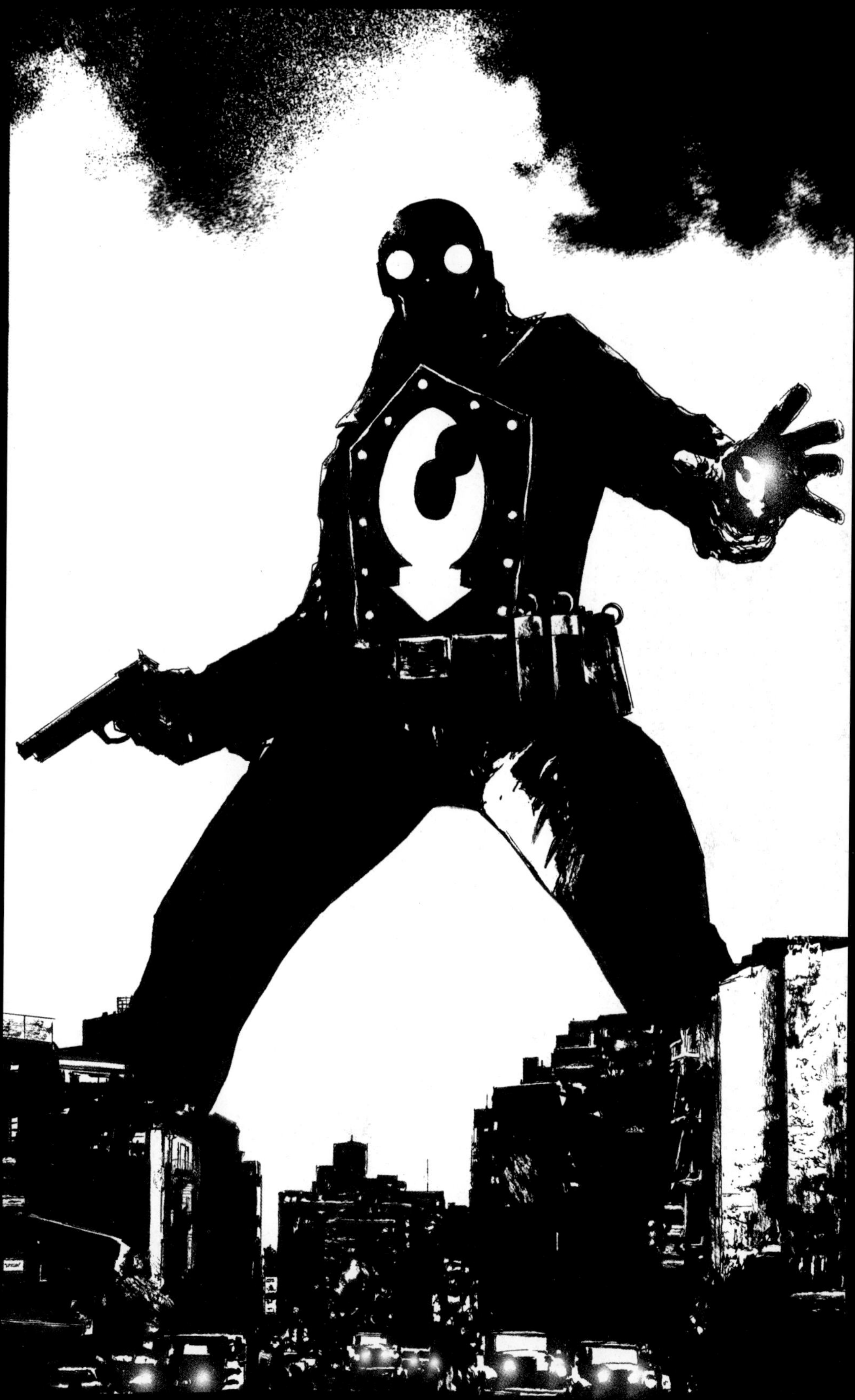

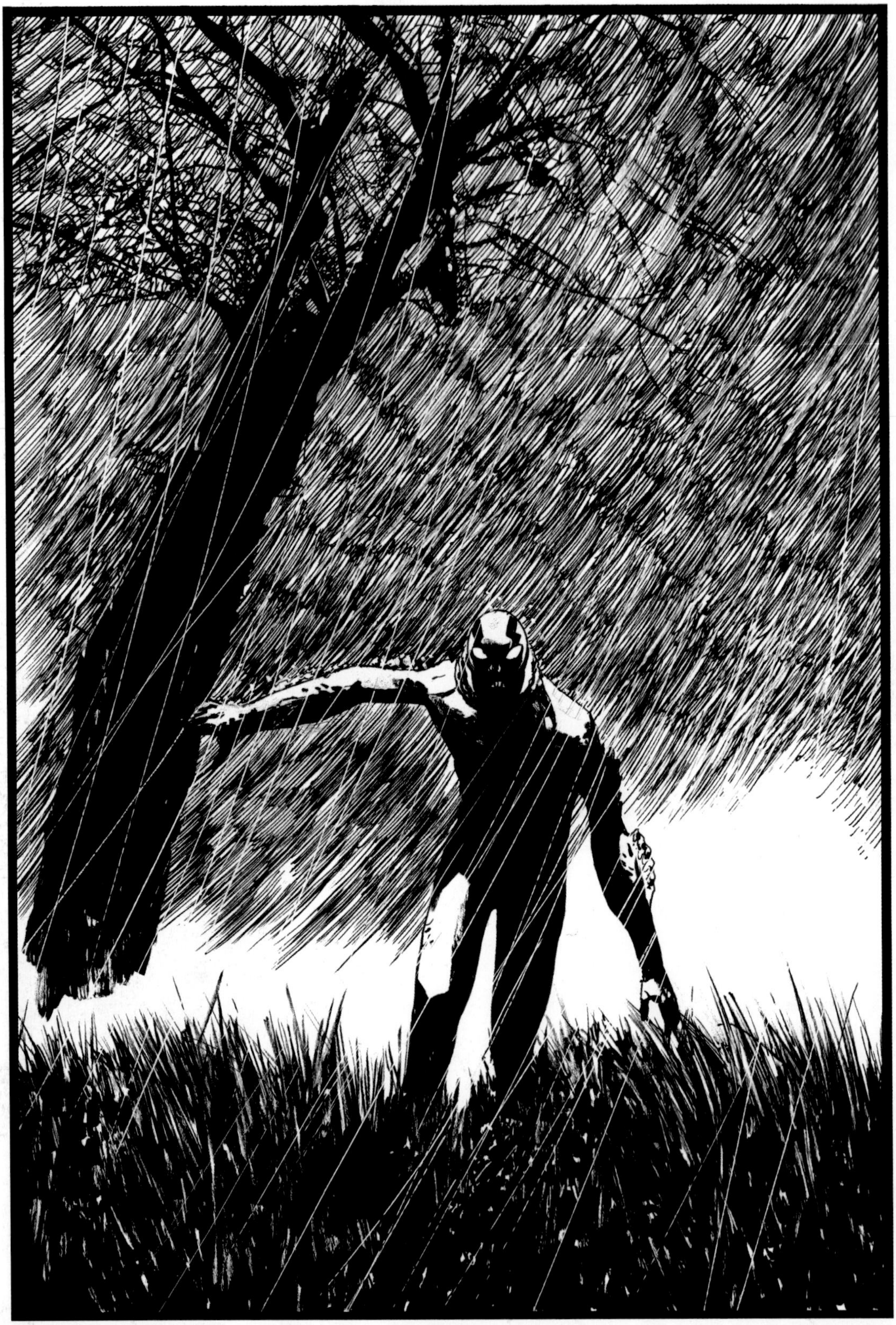

# *Also by* MIKE MIGNOLA

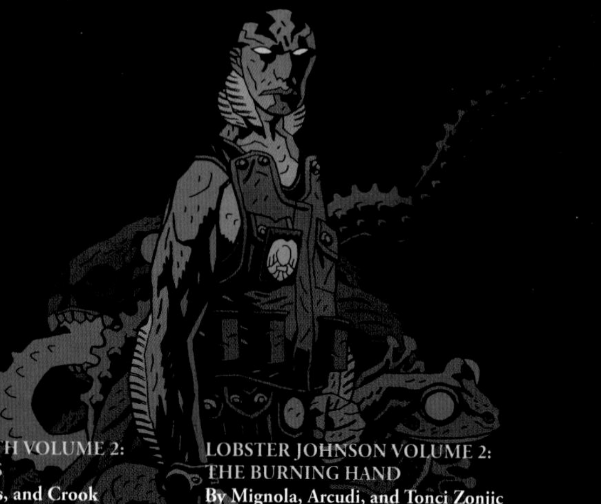

B.P.R.D.: PLAGUE OF FROGS
Hardcover Collection Volume 1
By Mike Mignola, Chris Golden, Guy Davis, and others
ISBN 978-1-59582-609-1 | $34.99

B.P.R.D.: PLAGUE OF FROGS
Hardcover Collection Volume 2
By Mignola, John Arcudi, Davis, and others
ISBN 978-1-59582-672-5 | $34.99

B.P.R.D.: PLAGUE OF FROGS
Hardcover Collection Volume 3
By Mignola, Arcudi, and Davis
ISBN 978-1-59582-860-6 | $34.99

B.P.R.D.: PLAGUE OF FROGS
Hardcover Collection Volume 4
By Mignola, Arcudi, and Davis
ISBN 978-1-59582-974-0 | $34.99

B.P.R.D.: THE WARNING
By Mignola, Arcudi, and Davis
ISBN 978-1-59582-304-5 | $17.99

B.P.R.D.: THE BLACK GODDESS
By Mignola, Arcudi, and Davis
ISBN 978-1-59582-411-0 | $17.99

B.P.R.D.: KING OF FEAR
By Mignola, Arcudi, and Davis
ISBN 978-1-59582-564-3 | $17.99

B.P.R.D.: 1946
By Mignola, Joshua Dysart, and Paul Azaceta
ISBN 978-1-59582-191-1 | $17.99

B.P.R.D.: 1947
By Mignola, Dysart, Fábio Moon, and Gabriel Bá
ISBN 978-1-59582-478-3 | $17.99

B.P.R.D.: 1948
By Mignola, Arcudi, and Max Fiumara
ISBN 978-1-61655-183-4 | $17.99

B.P.R.D.: BEING HUMAN
By Mignola, Arcudi, Davis, and others
ISBN 978-1-59582-756-2 | $17.99

B.P.R.D.: VAMPIRE
By Mignola, Moon, and Bá
ISBN 978-1-61655-196-4 | $19.99

B.P.R.D. HELL ON EARTH VOLUME 1: NEW WORLD
By Mignola, Arcudi, and Davis
ISBN 978-1-59582-707-4 | $19.99

B.P.R.D. HELL ON EARTH VOLUME 2: GODS AND MONSTERS
By Mignola, Arcudi, Davis, and Crook
ISBN 978-1-59582-822-4 | $19.99

B.P.R.D. HELL ON EARTH VOLUME 3: RUSSIA
By Mignola, Arcudi, Crook, and Duncan Fegredo
ISBN 978-1-59582-946-7 | $19.99

B.P.R.D. HELL ON EARTH VOLUME 4: THE DEVIL'S ENGINE AND THE LONG DEATH
By Mignola, Arcudi, Crook, and James Harren
ISBN 978-1-59582-981-8 | $19.99

B.P.R.D. HELL ON EARTH VOLUME 5: THE PICKENS COUNTY HORROR AND OTHERS
By Mignola, Scott Allie, Jason Latour, Harren, Max Fiumara, and Becky Cloonan
ISBN 978-1-61655-140-7 | $19.99

B.P.R.D. HELL ON EARTH VOLUME 6: THE RETURN OF THE MASTER
By Mignola, Arcudi, and Crook
ISBN 978-1-61655-193-3 | $19.99

B.P.R.D. HELL ON EARTH VOLUME 7: A COLD DAY IN HELL
By Mignola, Arcudi, Peter Snejbjerg, and Laurence Campbell
ISBN 978-1-61655-199-5 | $19.99

ABE SAPIEN VOLUME 1: THE DROWNING
By Mignola and Jason Shawn Alexander
ISBN 978-1-59582-185-0 | $17.99

ABE SAPIEN: VOLUME 2: THE DEVIL DOES NOT JEST AND OTHER STORIES
By Mignola, Arcudi, Harren, and others
ISBN 978-1-59582-925-2 | $17.99

ABE SAPIEN VOLUME 3: DARK AND TERRIBLE AND THE NEW RACE OF MAN
By Mignola, Allie, Arcudi, Sebastián Fiumara, and Max Fiumara
ISBN 978-1-61655-284-8 | $19.99

LOBSTER JOHNSON VOLUME 1: THE IRON PROMETHEUS
By Mignola and Jason Armstrong
ISBN 978-1-59307-975-8 | $17.99

LOBSTER JOHNSON VOLUME 2: THE BURNING HAND
By Mignola, Arcudi, and Tonci Zonjic
ISBN 978-1-61655-031-8 | $17.99

LOBSTER JOHNSON VOLUME 3: SATAN SMELLS A RAT
By Mignola, Arcudi, Fiumara, Joe Querio, Wilfredo Torres, and Kevin Nowlan
ISBN 978-1-61655-203-9 | $18.99

WITCHFINDER VOLUME 1: IN THE SERVICE OF ANGELS
By Mignola and Ben Stenbeck
ISBN 978-1-59582-483-7 | $17.99

WITCHFINDER VOLUME 2: LOST AND GONE FOREVER
By Mignola, Arcudi, and John Severin
ISBN 978-1-59582-794-4 | $17.99

THE AMAZING SCREW-ON HEAD AND OTHER CURIOUS OBJECTS
Hardcover Collection
By Mignola
ISBN 978-1-59582-501-8 | $17.99

BALTIMORE VOLUME 1: THE PLAGUE SHIPS
By Mignola, Golden, and Stenbeck
ISBN 978-1-59582-677-0 | $24.99

BALTIMORE VOLUME 2: THE CURSE BELLS
By Mignola, Golden, and Stenbeck
ISBN 978-1-59582-674-9 | $24.99

BALTIMORE VOLUME 3: A PASSING STRANGER AND OTHER STORIES
By Mignola, Golden, and Stenbeck
ISBN 978-1-61655-182-7 | $24.99

## NOVELS

LOBSTER JOHNSON: THE SATAN FACTORY
By Thomas E. Sniegoski
ISBN 978-1-59582-203-1 | $12.95

JOE GOLEM AND THE DROWNING CITY
Deluxe Hardcover
By Mignola and Golden
ISBN 978-1-59582-971-9 | $99.99

AVAILABLE AT YOUR LOCAL COMICS SHOP OR BOOKSTORE! • To find a comics shop in your area, call 1-888-266-4226.
For more information or to order direct visit DarkHorse.com or call 1-800-862-0052 Mon.–Fri. 9 AM to 5 PM Pacific Time.
Prices and availability subject to change without notice.

DARK HORSE BOOKS

# HELLBOY

## by MIKE MIGNOLA

**AVAILABLE AT YOUR LOCAL COMICS SHOP OR BOOKSTORE!** • To find a comics shop in your area, call 1-888-266-4226.
For more information or to order direct visit DarkHorse.com or call 1-800-862-0052 Mon.–Fri. 9 AM to 5 PM Pacific Time.
Prices and availability subject to change without notice.